EXPLODOBOOK

THE WORLD OF 80s ACTION ACCORDING TO SMERSH POD

JOHN RAIN

POLARIS
PUBLISHING

First published in 2021 by

POLARIS PUBLISHING LTD
c/o Aberdein Considine
2nd Floor, Elder House
Multrees Walk
Edinburgh
EH1 3DX

www.polarispublishing.com

ISBN: 9781913538187
eBook ISBN: 9781913538194

Designed and typeset by Polaris Publishing, Edinburgh
Printed in Great Britain by CPI Group (UK) Ltd, Croydon, CR0 4YY

For James and Alex
-- and Ron from Tapes Video Shop, Carpenders Park,
Watford, without whom none of this would be happening.

Thanks to:
Paul Litchfield, Tom Neenan, Dan Thomas, Dean Burnett,
Scott Innes, Tara Court, Peter Burns, Alison Rae, Sean Longmore,
The JP Special crowd, Elly, and Mum, Dad and Chris, my classic family.

CONTENTS

INTRODUCTION

THE EIGHTIES.

A time of fear – fear of the unknown, fear of your neighbours, fear of drugs, fear of sex, fear of strangers, fear of videos, and the very real fear that the world might end at any moment in an awful, and very sudden, nuclear attack.

However, in those times of turmoil and worry, there was a comfort that soothed the mind: action movies. Video shops were bursting at the seams with rampant gunfire, sex, drugs, rock, roll, cars on fire, people on fire, guns, bombs, and people dressed in army fatigues (and that was just the staff).

My personal nirvana was tucked away in a small cluster of shops, located in a tiny place called Carpenders Park – a leafy suburb of Watford. 'Tapes' was a temple of dreams; decked in wonderfully gaudy orange, from the exterior sign (where the logo had cleverly incorporated a spooling video tape), to the lush interior carpet, that also went part way up the walls to meet the shelves, in a satisfying act of interior design. The walls were floor to ceiling with video boxes, and there were more literally under the counter in a glass display case (mainly the more artistic foreign films, and certainly nothing untoward). The windows were covered in wire mesh, with a cacophony of posters competing for space, while also blocking out most of the daylight. Upon walking in, two things would immediately strike you: the strong smell of freshly made coffee, followed by the faint suggestion of cigarette smoke. Both blended together to form a satisfying aroma that when placed side-by-side formed an almost hypnotising scent that only enhanced your browsing experience. Tapes was run by a brilliant man by the name of Ron, and when we moved to the area in 1983, it became clear to my parents, who for some reason would sit me down with them when they watched everything (from cartoon to action, to horror film), that I loved being in that shop more than any other.

One day they told Ron that even though it was technically against the law, I had their blessing to be allowed to rent out anything I fancied, no matter the certification. With an untold tap of the nose, Ron had my back, and a good deal of my childhood (from 1983 to 1989, when we moved away), was spent in Tapes, endlessly browsing, chatting about movies, reserving future titles in his giant book, and renting everything I could get my stupid, tiny hands on.

He sold up in the early 1990s, and went on, as far as I understand, to open a florist in Watford. Tapes was taken over by an off-licence, that also pretended to be a video shop, and renamed 'Hollywood Nights', replacing walls of videos with a small corner of plastic jewel cases that you could leaf through in a fairly unsatisfying, noisy manner. It was the start of the slow death of the independent video shop, all eventually eaten up in Pac-Man-esque exuberance by Blockbuster, who themselves eventually were eaten up by the ghost of Netflix (a company they could have acquired), offering a stark reminder that nothing lasts forever.

But in the eye of the cyclone of eighties domestic video rentals, heroes were born shrouded in fire and violent revenge. They were not only armed with guns, but also red-hot quips, that served as a muscly arm around the shoulder, and a wink said that everything was going to be OK.

Together we would be OK, and together we got through it, with the help of a select band of freedom fighters, without whom the whole era would have been a truly miserable place.

Thank you Ron, Arnold, Sylvester, Sigourney, Bruce, Eddie, Charles, Patrick, Mel, Chuck and everyone else that made it happen. You saved the world, in your own inimitable way.

Join me as we go back and examine a choice selection from the decade where the explosion truly was king.

J.R.
2021

ONE

1981

JUST ONE MAN CAN MAKE A DIFFERENCE

WE START OUR GREAT adventure through 1980s action in . . . the future. The world is a blighted wasteland of chaos and wasted dreams. War broke out, the cities exploded and society collapsed. Oil, the black fuel, is the most precious commodity, and the roads, 'a white-line nightmare' of gangs and looters. Basically, Watford. A narrator tells us it was a bit of a difficult time, to put it mildly, but one man stuck out in his mind more than others: the Road Warrior, the man they called 'Max' (Mel Gibson). As the narration gets us up to speed with Max's desolate past and telling us how great he is, we cut to the man himself in his Pursuit Special, slightly tattered and less shiny and sexy than when last we saw it, but still one of the coolest cars ever seen onscreen.

Max and his dog (the very definition of a 'good boy') are being pursued by mad sods in beaten-up vehicles, who look like they've just ram-raided a leather daddy convention. They obviously don't know who they're dealing with. Within moments, all but one vehicle is written off, and as Max gets out to gather the petrol spoils from the fallen few, Wez (Vernon Wells), the last survivor

1

of this surprise attack and a man who looks like a quarterback who's pushed his head through a crow, watches. He and his backseat passenger, a blond slip of a Marc Almond impersonator named 'The Golden Youth', observe Max laying out pots, helmets and bowls to catch dripping petrol. Wez lets Max know that he's slightly put out by what has just occurred via the medium of screeching like a pig on Haribo, before speeding off and doing a wheelie – the big show-off.

Max checks out the roadside wreckage, and among the broken cars, trucks and bug-eyed corpses, he finds a tiny music box: a delicate, sweet symbol of a lost world of beauty and innocence. He smiles fleetingly as it tinkles out 'Happy Birthday', and breathes in a moment of normality before pocketing it and driving away from this site of carnage. However, this being the world it is, it's only a short drive before he encounters more carnage. This time, it's in the shape of a vacant gyrocopter, which certainly catches Max's attention. If he'd only known that anyone who owns an actual gyrocopter, or any kind of extreme sports vehicle or apparatus, should be avoided at all costs, he'd have been spared several annoying entanglements in the coming days. But Max lives in a world powered by scavenging, where mobility is key, and an abandoned vehicle, as anyone who's played a Fallout game will tell you, could be a goldmine of treats.

He approaches the flying shit-heap, ready to strip it for fuel and treats, but it has a big snake on it, hissing menacingly as he approaches. Max, though, is not one to be scared by a snake, what with him being Australian and used to living among creatures who want to kill you. As he subdues the snake, a worse threat emerges from the ground, like a hyperactive gopher: the Gyro Captain (Bruce Spence), looking every inch like Stephen Merchant's stunt double. He points a crossbow in Max's confused face, disarms him, and is about to steal his gasoline when Max's super-dog jumps to his rescue and downs him. As he begs for his life with Max's knife to his throat, he reveals that, just 20 miles away, there's an oil refinery with a limitless supply. The catch is that it is also heavily armed and patrolled. For mere mortals this place is a death zone, but it shouldn't be hard for a man like Max to find a way in and help himself to as much as he wants.

As Max watches through binoculars, the Gyro Captain tells him more about the refinery. It's a constant, pumping motherlode, with a tanker full of thousands of gallons and enough fuel to power Rod Stewart's groin for a month. There's only one small problem: it's under constant attack from marauding gangs, led by the wonderfully named Humungus (Kjell Nilsson), a vast, muscle-bound, *Guardian*-reading hulk, with a hockey-masked face and neck brace – sort of a post-apocalyptic Dominic Littlewood with a hangover. Among the many marauders, Max spots Wez and his beautiful Golden Youth chatting with the boss, so he decides to set up camp on the top of a cliff, to watch and learn about the set-up below.

By sunrise, the marauders have dispersed, and Max is woken by some vehicles leaving the compound, in what seems, on the face of it, a bit of a dangerous move. But there is method in their madness, as these vehicles are merely serving as a distraction, so another can slip away in the opposite direction. A brilliant plan, eh? No. It fails dismally, and they are captured immediately, with one mortally wounded and the other sexually assaulted, then murdered, with Wez overseeing the whole sordid affair. This makes Max, well, mad, and he races to his car to go down there and rescue the survivor and take him back to the refinery.

Max's car pulls up outside the fortified gate, and he emerges carrying the wounded man, with his hand in the air as he does so. He's allowed in, and the medics get to work at once on the survivor. A man called Pappagallo (Michael Preston) approaches. He's the leader of the refinery crowd, and he also happens to look a lot like Geoffrey Hayes from *Rainbow*, so it's tempting to think that somewhere, out in that wasteland, Bungle, Zippy and George lie dead in a burnt-out Ford Capri, and this thirst for vengeance fuels his ambitions for survival. Max explains to Pappagallo that he had a deal with the survivor that if he brought him here safely, he could have some fuel, but the leader and all the people in the refinery are not interested in helping him out, especially as the survivor dies just as they tell him as much. They tell him to leave, but before he does so, a worried call is heard: the marauders are coming back. The compound erupts into chaos as men and women dressed like dystopian aerobics instructors rush into place to man guns, flamethrowers, pigs, rabbits and rocks.

The marauders have brought thoughtful house-warming gifts – all the people who tried to make a break for it earlier, strapped to the front of their vehicles. They pull up outside the gates and shut off their engines in unison. Toady, a man who looks like Don Estelle if he joined the Manson Family, makes an announcement. We will shortly be hearing from Humungus, who is introduced as 'The Lord Humungus, the Warrior of the Wasteland, the Ayatollah of Rock and Rolla', but, disappointingly, doesn't give us a blast of 'Whispering Grass'. Humungus has his own PA system, and he gets to his feet to tell the refinery gang that he's disappointed that he's had to unleash his Dogs of War again. He says he knows all about their puny plans to make a break for it with a tanker full of gas, and as the prisoners object and tell their fellow refinery friends to ignore what he's saying, Wez steps in and headbutts one into silence, much to the enjoyment of the gang. Watching with disapproving eyes is the Feral Kid (Emil Minty) – think Nick Cave as a five-year-old. The little mite has seen enough. He unleashes his metal boomerang of death right into the Golden Youth's skull, killing him instantly, which understandably causes Wez to have a bit of a meltdown, and results in him having to be put into a chokehold and restrained by Humungus. He tells him they will get revenge, but they will do it his way. 'Just walk away, and there will be an end to the horror,' Humungus tells the refinery gang, giving them a day to decide.

As the Dogs of War make their exit in a cloud of dust, some of the refinery folk begin to have rumblings of dissent and fear, feeling that maybe giving up and leaving will be the safest course of action. But Pappagallo has to remind them that these lads are a bit on the homicidal side and will probably murder them all, like they did to Rod, Jane and Freddy. As he tries to calm down the guys and explain that the tanker represents a lifeline for them to get away from the marauders, Max watches from the sidelines and notices the Feral Kid emerging from a hole in the ground with his boomerang, still covered in the blood of the Golden Youth. The kid is intrigued by Max, and who wouldn't be? He's cool as fuck, and looks like Johnny Cash's stylist – I'd want to hang out with him all day long.

Max, being the bereaved father that he is, senses the innocence and lost childhood in the Feral Kid, and reaches into his pocket to retrieve the music box he found earlier. As he slowly turns the tiny handle and peals the delicate sounds of 'Happy Birthday', the boy becomes filled with excited wonder, and then runs off in honking glee when Max hands him it.

Max is tired of the refinery lads panicking and their defeatist talk. He whistles to get their attention and says that two days ago he saw a vehicle that will pull the tanker, and he may be their best hope of survival. His offer is that he'll go out and bring back the vehicle, if, in exchange, they give him as much fuel as he can carry. They accept his deal readily. As Max strides out into the darkness, with four cans of diesel on his shoulders, Pappagallo and the guys watch with faces of tense hope.

After a long walk into the morning sun, Max once again bumps into the Gyro Captain, who's staggering around the desert, still chained to the log he left him with. The gyrocopter is still in place, protected by the Gyro Captain's carefully placed snakes, so they fly the rest of the way. With the truck up and running, he gives the pilot his freedom by throwing him the keys to the lock, before starting the long drive back to the compound, but to Max's surprise (and probable intense disappointment) the pilot announces that they are now partners. Thus, he joins this arduous trip, and, together, they plough their way through the Dogs of War before finally getting the truck inside and sending the gang running.

The bad news is that, during the battle, Pappagallo got an arrow in the thigh for his efforts, and he can't even blame Zippy for it. As he struggles with his injury, he tells his guys to get ready to leave in the 12 hours it will take to fix the truck after the attack. Despite offering him the chance of living in paradise 2,000 miles away with everyone, Max has no interest in driving the rig. He's a loner. He just wants to take his fuel and leave, much to the regret of everyone in the refinery. They were quite keen on the idea of him taking the wheel for their escape attempt. He jumps into the driver's seat of his fully fuelled Pursuit Special, heads out into the wasteland, and leaves the cause behind, disappointing everyone as he does so, like a one-man personification of all our hopes and dreams.

It's really not long before he encounters the Dogs of War and is quickly driven off of the road, into a twisted wreck of broken metal and glass. They set upon him, steal his gas, and murder his very good dog. Unfortunately, they fail to realise his gas tanks are booby-trapped, so they're killed in a massive fireball. Max crawls away from the wreckage, thankfully being rescued by the Gyro Captain, who saw the explosion through his telescope. As Max is airlifted back to the haven of the compound, he's forced to reflect on one of the truisms of life: when things seem too hard, just don't bother trying.

He awakes, wounds treated and bandages applied, and staggers out to see Pappagallo briefing the team on how the tanker charge will go. He's telling his team he will drive it, but Max breaks up the conference to say: 'Can I shock you? I like driving tankers, despite what I previously said before I drove off and was nearly killed.' Pappagallo attempts to make him work for it, but quickly realises that Max is their best shot of getting out of there in one piece, so hands him the keys and the shotgun, and everyone tools up for the harrowing journey that awaits them.

There are changes afoot outside, as Wez is now being held by Humungus via a chain, suggesting that he's been reprimanded for losing the tanker, or it's just something he's into – both are possible at this point. Max's truck, which is now heavily armoured and staffed with makeshift warriors, ploughs out of the compound and through some of the Dogs, with the rest giving chase as it motors away. Seeing the compound now abandoned, some of the gang drive inside to celebrate the seizure of a never-ending supply of oil. But it's booby-trapped – will they never learn? – and kills them all in a raging, righteous explosion.

The truck bombs along the open road, flanked by many foul motorbikes, dune buggies and hot rods, all wanting to take it down for good. Humungus releases Wez, and the mad bastard sets about joining in with the rest of the Dogs to kill everyone they encounter. Extreme motor chaos breaks out, with one crash in particular giving cinema the greatest accidental spectacular stunt in history; a stuntman, who was meant to just go over a bonnet of a crashed vehicle, actually ended up somersaulting many times towards the camera, in a stunt that nearly killed him. Thankfully, he only broke his leg, and so it was kept in the film. As the (frankly useless) refinery gang are slowly picked up and thrown under wheels, and the gyrocopter is downed, it's up to Max and the Feral Child in the cab of the truck to form any kind of resistance. As Wez has them pinned down, Max has the clever idea of turning the truck around and going back in the opposite direction, ploughing the super-rig right through Humungus's oncoming vehicle, killing both him and a wailing Wez, who was hanging on to the truck for dear life.

Sadly, Max's truck of death is also sent tumbling in the process, and as the wreckage settles in the fractured ground, the remaining Dogs of War – and Max, to his annoyance – discover that it was full of dirt, merely an elaborate decoy.

As he reflects on what just happened, and maybe how Geoffrey from *Rainbow* will be happier in heaven with the rest of the gang, the Gyro Captain arrives right on cue, offering Max an opportunity to crack his second smile in about fifteen years – an opportunity he takes up with pleasure, slumped by the side of the downed tanker.

As the Feral Child is loaded onto the compound school bus, which is packed full of oil drums, the narrator from earlier informs us that they will now begin their long journey to paradise, with a new hero – the man who fell from the sky – and it's not Bowie, but the Gyro Captain. He has managed to get himself well-in with the refinery guys, and is somehow seen as a beacon of hope, though he's sure to be ejected from their good graces swiftly when they discover that he is the pervert he clearly seems to be. I mean, that gyrocopter is *plastered* with porn. We also discover that the narrator is none other than the Feral Child, proof, if ever it were needed, that it's never too late to follow your dreams and get a voice-over gig.

As for Max, we're told that he was never seen again, but will live for ever in their memories, as the man in black, who barely said anything, had a grumpy personality, but was really, really good at driving, thus inventing the legend of Nigel Mansell.

TWO

THE TERMINATOR

1984

IT CAN'T BE BARGAINED WITH. IT CAN'T BE REASONED
WITH. IT DOESN'T FEEL PITY, REMORSE, OR FEAR.

LOS ANGELES, 2029. A terrifying future where humans are hunted to the point of extinction by robot versions of the skeleton from the Scotch videotape adverts. Humankind's puny firepower is no match for their red-hot lasers and flying hoover planes. Something must be done. The opening caption tells us that the 'machines rose from the ashes of nuclear fire', which reads like it was written by Matt Bellamy for a long-abandoned Muse album. After witnessing this future dread and the hopeless scramble for life of our future cousins, we then arrive in the Los Angeles of 1984, naïvely busying itself for the arrival en masse of performance-enhanced Olympians. On the dark streets of the city, a yellow dumpster is trying to empty its load. But there's a sudden burst of cartoon electricity, and out of it rises a very large, naked body builder, one who isn't on his way to the shot put quarter-finals. It's a T-800 Terminator (Arnold Schwarzenegger), and it's here on a mission to stop the future. It wanders out to Griffith Observatory, completely billy-bollocks, and bumps into some street punks (including a young blue Mohican-toting Bill

9

Paxton and Brian Thompson), who, justifiably, ask if everything is alright and proceed to give him a light ribbing about the fact that he's wandering around in the nude. These days, of course, they would have filmed the entire encounter, and 'Confused Nude Body Builder' would very much be a meme for the ages. Rather than humouring them and laughing along with their banter, though, he murders them and steals their clothes.

Across town, in a dark, litter-strewn alley a drunk homeless man curses the world by saying the word 'bullshit' over and over again, and, brother, I hear you. His TED talk is disturbed by some more cartoon lightning and the landing of a very naked Kyle Reese (Michael Biehn) onto the pavement in front of him. Moments later, some police arrive to find Reese stealing the homeless man's trousers, so he does the decent, albeit undignified, thing and runs away. A policeman pursues, but he is accosted from the shadows by Reese, who takes his gun and asks him what day it is (it's the twelfth of May, a Thursday, if you're interested), and then confuses the man by asking what year it is, clearly hoping he doesn't say 2020. As a patrol car approaches, Reese again hotfoots it, but this time creeps around inside a department store, where he picks up a nice coat and a natty pair of Nike trainers – but doesn't think about swapping his piss-soaked trousers, which he will surely regret later. As the cops conduct a half-arsed search of the store, Reese is off down a fire escape and out into the night, stopping briefly to steal a shotgun from the patrol car and then look up a name in a phonebox directory.

The next morning, Sarah Connor (Linda Hamilton) parks her moped outside the burger joint where she works, securing it with a chain that, if you ask me, will offer no protection from theft whatsoever. She asks the giant burger-wielding mascot outside to guard it for her, and then makes her way inside to begin her shift. It's one of those days. She mixes up orders, spills drinks on laps, gets hassled for coffee, and then a small child plants a scoop of ice cream in her pocket. They say animals and children can sense trouble, and perhaps this ice cream was a warning that the world is in very real danger. We will never know.

Across town, the Terminator, now sporting some natty LA punk gear, has stolen a car and found a gun shop owned by Dick Miller in which to arm himself to the teeth. He puts together a massive order of weaponry, including a gun with a laser sight. He then gives himself away a bit by asking for a plasma rifle, which confuses Mr Miller, as he's just a simple gun-shop owner from 1984. After stacking the counter with nearly everything he sells, Miller asks what he'll be buying, and he says he'll take it all. Dick is excited by this news but warns him that there's a 15-day wait for the handguns. He can take the rifles now, though – ah, America, never change your mad gun rules. While he's prepping the paperwork, the Terminator begins to load the shotgun. 'You can't do that,' suggests Miller, but his mind is quickly changed when he is shot to death. The Terminator then grabs a page from the phonebook and heads for the first stop on his mission.

On arriving in suburbia, having crushed a kid's toy truck with his front wheel, he knocks on a door and asks the lady who answers if she is Sarah Connor. She says yes, and he shoots her many times. (He was subsequently fired by Avon.)

At work, the real Sarah is grabbed by her colleague who excitedly shows her the TV news broadcast. It would appear another Sarah Connor was murdered in her home. 'You're dead, honey,' her friend lovingly tells her, and with colleagues like these, it's no wonder a pocketful of ice cream isn't a problem.

Reese, meanwhile, has found himself a car in a scrapyard, and as he finishes hotwiring it, he watches the diggers and machines at work around him. This sends him into a flashback/forward showing us the very real war against the machines. Reese and his men are clearly up against it, having a terrible time fighting the very right-wing robots from the future while lying in piles of crushed skulls. At the point of this memory where he's about to burn to death, he awakes back in good old 1984 and drives away into the night, probably wishing he could just stay there and have a nice time eating crisps and watching *Ghostbusters*, which is what

I would do. But this is why I haven't, as yet, been asked to go back into the past and stop something from happening.

The real Sarah and her flatmate Ginger are getting ready to go out, which means lots of awkward dancing in knee socks and really long T-shirts and massive hair. It's 1984, so there's rubbish battery-powered hairdryers and Walkmans to get into the groove. They check the answer machine and Sarah receives more bad news: her date for the evening has cancelled on her, so she's going to have to change back into her old, stonewashed jeans and go and see a movie instead. Ginger's staying put, as her pervert of a boyfriend, Matt, is coming over. As Sarah leaves on her moped, Reese starts his car, and follows on behind.

At the police station there's concern: reports have come in that two Sarah Connors have been horribly killed, and it would appear they have a serial killer on their hands. This is particularly annoying as the police hate paperwork, and copy-and-paste hasn't been invented. The press have arrived, and they want comment, but Lieutenant Traxler (Paul Winfield) and Vukovich (Lance Henriksen, who Cameron initially wanted to play the Terminator, fact fans) are keeping schtum. They're trying to reach the last Sarah Connor in the phonebook to warn her, but as we know, she's at the movies and Ginger and Matt are in the next room listening to music and having it off, so they get the answer machine. The pill-popping, chain-smoking Traxler decides to make a statement to the assembled press, and the statement may well be on his appearance, because, as Vukovich tells him, he looks like shit.

While sitting on her own in a pizza restaurant, Sarah sees a TV news report about the two dead Sarahs and is rightly worried. She tries to use the phone, but it's out of order, so she leaves to find another. As she gets outside, she notices – undoubtedly owing to the stench of old piss – Reese following her. So, she ducks into Tech-Noir, a happening neon bar down the street. Reese knows he's been spotted and kicks himself about wearing those trousers, so he walks past to avoid suspicion. Sarah runs to a phone to call the police, but all the lines are busy, and the message tells her to stay on the line if she needs a police car, which is reassuring.

Ginger comes out of the bedroom, still wearing her headphones, to make a much-needed midnight snack after hours of rumpy-pumpy. Matt is sleeping, clearly spent, and doesn't notice the sliding door open and the Terminator wandering in. His dreams of ice cubes on his knackers are quickly ended when a knife narrowly misses his head and stabs the pillow next to him. He gamely tells the Terminator he will 'mess him up', and if the Terminator were capable of laughs, I am sure he would have been chuckling as he tosses Matt around the room like a rag doll in a tumble dryer. Ginger is oblivious to the racket, though, as she's still plugged in to her music while making a gigantic post-sex sandwich with celery and peanut butter. It's only when poor Matt's bloodied corpse flies through the door that she notices something is wrong, and before she can do anything about it, she's shot dead. Just as the Terminator is about to examine her questionable post-sex snack, the phone rings. It's Sarah leaving a message for Ginger and Matt, telling them she's scared; she thinks someone is following her, she's at Tech-Noir, and she wants them to pick her up. This should lead to a comedy moment where the Terminator looks down at their dead bodies and then breaks the fourth wall and says, 'Well, that's awkward', but in this unjust world, it doesn't. He grabs a photo of Sarah and heads out to find her.

Sarah finally gets through to the police, and Traxler picks up. She tells him she's in a bar called Tech-Noir, and he says, with whole-hearted confidence, that he knows it. He reminds her that she's in a public place so she should be safe, but don't leave or go to toilet or anything; he'll arrange for a car to pick her up in a minute. She returns to her seat to panic quietly over a drink. Meanwhile, the Terminator has arrived at Tech-Noir. He marches past the front desk without paying, which leads to his being accosted by a giant bouncer with a splendid moustache, whose hand he breaks. He spots Sarah sitting at the table on her own and approaches through a group of dancers with his dead eyes fixed on her. As he reaches her table, he pulls out his pistol, loads it, and aims the laser sight directly at her forehead. However, before he can end the future, Reese appears from the bar, having just finished a much-needed pint and some crisps, and unloads his shotgun into him, sending him sprawling to the ground like a big post-sex sandwich. But, as this is a Terminator, he stands up again and begins to spray his Uzi 9mm around the bar, sending panicked Lycra-clad patrons flying in a hail of gunfire. Reese sends him flying through a window with further shotgun blasts and then grabs Sarah's arm, uttering the immortal line: 'Come with me if you want to live.' Which is the best offer she's had all night. As the Terminator gets to his feet once again, they run for it, stealing a car and speeding off into the night. The Terminator takes out a policeman and steals his car in order to pursue the pair.

As they drive away, Reese tells Sarah that she must do exactly what he says, that he's here to protect her, and that she's been targeted for termination. She says she didn't do anything, and he tells her she will. The man hunting her is not a man, but a machine – a Terminator, a cyborg assassin. They pull over, and he tells her that these machines are so advanced they sweat and have bad breath – this coming from a heavily perspiring man with the foulest of trousers. She tells him she's not stupid and that such a thing doesn't exist, but he informs her that it won't for about forty years. She doesn't believe him, and he makes her feel better by telling her that the cyborg will never stop until she is dead. She asks if he can stop it, and he eases her mind by saying, hmm, he doesn't know. He goes on to explain that in the future there will be a nuclear war and everything will be gone. The computers and machines got smart and took over the world, exterminating everything that was left. He grew up in the ruins, starving and fighting against the 'hunter-killers' to stay alive, and one man taught them how to survive and started a rebellion. His name was John Connor, her unborn son.

The Terminator enters the car park in his stolen police car, and it has to be said that he's doing a better job of looking for them than the police are. Instead of driving up and down occasionally shining a torch, the T-800 is using his super-robot eyes and looking for them in every car. Reese, meanwhile, has hotwired a new one and is about to speed off when the Terminator spots him, and so a new car chase begins, this time with them taking shots at each other between cars on the street while driving at very high speeds. Sadly, for our robot chum, it culminates with him driving headlong into a wall. The real police arrive quickly on the scene and arrest Sarah and Reese, but the Terminator has already fled the scene.

Traxler hands Sarah a Styrofoam cup and tells her to drink it. Though we don't really know for sure what's in it, I will assume it's Tizer until someone tells me different. He breaks the bad news to her that Ginger has gone to sex heaven, and Sarah doesn't take it very well. As she's crying about the loss of her best friend, he introduces her to psychologist Dr Silberman (Earl Boen) and asks her to tell him everything Reese told her. She asks him if she thinks Reese is crazy, and Silberman assures her he will find out, through the medium of a big yawn.

The Terminator arrives back home to his squalid bedsit a bit worse for wear. How he has managed to rent this living space, negotiate the lease, and pay a deposit with his limited use of the English language and money is anyone's guess. Putting the fate of the world to one side for a moment, one thing's for sure: London estate agents would kill to rent places like this to Terminators. He sits himself down at a table, and begins to assess his damage and repair what he can. He has a mild bad arm that he tinkers with before approaching the mirror to remove his dodgy eye with a scalpel, revealing his sinister red laser robot eye. To hide the damage, he puts on a cool pair of shades, then checks his hair briefly, grabs two machine guns he's stashed under his mattress, and heads out the window.

Dr Silberman gets the lowdown on the future from Reese. To say he is not convinced is an understatement, though he may be more convinced than Vukovich and Traxler, who roll their eyes and cackle from behind the two-way mirror. Reese explains that

Skynet, the creators of the Terminator, have to kill Sarah in 1984. It is the only way to win the war and stop John Connor ever existing. He explains that he was sent through a time machine to follow the Terminator, and the machine was then destroyed, meaning there is no way he can get home. They then show the footage to Sarah, and Silberman is so excited at meeting someone so utterly off-the-scale bonkers, he forgets to pause the video at the part when Reese begins screaming that the Terminator will pull her fucking heart out and will never stop looking for her. Silberman tells Sarah that his diagnosis is that Reese is a 'loon' and that she shouldn't worry about what he says. Which begs the question as to why no one has asked her about the other guy who has been shooting at her and who has been killed at least three times, but I guess they'll get to that in a bit. Traxler gives her a bulletproof vest and says it will stop 'most' bullets. So that's a comfort. He then tells her to go and have a snooze on his couch, reassuring her that she'll be very safe as there are 30 cops in the building. And I am sure nothing will go wrong at all.

As Silberman leaves for the night, he passes a visitor at reception. The Terminator is asking the policeman on the front desk if he can see Sarah Connor; he's a friend. 'Did she not mention her giant Austrian friend who looks like death? Oh, weird?' The desk man tells him she's making a statement and he can wait if he wants. The Terminator gives the room a once-over before leaning ominously into the glass and growling those infamous words: 'I'll be back.' A line that has served Schwarzenegger so well you can be sure it will be on his gravestone. Seconds later, a car bursts through the front of the police station and runs the desk man over. There then begins a large-scale killing spree, with the Terminator wandering through the building machine-gunning anyone who crosses his path, including poor Traxler and Vukovich. In the chaos, Reese manages to unlock his own handcuffs (always impressive), find Sarah, grab a car, and escape the carnage.

They dump the car and hide under a bridge while Sarah bandages Reese's bullet wound. He tells Sarah how he volunteered for this mission so he could meet her, as in the future she's something of a legend, and I suspect he definitely fancied her. He gives her a message from John: basically, thanks for being a great mum, that the future is not set, and she must survive, or he won't exist. Nothing emotional or nice, as you can't show emotion in front of your men, though a quick 'Love you, Mum' wouldn't have gone amiss, John. She asks Reese where he's from, and he tells her all about how harrowing the future is, and how they're hunted day and night, and we get another flashback/forward where everything looks utterly dreadful and awful and smoky, and grubby little waifs eat rats. But in the midst of all this horror, he has a pretty photo of Sarah that he clings to, and I am guessing that it's laminated.

Back in his bedsit, the Terminator is scanning the address book he stole from Sarah's apartment with his robot eyes. He's interrupted by a janitor outside who asks if he has a dead cat in there, thus giving credence to the earlier statement from Reese that these things can really stink if they feel like it. He runs a list of appropriate responses through his robot brain, and settles on 'Fuck you, asshole' (which I believe was taken from a Judith Chalmers remark in an episode of *Wish You Were Here '84*, when she was asked by a fellow holidaymaker if her hotel room was nice). He finds an address, 'Mom's cabin', and once again tools up and heads out.

Sarah and Reese have found themselves a motel room. While he heads out for supplies, Sarah calls her mother at the cabin to tell her she's alright but that she can't tell her where they are. Eventually her mum talks her into it, but what Sarah doesn't realise is that it's not her mum on the other end of the line. It's the Terminator, using her mum's voice to fool her, finally confirming my theory that Rory Bremner has been sent from the future to kill us all. Reese returns with a couple of giant brown bags full of common household supplies in order to build explosives. 'Moth balls, corn syrup, ammonia – what's for dinner?' jokes Sarah. He explains sternly that he learned how to make bombs when he was a kid (I could barely make toast), and they then build pipe bombs and fuses together, before it's established that Reese is a virgin and he loves her, and they retire to bed for some retro nookie.

However, as they are getting dressed and awkwardly exchanging small talk, they hear a dog barking outside, and as Kyle told Sarah earlier, they are very good at spotting Terminators. They make a break for it in a pick-up truck, and the Terminator gives chase on his motorbike, taking shots at them as he follows. Kyle responds with pipe bombs, but misses every single time, ultimately getting shot as he hangs out of the window like a doofus. Sarah runs over the Terminator in retaliation, but in doing so flips the truck. They are sitting targets now, but luckily a massive speeding truck runs over the recovering cyborg. It's just not his day. As the driver stops to investigate, the Terminator emerges and murders him. He is now visibly worse for wear, with his leg buckled and his face mostly removed, exposing his spooky robot features. He climbs into the big truck and hits the gas, chasing Sarah and Reese as they try to hobble away. Always the tactician, Reese lets the truck chase Sarah while he slides a pipe bomb into the back of the truck, before jumping in a bin as it explodes in a ball of flames. They watch as the scary robot from the future falls to his death in the inferno. Phew. *Definitely* this time . . .

No. Just as Sarah and Reese are celebrating their victory with big cuddles, this unstoppable killing machine from the future emerges from the fire. And now he's a full-blown robot with a full set of teeth, red evil eyes and a bad leg. They race into a nearby factory, and the thing hobbles after them. Reese turns on all the machines in the factory to distract it, while he and Sarah skulk in the shadows trying not to be discovered. But it's too late. It's found them. Reese tells Sarah to RUN while he engages in hand-to-hand combat with the robot – well, he hits it with a metal pole – and as he's getting beaten up, he reveals the plan he had up his sleeve, another pipe bomb, which he slides into the robot's chest. It explodes, regrettably sending a large piece of shrapnel right into Sarah's leg, which she bravely removes. Legend. She crawls over to check on Reese, but he is sadly dead, killed in the explosion. She doesn't have too much time to mourn, though, as the robot, much like the Black Knight from *Monty Python and the Holy Grail*, is still ready to fight, despite having no actual legs. Sarah crawls through the factory to get away, and eventually leads the annoyingly persistent Terminator into a crushing machine, where she traps it behind a grille, presses the button, and proclaims, 'You're terminated, fucker,' as the crusher swiftly descends. Cartoon electricity shoots out as the industrial machine flattens the T-800 in one smooth go – for good.

We next see Reese being zipped into a body bag and Sarah being stretchered from the scene.

Sarah's driving a jeep along a long deserted Mexican highway, a big Terminator-aware dog sitting beside her. She's dictating into a tape machine, recording her story for John, who, judging by the flowing smock she's in, she is clearly carrying – that or she's been downing too many midnight snacks to recover from her trauma. She pulls in at a petrol station, and as she's being refilled, she starts to talk about Kyle Reese, and how it's a bit weird that he has to send his own dad back from the future (I smell a sitcom!). She goes on to say that in the few hours they had together, they loved a lifetime's worth of time. Eeuwww, Mum?! As she's finishing up telling John way too much information, a small boy appears and takes a Polaroid snap of her, asking if she wants to buy it. She does, knocking him down from five dollars to four, and we see that it's the same picture of Sarah that Reese had in the future – before it was laminated. She pays for the petrol and then hears from the kid that a storm is coming. Sarah agrees and drives away into the scenery, full to the brim with trepidation about the horrifying future that is yet to come. While she's thinking of the incoming nuclear destruction and robot apocalypse, we, the audience, are left to contemplate how this franchise just refuses to die and will keep coming back and back until we are all dead.

THREE

1985

THEY SENT HIM ON A MISSION AND SET HIM UP TO FAIL.
BUT THEY MADE ONE MISTAKE.
THEY FORGOT THEY WERE DEALING WITH RAMBO.

A MASSIVE EXPLOSION. THAT'S how you set your stall out early. The quarry underneath is draped in a blanket of dust as the prisoners doing hard time break rocks in the hot sun. They fought the law, and the law very much won. Among the sweaty criminals is one sad-eyed man who very much did just that, and blew up the town in the process: John Rambo (Sylvester Stallone). He's three years into a prison sentence, and looks to be not enjoying himself very much. His work in this hellhole is stopped when a visitor wants to speak with him. It's his old commanding officer, Colonel Trautman (Richard Crenna). They meet at the mesh gate, and Trautman breaks the ice by asking how he's doing. 'Good,' says Rambo. After exchanging further pleasantries, Trautman gets to the point. He has a proposition for Rambo: stay breaking rocks for another five years or go on a covert mission to the Far East to do some recon for a bunch of US POWs who are still in Vietnam – in the same camp Rambo escaped from in 1971. No one knows the terrain better than he does, though the risk factor is very high. Rambo stares into space

20

for an hour. At least when he's breaking rocks he knows where he stands (by a rock), but Trautman tells him he'll be reinstated in the Special Forces and, if successful, there may be a presidential pardon in it for him. This convinces our man, and as Trautman leaves, he asks if they get to win this time, to which Trautman replies that it's up to him – it's his film.

After soaring over paddy fields and Buddhist shrines, with Jerry Goldsmith's theme being epic in the background, Rambo's chopper lands in Thailand. He's greeted by Ericson (Martin Kove), who takes him to see Major Murdock (Charles Napier) and Trautman in an office that looks like a branch of Kwik Fit with a handy, and prominent, Coca-Cola vending machine for guests. Murdock reads through Rambo's file, listing his many honours and murders, and then tells him they need conclusive proof that there are still men at the POW camp. Rambo is a bit surprised when he's handed a camera and told he's only to take pictures, and even more so when they tell him that he must chop down the tallest tree with a pickled herring, but he's informed in no uncertain terms that he must *not* engage the enemy. Trautman will return to perform the Phase Two extraction later.

In the operations centre, Murdock, surrounded by chirping terminals, tells Rambo that he can relax, he'll have the most advanced weapons in the world available to him, and with the loud beeps those machines make, you can be sure of it. Rambo tells him that he's always thought that the mind was the best weapon, which to a certain extent is true, but I've never seen one blow up anything. Trautman tells him that, upon insertion, he should rendezvous with his ground contact, which sounds like they'll have a lovely candle-lit dinner. Worried that Rambo seems 'unbalanced', Murdock pulls Trautman to one side and asks if he's sure he's up to it, as he seems stoned as fuck. Trautman tells him that what he chooses to call 'hell', Rambo calls 'home', which explains why he lives in Watford.

While the ground crew ready the jet, Rambo readies himself in the dark: flexing his muscles, sharpening his knife, tying his laces, boxing his explosives, packing his arrows, loading his guns, packing his extra knives, his lucky gonk and his spare lucky gonk, and zipping up his jumpsuit. He has 36 hours to get in and out, and as he says goodbye to Trautman, he mentions that when Murdock told them which battalion he was with in Vietnam, he gave the wrong location, so Trautman is, once again, the only man he trusts.

The green light pings into life, and Rambo knows it's time to jump. He puts on his Biggles mask, straightens his goggles, and then heads for the open plane door. However, there's a problem. When he jumps, he turns into Frank Spencer and is 'hung up' – a Special Forces technical term meaning he gets a strap caught on the plane and is left dangling out the side like a sock caught on a stick in a high wind, shouting about Betty and how the cat did a whoopsie in his parachute.

Eventually, he uses one of his many knives to cut himself loose, but in doing so loses all his meticulously packed weapons and equipment. As he tumbles down into Vietnam, Murdock tells Trautman that if it were up to him, he'd abandon the mission, but Trautman believes in his man, and he's sure that Rambo will get the job done.

On the ground, Rambo races through the jungle, and after a brief encounter with a snake, notices that he's not alone. He tracks the person in the straw hat and jumps them, wielding his giant knife, but it's not an enemy. It's Co (Julia Nickson), his contact, and she notes his surprise that she isn't a man. He reflects for a moment on how awful the patriarchy is, before recommending that they keep moving. She says she'll take him to the river, she's arranged a boat for them, and mentions that he's come a long way to look at an empty camp.

They arrive at the boat, and Rambo is disgusted that it's manned by dodgy-looking pirates, and even more disgusted when the captain later shows him his Russian rocket launcher. Say what you will about John Rambo, but if he's going to blow people up, he'd rather do it with American rockets.

The boat putters down the river, giving Rambo and Co a chance to exchange small talk and take in the beautiful sights. She asks for his life story, and he tells her that after he left the army, he got home to find another war going on: a war against the soldiers returning from battle, the kind of war you don't win – like male pattern baldness. Co tells Rambo how she took her father's place in the intelligence agency after he was killed – aptly demonstrating that it's not what you know but who you know – and that she's sick of killing. She sagely observes that there's too much death. Co just wants to live, and go to America to live the quiet life (has she seen America?), maybe even go to Disneyland and do the log flumes. Rambo says he wants to win, to survive, and that to survive a war, you have to become war. He mentions that he was picked for this mission because he's expendable, explaining that it's like if you're invited to a party and you don't show up, it doesn't matter, which sounds less like 'expendable' and more like being Matt Hancock. He also likes her necklace, which she says brings her good luck, so in terms of portents, she's really pushing her luck.

They arrive ashore and carefully traverse their way through the jungle foliage as darkness falls. The camp appears empty, just as Co predicted, but as they move closer, they notice guards in towers and in huts, so Rambo starts to build his bow and arrows. Co asks about his order to only take pictures, but Rambo, much like a chef on a fag break, is no longer interested in orders. He creeps off into the undergrowth to get a closer look at what exactly is going on in this camp. After skulking around under the floors and behind rocks, dodging guards, he comes upon a bamboo cage, and is shocked to find it full of shivering and broken-looking POWs, one of whom has a big spider on him. Others have rats casually wandering around their person – these horrors of war making for sobering imagery. Rambo makes his way further into the camp. He finds another POW on a crucifix, so he decides to free him, kill a few guards with silent arrows and knives, and walk him slowly into the jungle, reassuring him that he'll return for the others.

As day breaks, the dead bodies littering the camp are discovered, and the alarm is raised, with soldiers being despatched into the jungle to find the people responsible. Co, Rambo and the POW, meanwhile, have left the area, but have to take a break so that the emaciated POW can rest and get his breath back. He tells them it's a good thing they arrived when they did; the prisoners are moved around camps a lot to harvest crops, and his captors only put him the right way up yesterday. He then asks what year it is, and looks suitably aghast on finding out it's 1985, as he had a book due back at the library in 1973 and the late fees are astronomical. However, before he can linger too long on the lost years, Rambo gets them moving again. But they have company. The camp guards have caught up with them, and they radio ahead as they see the boat pull away with our heroes.

On the boat you can cut the tension with a very small knife, as it immediately becomes clear that these no-good pirates have sold our heroes down the river. A patrol boat approaches, and Rambo realises that a very special form of diplomacy may be the best course of action, so he murders all the pirates on board and tells Co and the POW to jump into the river. As they swim to safety, Rambo dives to the deck floor as the boat is reduced to splinters by gunfire. It's not looking good for him, but then he remembers that there's a massive Russian rocket launcher onboard. He jumps to his feet and blows the tailing boat to smithereens before joining his companions onshore. As the three soaked freedom fighters unite and their enemies' charred corpses sink to the riverbed, there's an air of *joie de vivre*. Rambo tells Co to leave. He's going on ahead with the POW to make the rendezvous with the chopper, oblivious to the watching prison guards headed his way. Co tells him he's not expendable, unaware that he would later make three films proving that he very much is.

Rambo and the POW scuttle through a paddy field as mortar fire rains down on them, and it's very much a race for survival. But hope is at hand, as Trautman, Ericson and his men arrive in the helicopter and even up the odds with machine gunfire. As

Rambo struggles up the hill with his bedraggled prisoner, like a parent dragging a toddler through an airport on the way back from holiday, word gets back to Murdock that not only is Rambo alive, he has a POW with him. He then jumps on the radio to tell his men to abort the mission immediately, causing Trautman to protest angrily. They're only a few feet away from a rescue, but one of Murdock's men points a gun at him and tells him to sit down. The helicopter banks away and heads off into the distance, with Trautman looking on mournfully and Rambo and his new friend staring in horror, laced with a dose of 'I knew this would happen'. Within seconds, the two men are surrounded, and Rambo drops his weapon, knowing the game is up.

Trautman bursts into Murdock's office to give the stinking bureaucrat a piece of his mind. This was never about a rescue; it was to take photographs of an empty camp to satisfy Congress that there was nothing there; and if the pictures had shown otherwise, they could have been buried. But now, with Rambo finding proof of life, and even rescuing one, it scuppered his plans. Murdock admits as much, saying he won't risk another war for a few forgotten ghosts, to which Trautman retorts that these aren't ghosts, they are men – and that ghosts are usually found in haunted houses or Demi Moore's apartment. Murdock tells him he'll forget this conversation ever happened, but Trautman is raging now; he calls Murdock a bastard and warns him that he's made an even bigger mistake: he's pissed off John Rambo.

Back at the camp, there's a bitter sense of familiarity for Rambo. He's once again a prisoner, and this is not the kind of camp you want to be stuck in. This is no Maplin's. There's no Ted Bovis or Gladys Pugh here, no yellow coats, and certainly no knobbly-knees contest. He's up to his nipples in horrible mud, covered in leeches, and tied to a big stick, so it's more like a Premier Inn. And he must watch helplessly as the POWs suffer in their bamboo cages, powerless to give them the freedom they so wholly deserve. And as if things weren't bad enough, the villainous Lieutenant-Colonel Podovsky (Steven Berkoff) descends from a Russian chopper and demands an inspection of Rambo. He removes a few leeches with Rambo's big knife as he introduces himself in an accent that veers wildly from Russian to German and back, and tells him that he will soon find out who he is.

In Podovsky's hut there's a more laid-back atmosphere, more of a velvet-glove vibe. He sits Rambo down and tells the Vietnamese guard to leave. He monologues away about how they are both comrades – warriors of battle – and have more in common than Rambo thinks. He tells him that, as nice as it is to meet him, he will regrettably need to interrogate him. He kicks off by asking his name, which Rambo refuses to provide. He then tries to get a rise out of him by saying that Rambo's capture is embarrassing (though not as embarrassing as when he fell out the plane) and that he will need him to radio his HQ and tell them he's been captured trying to free war criminals, and that no one should try to repeat his mission in the future. Rambo refuses. So, torture it is.

Later that night, Co arrives on a moped disguised as a humble sex worker, which gains her entry to the camp without any questions. Rambo, meanwhile, is strapped to a rusty, old, upright bed frame, electrocuted slowly, and told there's no shame in screaming. As if . . . Realising he won't talk, Podovsky decides to turn the screw by reading out an intercepted radio communication between Murdock and the helicopter pilot with the order to abort the mission. Thus, Rambo finds out he was abandoned and expendable. Why bother protecting these people? asks Podovsky. Rambo stands firm, so it's time to increase the voltage. But he will not make that radio call, so a POW is brought in, and Rambo has to watch as they direct a hot knife to his eyeball. Rambo appears to cave in, fumbling at the radio switches until he locates the frequency, and then begins his message to base. Back at Murdock's operation centre, they read the message and ask for his position. Podovsky tells him again that if he doesn't reply, the POW will die. Rambo grasps the mic firmly in his manly hands and brings it to his face. 'Murdock . . . I'm coming to get you,' he growls, before slapping everyone in the room, pushing his torturer onto the bed frame and turning it up to eleven, and allowing Co to fire her machine gun into the hut. He grabs some explosive things and vaults through the window before Podovsky knows what has happened.

Spotlights fire into action, helicopters boot up their engines, and Podovsky points at men, ordering them to give chase. Rambo and Co race into the jungle, splashing through rivers and shooting everything that moves as they make their escape.

The following morning, Co tends to our hero's wounds with a piece of her dress as they take a breather, knowing that the coast is clear for now. He tells her he will never forget what she did to save him, and thanks her by snogging her to swelling music. Having found eternal bliss in the arms of John Rambo, she asks him to take her to America, so she can live forever in happiness and peace, and go to Universal and see the *Jaws* shark. He's very much into the idea, and as he basks in the warm glow of her smile, they decide to keep moving. However, as soon as they stand up, Co is machine-gunned to death by the camp commandant and his men, falling into the river as Rambo returns fire and murders most of them in retaliation. As he cradles her bullet-riddled body, he tells her he will never forget her. He lets out a tear as she slips away into the afterlife, knowing full well that she will never see a proper Superbowl game. Suitably recovered, and after burying Co in a pile of mud, Rambo redresses his outfit, using a strip of Co's dress as his new headband and her 'lucky' necklace. If it's a war they want, it's a war they'll get. Again.

Podovsky's men and the camp guards patrol the undergrowth, searching for their quarry, unaware that he is doing the same to them. He pops out of the jungle to despatch them silently, one by one, utilising the surroundings and his silent methods of death. After killing most of them with consummate ease, Rambo races out of the green blanket of death that is the jungle and back towards the camp. More soldiers are murdered with ingenious traps and multiple explosive arrows before he comes face to face with the camp commandant at a waterfall. As the commandant draws his pistol and begins firing directly at him, Rambo draws an arrow from his back and slowly places it in the bow. The bullets are pinging around him like balls in a pinball machine, but not one hits him. It just isn't the commandant's day. Rambo releases the arrow and the commandant explodes in a fiery puff of clothes and blood. That's for murdering the only woman who ever liked me, and ever will, because I am really weird.

Rambo cannot rest on his laurels, though. A Russian helicopter appears overhead, dangling a large bomb from its belly. He races away from the water as fast as he can, and as the bomb drops into the water, he jumps over the edge, just as the fire licks the surface for miles around. Happy that Rambo is dead, they stop shooting and peer out into the depths in the hope that a body pops up to the surface. They get their wish, but not in a good way. Rambo leaps from the surface like a fucked-off salmon and pulls the gunner into the water. A wrestle with Podovsky's giant henchman commences as the chopper continues through the sky, but Rambo sends him flying out the open door and takes control of the helicopter, with all the urgency of a man who wants to drive to Durham during a global pandemic to test his eyesight.

Back at the camp, he makes good use of the onboard explosives and guns to take out many guards, screaming as he does so, as if he's walking on Lego. Once landed, he takes a machine gun with him and proceeds to kill everything in his path before liberating the POWs. With everyone safely on board and en route to freedom, they're about to break out the Baby Ruths and hotdogs when a cackling Podovsky comes swinging over the horizon in a giant Russian gunship and gives chase.

Eventually, Rambo's chopper takes a critical hit and has to crash-land in a river. Podovsky licks his lips as he hovers overhead and readies his finger over the rocket-ignition button. Rambo is out cold in the driver's seat, and it's not looking good for our hero and his newly rescued brethren; however, there's life in the old warrior yet. He leans out the broken window of his downed vehicle and fires a rocket launcher right into Podovsky, taking him down in a giant inferno of death.

Rambo slumps in his seat in relief, before firing up his chopper, which it turns out can still fly, and radioing to base that he's bringing the POWs back home and will need help with an emergency landing. Everyone back at HQ bursts into rapturous applause, everyone that is except for Murdock and his men, who must know a serious ass-whupping is coming their way.

After the smoking, broken chopper lands at the base in Thailand and the ground crew race to retrieve the wounded men, Rambo jumps out and grabs his trusty giant machine gun, with ferocity. Trautman and Ericson meet him outside the hangar, and as Ericson congratulates him for making it back, Rambo knees him in the balls and knocks him out. Trautman, entirely used to this behaviour, watches Rambo stomp into the hangar and fire a lot of bullets into the wall of expensive, beeping equipment for a solid hour while screaming like he's just read the script for *Last Blood*. After running out of ammo, he dumps the gun and races into Murdock's office. There, he finds the conniving worm shitting his pants and trying to explain that he was just another victim of red tape, like him, y'know, and aren't we all at the end of the day? Rambo demonstrates his disagreement by pulling out his giant knife and pinning Murdock to his own desk. 'Mission . . . accomplished,' he murmurs. He then tells Murdock to save the rest of the POWs, or he'll come find him.

As Rambo walks away from the smouldering wreckage, watching the POWs being whisked away to hospital, Trautman tells him that he'll probably get another medal of honour and, despite everything that happened, he shouldn't hate his country. Rambo passionately tells him all he wants is for his country to love its soldiers as much as they love their country (history suggests this is unlikely), and that he is busting for a wee as he hasn't had one in 36 hours. He tells Trautman he's going to live day by day, and maybe he'll make a few more of these movies, and they'll all be sort of the same film over and over again, reminding us all that war is hell, but not nearly as hellish as enduring the same film over and over again, with diminishing levels of quality and craftsmanship.

four

INVASION U.S.A.

1985

NO ONE THOUGHT IT COULD EVER HAPPEN . . .
AMERICA WASN'T READY . . .
BUT HE WAS.

AS THE CANNON LOGO leaves the screen, like a killer leaving a calling card at a gruesome murder, we know we're in for a treat, because if there's one thing that movie studio gave us that we should forever be thankful for, it's putting a pair of Uzis in Chuck Norris's hands.

A boat slips silently across the open waters of the Florida Straits. Onboard are many Cuban refugees, hoping for a better life in America, where they can meet Mickey Mouse, eat a banoffee pie, and maybe even have a nice, honest cup of joe. Suddenly, there is hope in sight when a Coast Guard vessel arrives to pick them up, but this isn't any Coast Guard boat; it's one captained by perennial bad guy Richard Lynch – a man who turned a mad, drug-fuelled rampage (during which he set himself on fire) into a profession, using his incredibly distinct look to carve out a career as a terrifying villain. Here, he's Mikhail Rostov, a Russian terrorist, and he's smiling at the sad, sunburnt people, welcoming them to America, causing the desperate passengers to cry out in joy at the thought of the new life that awaits them. However, their joy is short-lived. Rostov has them all shot, then steals the vast amount of cocaine that was hidden below deck – so much for the American dream.

Meet Matt Hunter (Chuck Norris), a man so comfortable in his own skin and muscle that he'll happily skate along the Everglades on an airboat with his shirt wide open and care not one jot that he looks like an arsehole, because he's 300% MAN, which means he can have an off day and still be more man than you'll ever be. He goes about his day, pulling doughnuts around the wetlands, before eventually helping his buddy rope an alligator and put it in a box. Imagine you doing that? Dream on.

Rostov brings his drugs to Mickey (Billy Drago), a drug guy who may look like a scumbag living in a tiny office, but would a scumbag really have three telephones in different colours on his desk? Mickey is a man with solid connections, and after he checks the coke and likes what he sees, he makes a call to give the green light to exchange it all for an arsenal of weapons. Rostov is pleased with the development, and celebrates by shooting Mickey in the penis three times, murdering his bodyguards, and throwing his mistress out of a window. That may be how you celebrate things in Russia, but what's wrong with a cake or something?

A rowing boat creeps along in the darkness, eventually settling right outside Hunter's waterside house. The suited occupant strides out of the vessel, not at all dressed for the job he's doing, and gingerly steps inside the silent home. To his left is an armadillo on a rug, and to his right is Hunter, all ten feet of him, who tells him immediately he isn't interested. It would seem that Hunter used to be in the CIA, and they want him back, as they've heard that his old enemy Rostov is back in the country. This can only mean something very bad is brewing, but Hunter doesn't even stop to think. He blithely tells his guest that Rostov is the CIA's problem now, and mentions that he wasn't allowed to kill him in the past, bloody do-gooders.

After a nightmare in which he recalls how Hunter stopped him assassinating a diplomat, Rostov wakes from his sleep and demands that Nikko, his right-hand man, kills Hunter before they begin 'their mission'. Hunter is the only man who can stop them, so he needs him eliminated as soon as possible. Nikko dismisses him as just one man, not a real threat, but Rostov corrects him, and proceeds to reel off all the Chuck Norris memes in order. Rostov is certainly a man who knows no fear, but he has felt it every time he looked into the eyes of Matt Hunter: the man, the myth, the American Noel Edmonds franchise.

The next morning, as Hunter chainsaws his way through a giant log (and he's not even wearing goggles), all seems well. The sun is shining, the birds are chirping, and his petrol-driven blade is in fine fettle. Nothing could spoil the vibes of this lovely day. Once the log is chopped, he's looking forward to a nice cup of coffee, a read of the funny pages, and maybe a quick wrestle of the bald champ. However, fate has other ideas. Rostov and his men begin coursing along the waterways of the Everglades in their airboats, armed to the teeth, and looking for Hunter's blood. As our man gathers his logs and heads inside, his pal John Eagle arrives for a chat and a catch-up. He spots the heavily armed militia parked outside, waiting to blow Hunter's house to pieces, so he warns his pal, but it's too late. Eagle is shot dead, and Hunter's home is blown to smithereens. After the debris settles, Rostov and his crew turn and go back to wherever they came from, and Matt emerges from the broken shell of his former house/shed. He pulls his friend's body from the water. They made a big mistake today, my friends; they messed with the wrong man. Luckily, his airboat is entirely unharmed, and after torching what's left of his waterside pile, he speeds off into the horizon, with revenge on his mind.

Rostov and Nikko take their seats at the waterside cafe and toast their victory with an American hotdog – symbol of the free West – but Rostov speaks of America through bitter, gritted teeth. He looks around at the simple folk of Florida and mocks their soft, spineless decadence and arrogance. He curses their freedom and relishes the idea of a forthcoming invasion. Here is a man who has bought himself the Haynes Manual on Evil Russians, and he's meticulously ticking engine parts off as he paints in the broadest of strokes and twirls the thickest of moustaches.

A loving couple emerge from the night sea and engage in some light petting on a towel by their portable TV. The night is calm, and the soothing wash of the tide fills the air. Nikko emerges from the darkness to watch them, but he's not a pervert – well, not on this occasion. He's there with one purpose in mind, so he murders them both, briefly stopping to watch their TV before happily witnessing his invasion force slowly glide out of the sea and storm the beach in heavy numbers. A fleet of trucks await them, and as they board the vehicles, Rostov watches with a smile on his face. He proclaims that in just 18 hours, America will be a different place – or very similar, depending on your point of view. It's Christmas time in suburbia, and as the simple people go about their simple lives of decking the halls, playing ball, necking in cars, and decorating their trees, Rostov and his men move into place. Rather than doing what any normal man would do – write a gritty play or musical about class war and the vast chip on his shoulder – Rostov chooses to fire a bazooka indiscriminately into the peaceful neighbourhood, blowing up every house that takes his fancy, leaving nothing behind but carnage and dead bodies as his truck peels away into the night. The random attacks carry on throughout the night in Miami, with Rostov targeting ethnic neighbourhoods to stir up internal strife.

One of Rostov's men ducks into a seedy bar for a little 'me time' with a lady friend. He's nursing an injured hand – the result of trying to destroy Hunter's home. As he readies himself for a rejuvenating passion session, a knife plunges through his damaged hand, and Matt Hunter is holding the handle. He wants information on Rostov, but this guy says he doesn't know where he is, he keeps moving, and he's too late anyway, but before he can explain why, a couple of thugs burst in, giving Hunter the opportunity to try out a line he's probably been working on for years: 'I'm gonna hit you with so many rights, you're gonna beg for a left.' It's a line that may work with your average scumbag, but it doesn't really wash with these brutes, so Hunter goes for Plan B. He kicks one of them out the room, then pulls a grenade, causing those who can to run for the exit. He takes out the pin and wanders over to his stricken friend, placing it tightly in his uninjured hand, and asks him to pass on a message to Rostov: 'It's time to die.'

It's a busy time at the shopping mall. The dulcet tones of festive cheer echo through the packed corridors of pedestrians sauntering along, bags in hands, looking for last-minute gifts, and soaking in the Yuletide cheer. However, one shopper has an ulterior motive. His bag was given to him by Nikko, and you can guarantee it's not a breadmaker. He places the bag down in the middle of a packed department store and makes his way back out into the crowd, not counting on a nice man picking it up and chasing after him to tell him he left it behind. Sadly, the only thanks he gets is to be gunned down by two mad bastards with heavy artillery, who then detonate the explosive and begin shooting up the mall. With the shoppers seemingly sitting ducks, and sure to be riddled with bullets and shrapnel, who will save them now? Well, as fate would have it, Matt Hunter will, by driving his truck through the doors of the mall and killing most of the bad guys with his patented twin-Uzi technique. The would-be bomber gets away in a truck, Hunter pursues him, and it culminates in an explosive finale that Jeremy Clarkson would watch, alone, with his trousers round his ankles. The police investigate the scene and are at a loss to work out just what is going on. The truck that caused most of the damage was impounded but then stolen back, there's mass hysteria and chaos on the streets, officers are phoning in sick to protect their families, and because so many citizens are arming themselves for protection, the National Guard has been deployed to protect the people and order them all to stay in their homes – presumably so Rostov can blow them up more easily.

As helicopters circle in the sky barking orders, families have gathered in a church, in search of refuge and the warm glow of shared faith. As they sing hymns and find solace, Rostov and his men plant an elaborate suitcase bomb outside, which, if you don't mind me saying, seems a bit small-time when we're thinking in terms of a full-blown invasion. Shouldn't you be storming the White House, rather than blowing up normal people's houses and churches? News reaches him via Nikko that his bomber is dead and Hunter is alive and well, so he and Nikko race to their car and leave this pointless church bombing in the hands of their goons. They set the charge, wind the fuse, and push the button. However, nothing happens, and as they inspect the device, Hunter appears on the rooftop behind them, throwing the suitcase down among them and blowing them all to pieces.

The next day, Nikko leads a small team of men, all in disguise as National Guards, to a small shop, where a small group of people are protesting the fact that the shopkeeper has no meat and will have to hand out rationed food. I mean, really, Nikko? Haven't you got better targets in mind than mom-and-pop stores with supply issues? It's not so much an invasion at this point, but more of an elaborate episode of *Beadle's About*. Just as the shoppers are reaching fever pitch when they find out they can't have hotdogs, Nikko and his men prepare to slaughter them all. But they forgot about one thing: Matt Hunter. He arrives at high speed in his death mobile and murders them all, before then going on to rescue a school bus full of kids from being blown up. In a plan more stupid than the last in the history of invasion planning, Rostov's team of bungling twats opt to drive up to the moving school bus and stick their bomb to the side. Hunter, being the smart man of action that he is, simply grabs the bomb from the side of the bus, catches up with the bad guys, and chucks it back into their car, blowing them up immediately.

However, even perfect men have limits, and as Hunter arrives at the ruins of a destroyed carnival, he examines the wreckage and realises, all too late, that he isn't a god after all. His CIA buddy tries to make him feel better by congratulating him on taking out Nikko, but Hunter is hard on himself. He knows he'll have to change his tactics, as for every terrorist he stops, hundreds more succeed. To be honest, any kind of plan would be welcome right now, as just turning up as they're about to carry out an attack seems a bit risky to me. He hands his CIA buddy a piece of paper and tells him what he needs to do, reminding him what's at stake. However, before anything can be looked at, the FBI storm Hunter's seedy hotel room and take him into custody for vigilantism, sternly reminding him that no one is above the law.

Hunter is open-shirted and shackled as he's brought into the operations HQ to be questioned by the media. He stops, looks coldly down the lens, and tells a watching Rostov that Nikko was easy and now it's his time to die. This special report doesn't go down too well with the Russian, and after he smashes up the TV, proving once and for all he's as easy to rattle as Kevin Keegan after 90 minutes of sheer hell, he rants that it's time to go and finish this once and for all. They're going to kill Hunter – properly this time. After securing a fleet of armoured trucks and boarding a helicopter, they all head for Atlanta to strike the final blow, although, knowing this lot, it probably means they'll be blowing up a small newsagent.

Chaos erupts in Atlanta, with Rostov's men slamming through the barricades and firing into the armed forces. They storm the operations building and, corridor by corridor, take charge of the building, shooting aimlessly into rooms as Rostov nods in approval. The building is completely empty, and Rostov realises, maybe a bit too late, that it's a trap: this must be Hunter's secret plan. When they turn to leave, they're met with a huge military ambush outside. Rostov heads up to the roof to meet his chopper, only to find that Hunter has blown it up and is waiting for him with his twin-Uzi response. He runs, and now it's Hunter's turn to stalk the building and kill every bad guy who crosses his path.

After murdering about thirty men, he eventually comes face to face with Rostov, and even though he is outgunned, he still manages to kick him in the face enough times for him to get the next one free. When Rostov stands up from his pummelling,

Hunter has vanished, so he grabs a bazooka and goes looking for him. With the invasion totally quelled outside, he knows he's fighting a losing battle, and as Hunter appears behind him, with his own bazooka, he must realise that the game is up. 'It's time,' Hunter says, before blowing Rostov into tiny pieces. Hunter is a man who will stick by his catchphrase, and if he tells you it's time to die, you know you're on a meter. As Rostov's burning limbs float out of the shattered window and the invasion forces below raise their hands in surrender, the USA can relax once more, knowing full well that if anything like this happens again, Matt Hunter will form a plan, at some point down the line, and it will work, eventually. Thank you, Matt. The world salutes you – now treat yourself to a new airboat.

FIVE

COMMANDO

1985

SOMEWHERE, SOMEHOW,
SOMEONE'S GOING TO PAY

WE BEGIN WITH AN act of terror that will send a shiver down the spine of any community-minded human being in possession of even the vaguest sense of innate decency. A man, waking up in a cold sweat, *nearly* misses getting his bins out for the garbage men. It's Tuesday and therefore bin day, so this is a dilemma that we've all had to contend with, and something that should be taken seriously. Had the man not had the courage and strong moral fortitude to rush out with the bags and newspapers, he may well have had to deal with a bin fixture pile-up – which is something no one wants, especially not in this heat.

Sadly, though, this act of thoughtfulness is not rewarded; in fact, if anything, it's punished. Upon seeing him amble down his driveway in his jammies, newspapers tucked under his arms, the garbage men produce Uzis from the lorry and pump him full of lead. I suspect the lesson here is: Do not *ever* make the garbage men wait, punk.

Later, in a car showroom, a salesman is boasting to a smart-suited customer (Bill Duke, who was one of the killer garbage men) about how American things are better than Japanese things as they stroll around a shiny new Cadillac. The customer agrees that it's a nice car and takes a seat inside. While the salesman dribbles on about how the best seats are vinyl (apparently leather is too hot and it cracks), the customer starts up the engine and looks impressed with the roar of it. The salesman's eyes light up like bonfires as he contemplates the cash, only to panic as the customer hits reverse and then careers through the showroom window, with the salesman on his bonnet. Possibly not the death Arthur Miller had in mind when he wrote his play, but this version would make a cracking stage show.

Bennett (Vernon Wells) arrives at the dock, dressed as a wellie-booted Freddie Mercury on his way to catch crabs. He sees the salesman-killer and his accomplice, and gives them a knowing smile, as if he knows what's coming. He pulls away in his little boat, and sure enough, Duke produces a remote control, flicks a switch, and the boat explodes. It all makes you sort of wonder who will be next on his list, given that we're only four minutes in.

The music takes a sinister turn as we're presented with a white-vested man walking through a forest. However, this isn't just any man; this is a man made of mountains and gristle, bathed in sweat, and looking every inch like he's just had a fight with Treebeard and smacked the living shit out of him. He has a massive chainsaw in one hand, a log over his shoulder, and you'd be forgiven for thinking this was Bigfoot's personal trainer. But it isn't. It's John Matrix, ex-Delta Force soldier, with a name that would seem ridiculous when handed to anyone else, but on Arnold Schwarzenegger fits like a big comfy boxing glove. He wanders to his cabin, gets his axe out, and sets about chopping up wood for the fire. A shadow begins to creep up behind him – obviously thinking they will catch Matrix out – but Mummy Matrix didn't raise no fool, and he observes the shadow in the reflection of his axe blade. He turns and scoops up his mystery stalker, and all is revealed. It's his daughter Jenny (Alyssa Milano), whom he has given the playful name of 'Chenny'. The music once again takes a sinister turn, pumping out

Disney-esque warblings as we're treated to a montage of Matrix and Chenny to show how much they are devoted to each other. They feed a deer, go fishing, cavort in a swimming pool, and she pushes ice cream into his face. He teaches her some killer martial arts moves – a touching family scene that melts the heart. They eat sandwiches together, and Matrix explains that 'Boy George should be called Girl George' before giving Chenny a potted history of his childhood in East Germany – all the while pondering just what it is that Chenny has put in this bread-born abomination he's eating. Luckily for her, however, this shit conversation is disturbed by the low rumble of an army helicopter. Chenny looks anxious, but Matrix promises her that he's not going anywhere.

It's Major General Franklin Kirby, Matrix's old boss. He tells his men to secure the area and then calls out for Matrix, who appears behind him and takes his gun. 'Silent and smooth, just like always,' says Kirby, like he's congratulating himself for farting in a lift. He tells Matrix his old badass army team are all being killed – even though they have new identities. He doesn't tell Matrix about the near-miss with the bins, which is good leadership: no sense panicking the man. Kirby doesn't know who's behind it all but offers that Matrix has made enemies all over the world, so basically it could be anyone. He warns Matrix that he's in danger, as it's surely him next on the list. He tells him that he'll leave two men with him that are 'real good' while he goes to the city to 'nail those bastards'. Matrix agrees and reassures Chenny that everything will be fine, and you know what? I reckon it will be.

He watches as the helicopter takes off and putters away towards the horizon, but suddenly his face changes. Without stopping, he picks up Chenny and runs inside the house as machine gunfire rattles around the front of his cabin, instantly killing one of the soldiers sent to protect him. The other soldier makes it into the house, where Matrix reveals that he 'smelt' the bad guys coming. He tells Chenny to go to her room and runs to his shed to get his rifle. Once inside, he unlocks his arsenal with the passcode of one followed by the number three: he really needs to rethink some basic security issues.

Now armed with his trusty rifle, Matrix races back to the house to find the second soldier dead (Kirby's two best men, gone in five minutes flat), and no Chenny. A mercenary is sitting in a chair and he tells him that his daughter will be safe, as long as he plays along. With what isn't made clear. Matrix mildly disagrees with him, and to prove his point, shoots him in the head – which obviously explains how he was the undefeated college debating champion for so many years. He sees vehicles driving down the hill and races to his truck, only to find that the bad guys have ripped the guts out of the engine. So, with the lemons of a dead car, he makes lemonade by pushing it down the hill and getting behind the wheel, steering recklessly through trees, bushes, hedges and panicking wildlife, and facing the very real possibility that he could plough into the car containing his beloved Chenny. His plan fails. He crashes into a ditch, and his car explodes, for no discernible reason other than this was the decade where everything exploded when it stopped. People could perform a perfect parallel parking manoeuvre, only to then be faced with the very real prospect of their vehicle exploding. After a brief scuffle with some random bad guys, Matrix is held down, and a face emerges. It's Bennett – no, not Lennie, host of *Lucky Ladders*, or Tony, legendary crooner and decent painter – but Vernon Wells's Bennett, who obviously staged his boat explosion earlier to fool Kirby and his 'friends in the city'. How best to describe Bennett? Well, he's the kind of man who wears a grey chainmail vest that doesn't fit too well (Wells was a last-minute replacement for the initial casting choice of Wings Hauser), a chunky padlock necklace and a thick moustache, and constantly mentions wanting to have someone's ass while simultaneously demanding to be taken seriously. Wells's performance is a joy, and so scenery-chewing that he can't open his mouth without bits of the set falling out. He tells Matrix that ever since he had him 'thrown out of his unit' (oo-er), he's wanted to pay him back via the method of revenge, and today is payday. He fires a tranquilliser dart into Matrix's guts and watches as he passes out.

41

When Matrix awakes, he's inside a shed, with four men staring down at him like they've just played a prank and had big fake boobs stuck on him for LOLZ. He recognises the leader immediately: it's Arius (Dan Hedaya), a former dictator from the South American country of Val Verde (a fictional place screenwriter Steven E. de Souza likes a lot; keen observers will note that it also turns up in *Die Hard 2*). He wants Matrix to go there and kill the President, so that Arius can lead a military coup and take over. Matrix rightly asks why he doesn't get Bennett to do it, as he'd probably 'get off' on it – which, judging by the way Bennett dresses, is an astute observation. However, Arius is insistent that Matrix must do it (apparently the President trusts him because he helped out during a revolution). Matrix thinks for a second and then gives his carefully considered riposte, which is 'fuck you'. To make sure Matrix plays ball, Arius wheels out Chenny and tells him if he doesn't do it, he'll mail his daughter to him in little pieces.

Loving father that he is, Matrix knows he has no choice. He is driven to the airport by Bennett, who leaves him in the capable hands of Sully (the diminutive David Patrick Kelly – quirky star of *Warriors* and *Twin Peaks*) and Henriques, who for some reason known only to himself has decided to dress like a Hawaii-based Victorian explorer-cum-pimp. Just before Matrix heads off for the plane, he compliments Sully on his sense of humour and then informs him he will kill him last – probably because he is the smallest, so he'll be sort of like an After Eight mint after a giant meal. Sully watches as Matrix and Henriques board the plane, and then wanders off to his tiny car. As they take their seats on the plane, Matrix asks for a blanket and a pillow, murders Henriques by snapping his neck, and then dresses him like an ornate sleeping pimp. One down. He then checks how long the flight is (exactly eleven hours), sets the timer on his watch, rips his way out of the cargo hold, and jumps out of the plane via the retracting wheels as it takes off, landing safely in a swamp.

Flight attendant Cindy (a very fun Rae Dawn Chong) is on a public phone speaking to a friend when Sully catches her eye and decides that now is as good a time as any to show her his moves, which are best described as 'predatory'. Cindy tells him to leave her alone, but he doesn't take the hint and follows her to a car park. She rejects him and he calls her a whore and walks off. Not sure that technique will ever work, even in his little Spandau Ballet-style suit and red-framed glasses. After bidding goodbye to her tiny menace, Cindy is about to get on with her day when Matrix emerges from the shadows, rips the passenger seat from her cute little Sunbeam Alpine, and tells her to follow Sully. He promises he won't kill her, but strangely enough, despite her claim to be a 7th Dan at karate, she still doesn't look convinced by this hulk who's just irrevocably damaged her car.

Sully drives to the Galleria shopping mall to look for more women to harass, with Cindy and Matrix in pursuit. Matrix finally tells Cindy what is going on and asks her if she'll use her womanly ways to lure Sully out into the open, so he can presumably beat some information out of him.

However, things go awry when Cindy alerts the security guards. They become suspicious at the sight of a sweating mountain of a man hanging around on his own, so they naturally ask him what he's up to – a problem he solves by beating them all up. Sadly, the commotion is witnessed by Sully, and he races away to his car in order to alert his bosses. Matrix and Cindy tear after him, and a car chase culminates in Sully rolling his Porsche. Matrix picks him up like an errant toddler and hangs him over the side of a cliff while enquiring about Chenny's whereabouts. Sully says that Cooke knows where she is, and he's off to meet him if he wants to know where; however, Matrix is one step ahead as he retrieves a motel-room key from his pocket. He then asks Sully if he remembers that he said he would kill him last, which thankfully he does, with the tragic kicker being that he lied. Matrix then drops Sully over the cliff to his death, presumably to be found years later, a tiny doll skeleton.

Cindy and Matrix arrive at the seedy Sunspot motel, and Cindy decides that she wants to help, after he gives her the full story, emotionally adding that 'all that matters is Chenny'. Sold on his enthusiasm and adorable mauling of language, she follows him to keep Sully's appointment with Cooke.

A short time later, Cooke arrives to meet Sully, and Cindy, after Matrix makes her rumpled enough for anyone to believe that Sully has had his wicked way with her (perhaps some crayon lines on her ankles would be more believable?), lets him in the room. It's a trap, as Matrix steps out from behind the door and thumps him. Cooke warns him that he should be scared, as he's a Green Beret, but Matrix scoffs at this, telling him that he eats Green Berets for breakfast, as well as seventy-five Shredded Wheat. As the fight progresses, we're reminded that it's the mid-eighties when they spill into a neighbouring room and disturb a couple (one of whom looks like that guy in Buck's Fizz) having it off, and some boobs are flashed for purely artistic reasons. Matrix throws Cooke onto a wooden spike and is about to ask for further information on his beloved Chenny, but it's clear that the man is as dead as disco. Cindy and Matrix flee the scene, presumably leaving the couple next door to quietly resume sex while knowing a corpse is lying outside.

In Cooke's car they find a receipt for aeroplane fuel. Luckily for Matrix, Cindy is training to be a pilot, so knows all about planes and fuel and stuff, and off they go to check out the warehouse on the paperwork. After some complicated map reading and fuel consumption calculations, they work out where Chenny is being hidden – a remote island off the coast – but before finding a plane to save her, Matrix decides it's time to go 'shopping' – by which he means breaking into a gun superstore, stocking up on every weapon known to mankind (plus a pair of flippers), and loading it into the car like the last booze cruisers out of Calais before Brexit. However, before Matrix can ride off into the night like Rambo's big brother who's just won the NRA *Supermarket Sweep*, the police arrive in response to the alarm and arrest him, loading him into an extra-big van. Luckily for Matrix, he has back-up. Cindy, who was out of sight when he was arrested, is following on behind and slows up beside the police van at a red light. The officers look over at her hornily, before realising that she has a bazooka (and that is not a euphemism), which she utilises to fire a giant missile at them (after 'reading the instructions'). Inexplicably, Matrix isn't disintegrated in the blast, and he emerges from the smoke like a hibernating Grizzly on twenty a day, to join her in the car and drive away to properly begin his mission of death and destruction.

Meanwhile on Chenny Island, Arius and Bennett check their watches and chew some more scenery – with Bennett looking more and more like he's eaten a row of pink tents. Matrix has two hours until the plane lands in Val Verde, and they're sure he'll play along, if he ever wants his kid back. Talking of which, Chenny has made like Andy Dufresne and started to chisel her way out of the locked room she's in, using a broken door handle.

Cindy is stressed. She's never flown the kind of seaplane they have found in the harbour: it's 'a canoe with wings', older than she is, and has no LED readouts. She is also stressed because Matrix is hanging out of the door firing a machine gun at a jeepful of very angry right-wing South Americans. She can't get the propellers to start and is just about to look for the Haynes Manual, when Matrix appears to punch the plane into starting, like it's an old shit television. Within moments they take off, and Matrix congratulates her on her flying skills. But they're flying over a Heavily Restricted Area and are informed over the radio that they'll be shot down if they proceed. No problem – Cindy's going to 'fly nearer the waves' to 'camouflage them'. And it actually works.

'Slitting a little girl's throat is like cutting warm butter,' a guard tells Bennett, which is the gross level of water-cooler chat you can expect at Arius's villa. Bennett is unimpressed with this banter and tells the guard to put his knife away, before popping over to taunt Arius about how pathetic his guards are, adding that if Matrix was there, he'd laugh too. Would he, though? I'm not too sure that Matrix would be tickled by talk about slicing up his little Chenny. Arius points out that all his men are patriots, but this holds no water with Bennett, who tells him that his soldiers are rubbish, and that he and Matrix could kill them all in 'the blink of an eye' – which would mean killing over 70 men in 100 milliseconds – and it's at this point that Arius should ask Bennett just what the fuck is he's going on about. However, Bennett has chilling words for Arius. He tells him that when Matrix finishes the job, he'll be back for his daughter, and whether she's alive or dead, he'll still want to kill him. Arius tells him he's scared, and Bennett rightly confirms that he is, because he's 'smart', but he has an edge: he has Matrix's daughter.

Cindy lands the plane near the beach, and Matrix pops himself into a minuscule pair of Speedos before loading a dinghy, and possibly sinking it, with his massive arsenal. He tells Cindy to contact Major Kirby and tell him that he's about to destroy an entire generation of humans, so they should send a digger and a lot of cleaning products. He tells her not to break radio silence until he's spotted at the villa and that 'all fucking hell is about to break loose'.

Over in Val Verde the plane has landed, and Henriques, snuggled under his cosy blanket and straw hat, is found to be very dead, and Matrix is found to be very missing, but we know where he is. He's on the beach tooling up with endless weaponry, tying grenades to himself, and painting needless black lines all over his body, like some sort of militant zebra hunting lions. He skulks up the beach and watches the villa through binoculars; it's heavily guarded, but to John Matrix, they're all just notches on his ginormous bed post.

Arius gets the call from his henchmen at the airport, and it's not the one he wanted: Matrix is not on the plane, and Henriques has lost the use of oxygen. However, before he can begin to hurriedly flick through the 'M' section in the *Yellow Pages* for another mercenary with a daughter, everything begins to explode outside. Matrix has started to despatch all of Arius's heavily moustachioed men with wild abandon, like a pissed Elmer Fudd during rabbit season. Some are shot, some are exploded (and through the shock of the blast turn into dummies nailed to posts), and some are scalped with circular saw blades (a moment cut from the original UK release). Bennett is given the order to kill Chenny, and as he approaches her room, he can hear the gunfire and explosions, which he seems to enjoy, even stopping to comment that it's good to have John back. If you missed him, it might be an idea next time, Mr Bennett, to just chew the fat over a half-shandy with him rather than abduct his daughter. And another plan has gone south for Bennett, as when he enters the room, he finds that Chenny has done a runner. As he races to the gap in the door, he sees her running down some stairs across the courtyard, so he gives chase.

Arius is not having a nice time. His beautiful villa is on fire, most of his men are dead, his garden has been shot to shit, all his flowers have been decapitated, and his decor is full of bullet holes. He's just about to console himself with the fact that he can at least shoot Matrix, when that small pleasure is taken away from him too. Matrix performs a forward roll through a glass door and pumps him full of lead. RIP Arius, you were one of the best South American stereotypical baddies there ever was. As Matrix watches him plummet over the balcony and into a garden that even the *Ground Force* team would struggle to salvage, he hears Chenny calling for him. He races downstairs.

In the dark and dingy steam-room basement, Chenny is grabbed by Bennett. He puts a knife to her neck and shoots Matrix in the arm, wounding him and causing him to drop his shotgun. He promises that if Matrix puts his head out, he'll shoot him and make it quick, just for old times' sake, a touching gesture that will surely have him up for a Nobel Peace Prize. But Matrix has a better idea: how about they just fight to the death? He reminds Bennett that he only has one arm, and that Bennett would probably prefer to stab him to death, and this is an idea that obviously appeals to him, as he lunges at Matrix waving a knife like a malfunctioning Magimix.

And so, the fight begins: two large men wrestling in the dark with knives by a flaming boiler, a nightmarish scene as if painted by Hieronymus Bosch on crystal meth. Bennett tells Matrix he feels good, but his joy is short-lived as Matrix lands 367 punches on him in four rapidly edited seconds. Knowing he's beaten, Bennett again reaches for the gun, telling Matrix he's not going to shoot him between the eyes, but between the balls – a humblebrag if ever I heard one. Matrix, though, has heard just about enough of this twaddle, so he wrenches a giant pipe from the wall and throws it like a javelin through Bennett's chest, adding the immortal words: 'Let off some steam, Bennett.' He must have been SO pleased with that one-liner. As Bennett gasps his dying breath, Chenny and her dad are reunited, and she seems perfectly fine after witnessing a horrifically violent fight to the death, so that's all good.

As father and daughter reach the beach, Major Kirby and his men arrive just in time to bury hundreds of dead people, which seems like a good use of US Special Forces manpower. Kirby asks Matrix if he'd be interested in starting up his unit again (not a euphemism), but he says this is the last time he'll be blowing up hundreds of men, and there's no chance he will do anything like this ever again, and Kirby, like us, doesn't seem too sure about that. Matrix takes Chenny to meet her new mom, Cindy, who will fly them all home. There, they can all share stories about the gargantuan amount of death they've all witnessed that day, and it will presumably end with Cindy making side-eyes at Chenny that suggest she is still terrified. And with good reason, frankly.

SIX

1985

HE'S BACK IN NEW YORK BRINGING
JUSTICE TO THE STREETS . . .

THE CANNON LOGO SINGES as it clashes in the centre of the screen, seemingly rattling as the eighties synth drums beat a tempo behind it. This serves on the one hand as a sign of brand identity, and on the other as a warning about what is coming up. A bus drives up a turnpike and turns towards New York. Paul Kersey (Charles Bronson) is onboard with his usual resting livid face – a face that looks like it's been stung by bees while trying to eat their nest, simultaneously pained and angry. And he should be angry, because the funk that's tooting out is like a bad porn theme played in a ping-pong factory. It's allegedly written by Jimmy Page – and there are some of Page's moody cues from *Death Wish 2* – but there's no way he created the abomination that's playing out over these credits. Credits that list the editor as 'Arnold Crust', the alter ego of the film's director, Michael Winner, which I am guessing sounded totally hilarious after that third bottle of red.

Kersey is in town to visit his old buddy Charlie, who it turns out lives in the worst place in the world – a corner of New York that we'll call 'Little Lambeth', seeing as it was all shot in London. 'Little Lambeth' is controlled by a gang of street punks, who patrol and intimidate the locals with bicycle chains, Mohawks and their painted faces – exactly the kind of menace a man in his fifties would imagine all miscreants having. Today, these punks have decided to menace Charlie in his home. They storm in, quickly overpower him and demand money. When he resists, they beat him up, and they seem to be having a jolly old laugh as they do it. This was the eighties, and there wasn't much else to do for street punks but beat up old folk.

Kersey, getting no reply on Charlie's phone, races in a cab to get to his apartment, gun drawn – as any normal person would do when a phone isn't answered – only to find Charlie in a bloody heap on the floor. As he cradles his old friend in his arms, Charlie looks up at him and says his last words, 'Paul, take care of my things, will you?', which one can only assume is code for 'For God's sake, hide my porn stash'. That, or 'Kill every last one of those motherfucking punks, old pal'. He then dies, and Kersey really must wonder if he is the living embodiment of the *Final Destination* curse. Everywhere he goes, someone dies – we really should be sending him to war zones. After being alerted by the neighbours, the police steam in and arrest Kersey, thinking that he is the murderer.

At the precinct, the assembled team of detectives decide to interrogate him with truncheons, but before they can beat any kind of confession out of him, Chief Shriker (Ed Lauter) strolls in and asks who the 'dude' is. He's told that Kersey doesn't want to talk, so they decide to beat him up – and this is exactly what Michael Parkinson used to do in the green room before shows. The Chief tells his men to leave, then reveals that he knows exactly who Kersey is. He was with the NYPD when Kersey did his first murderous rampage ten years prior. He tells him firmly that the last thing he needs is a vigilante on his patch and asks what he was doing in the area. Kersey explains that he was visiting a friend, and he found him dead. When he requests a lawyer, the crooked

Chief tells him he can't have one and then steps on a cockroach, to underline just how much he hates any kind of punk. He suggests that he could have Kersey killed, which as a statement comes rather out of left field. When Kersey points out that that could be deemed as a violation of his constitutional rights, the Chief punches him in the face, whereupon the constitutional rights stand up and declare that they'll get their coat. Kersey fires back with a kick to the balls, whereupon the other police officers come running back in, presumably to place bets. While doubled over, holding his crown jewels, the Chief demands that Kersey be put in jail at once.

Kersey is placed with the worst of the worst, all of whom want to be top dog, or even Top Cat. One man in particular decides to lay out his credentials by showing Kersey the en-suite toilet and confessing that he tore it out, probably with his teeth. He lunges at our hero, but soon comes to regret it when Kersey rams his head through the prison bars, much to the delight of the other prisoners.

Seated amidst the rabble is Manny Fraker (Gavan O'Herlihy – son of Dan, the Old Man in Robocop), who looks a bit like a dystopian Neil Kinnock. He has the familiar shaved parting in his hair and an ominous tattoo, and we soon find out that he's the leader of the Little Lambeth street punks, and presumably did all their haircuts, too. He doesn't like the cut of Kersey's jib, and as they lock eyes, the rest of the world is left in no doubt that the fate of this broken city rests with these two angry white men.

The following morning, Kersey is in the corner, head in hands, looking every inch like he's just found out he's in this film, when the prisoners decide to make their move on him. As they all stand around kicking him as he rolls on the floor, Fraker tells him he always wins, only for Kersey to stand up and thump him, in lieu of a witty comeback. The guards come in and break it up, just as Fraker makes bail (his lawyer is played by Billy J. Mitchell, who also played Nick River's agent in *Top Secret!* and Admiral Chuck Farrel in *GoldenEye* – making him the only man, that we know of, in this film to have died in other films via a defective anal sex toy and during harsh sexual intercourse). As Fraker walks out of the cell, he tells Kersey he would have killed him if he hadn't been stopped, and, as a parting gesture, he'll kill a little old lady just for him, which in some cultures would be seen as quite a nice gesture.

As the Chief wanders through the precinct, probably looking for more cockroaches to crush, Kathryn Davis (Deborah Raffin), a hot-shot lawyer, arrives to ask why he's keeping Kersey in jail. The Chief readily admits there are no charges, but he just likes keeping him in jail, which can be seen as something of a no-no. She advises that Kersey could easily sue, because he has a strong case for right violations, but the Chief doesn't give a flying fuck about hippies and their rights, and shrugs it off as he walks away. He has plans for Kersey. Crime rates are through the roof, the police are seemingly helpless to stop the growing problem of Neo-Kinnock and his mad gang, so, he has a proposition. If Kersey wouldn't mind dusting off his vigilante hat and cleaning up the streets, he'll turn a blind eye to it. Kersey tells him he's 'through with all that', like he's talking about collecting football stickers or country dancing, but the Chief tells him he's working for him now and he'll have to start killing creeps, or he'll stay in jail for ever. Kersey reluctantly agrees, and is set free to return to Little Lambeth.

Fraker returns home to his gang hideout under cover of night, clearly wanting to surprise the Neo-Kinnocks. He finds fellow punk Hector throwing his weight around, giving orders to his men, and he doesn't really like what he sees. They hold Hector still while Fraker pulls out a flick knife and says the immortal words, 'This is a sticker, Hector, and you're the stickee' – a line surely Shakespearean in origin. With Hector now dead, Fraker can lead the gang to glory and further terrorise a neighbourhood that is sick to the back teeth of them.

Kathryn tells Kersey he's free to leave, and as he gathers his things together, she asks why he doesn't want to press charges for the way he's been treated by the police. Kersey insists he's fine with being beaten up and put in a cell with punks, as it's sort of his thing anyway. She gives him her card and tells him to call should he need anything, and it's at this point that he should warn her that she will now almost definitely be killed. He wanders back to Charlie's patch and takes in the sights of punks running around shouting and picking on strangers, before then witnessing the Giggler rob a lady's purse and run like a gazelle with an ASBO into the night.

Meanwhile, Maria Rodriguez (Marina Sirtis) is driving through the neighbourhood when she finds a punk (played by Alex Winter, slacker Bill in *Bill & Ted's Excellent Adventure*) on her bonnet, shouting into her windscreen that he wants to 'eat her' and calling her a 'bitch' (essentially being a man on Twitter). She drives into a garage and stops, throwing him from the car, which he isn't best pleased with. However, before he can exact revenge, he comes face to face with Paul Kersey, who smashes him in the face with an iron bar, sending him running as fast as he can. As Kersey exits the garage a voice shouts down from yonder window; it's Bennett (Martin Balsam), an old man who lives in Charlie's block. They find that they had a mutual friend in Charlie, and Bennett invites him up to his apartment. He tells Kersey how awful the neighbourhood is and then mentions that Kersey missed Charlie's funeral, even though he's only been gone for one day – did they just chuck him in a bin? He shows Kersey pictures of he and Charlie when they were in the army together. Kersey tells him that he got a letter from Charlie a few days ago, and he sounded really scared – could it maybe have something to do with the guys who keep breaking into his apartment and beating him up? Bennett tells him that Charlie didn't pay the punks and wouldn't let them take his things, so they killed him, and he then goes to the window and points out exactly who did it, like a grass. Kersey asks what Charlie meant by 'take care of my things', as if it's some sort of mysterious request, and Bennett hands him Charlie's keys. The rent is paid until the end of the month, so Paul moves in and wanders around the ghostly apartment. While he's inspecting the photos and reliving fond memories, he hears a disturbance outside. The street is full of scum, roaming and attacking innocent people, and someone will need to clean it up. He knows just the man to do it – a 64-year-old white man who looks like he was at Orgreave.

The next morning, there's a playful knock at Charlie's door, and Mr Rodriguez walks in, all smiles, with his wife Maria. He thanks Kersey for saving her the night before, which Kersey bashfully accepts. Rodriguez admires him as he's 'a man who doesn't run', although that may well be more to do with his age than anything else. He tells Kersey that if there's ever anything he needs, all he has to do is ask. As he leaves, Kersey gets a very exciting phone call. He announces to Bennett with glee that his friend Wildey is coming and that he'll help out, though when Bennett asks just what the fuck is he talking about, Paul essentially taps his nose and tells him to take it easy – this is all his problem now.

Kersey begins his planning in earnest, renting a PO box and buying a used car in cash, which he then drives into the neighbourhood and parks right outside his building. You can tell he knows he's going to murder someone soon, as there's a real glint in his eyes when he tells Bennett that the car is 'bait'.

Kersey is introduced to the Kaprovs, a pleasant Jewish couple on the first floor, and he tells them he's a real fan of their cooking, which it turns out is stuffed cabbage – a look Charles Bronson's face is vehemently aiming towards. The Kaprovs invite Kersey and Bennett for dinner, and Kersey accepts happily, even smiling as he does so, which basically cracks his face in half. The banter flows over dinner, with Mrs Kaprov sinking a few zingers about her marriage. The room erupts with laughter, but those laughs don't last very long, as they're interrupted by the sound of smashing glass and swearing outside. The punks are trying to steal Paul's sexy new ride, and he loves it. He excuses himself from the stuffed cabbage and steps outside to ask the punks what they're doing to his awesome automobile, but they give him short shrift and a knife is pulled, so he shoots them both dead before heading back upstairs to enjoy more cabbage and banter – which should have been the working title for this picture.

The next day, Mr and Mrs Rodriguez are out shopping when a punk, who looks like an out-of-work background dancer from *Cats*, starts hassling them, asking what they're looking at, and if they've seen Macavity the Mystery Cat. He threatens them and orders them to hand over money, before pushing Rodriguez to the ground, but he doesn't count on Paul Kersey arriving and giving him a proper thump in the face. As the punk runs away, the entire neighbourhood comes out to thank their new vigilante friend, like he just slayed a dragon in Skyrim and saved their crops. Fraker watches on, fixing him with an evil stare, and tells his men he'll take him out himself.

Later that day, back in his apartment, Kersey does push-ups on his own, but he's not showing off. The phone rings, and it's Fraker, who tells him he's watching him and that he'll soon be dead. Kersey doesn't think to ask how he got the number; instead, he goes to the kitchen and, under a fog of jaunty sitcom music, lays a trap for any would-be intruder wishing to jump in through his window: a plank of wood filled with sharp nails. After smugly laying it on the kitchen floor, he steps outside for a wander and bumps into the Chief down an alleyway. The Chief wants something from Kersey, for the press. He wants a bust, saying it will make him look good, and I think we can all agree that a pair of breasts would improve him immeasurably. However, he actually means a high-profile arrest, and he wants Kersey to give him one. Kersey, though, is in no mood to help. He tells the Chief that the only thing he knows is that Fraker is the head of the punks, and it's about time he busted him. But the Chief says Fraker has a cleaner arrest record than him, even though he was in jail earlier. After telling the Chief he can't help, he wanders back home to the kitchen and that jaunty music, to find bloody footprints and an even bloodier nail plank.

Fraker and his boys seem spooked by a man in his sixties thumping them, which just goes to show how much resistance they have faced thus far. They sit around in their hideout cursing Kersey, but they don't actually decide to do anything about it, and you have to applaud how utterly useless they are.

The next day, an old lady is being hassled by a punk, and Kersey and Rodriguez witness her telling him to leave her alone and slapping him in the face, which pleases them both, as it means the residents are no longer afraid of these unemployed dancers who haven't had to deal with a fight since *West Side Story* closed. Kathryn arrives in a cab, and asks Kersey to have dinner with her, suggesting that both her paddles aren't exactly in the water. She asks if he's free on Friday, and he says he's not killing anyone that night, so he can make it to her place for an erotic meal. She asks why he is in this godawful neighbourhood, and he explains that his friend was killed and he's going to find out what happened by murdering everyone.

The Kaprovs are in trouble with the police. It seems that one of the punks complained to the cops when he tried to burgle their house and Mr Kaprov pointed a gun at him, so they have come to take the gun away, as they're illegal, and I'm taking a second to process this information. Kaprov hands over the gun, and then later on has to watch helplessly as some punks jump in through the window and take things while laughing and taunting him. Kersey is livid when he hears about this, and fixes the problem for them by installing a spring-loaded plank of wood beneath the open window – and it's at this point that we have to wonder if he is Kevin McCallister's grandfather. Amazingly, this little ruse works, and later that night they find the plank trap has been activated and a pair of teeth are embedded at the top.

The next day, there is much excitement in the Kersey household, as Wildey has arrived to help. However, Wildey is not a man; he's a gas-operated, double-action/single-action pistol. Essentially, it's a giant hand gun, and Kersey excitedly tells the assembled masses that it makes a real mess. The excitement doesn't last long, though, as later that evening Maria is set upon by the punks, taken to the garages, and brutally attacked. Kersey calls the hospital while Rodriguez tries to come to terms with what has happened to his wife. Kersey tells Bennett to get them a cab, and passes on to Rodriguez that the hospital say she'll be fine – she just has a broken arm. However, when they arrive at the hospital the doctor informs them that she has 'expired', which doesn't seem like the most sensitive terminology in this scenario, what with her being a human being and not a packet of mince. It transpires that the broken arm was fatal – due to blood clots, apparently – and as Rodriguez collapses in tears, Kersey welcomes that familiar feeling he always gets when people he knows are brutally murdered.

After manufacturing his own giant bullets, Kersey decides to buy an ice cream while dangling a brand new camera over his shoulder, once again becoming the Quint of crime. As he enjoys his tasty choc ice, the Giggler spots the camera. It all seems too easy. He shoves Kersey and whips the camera from his hand. Kersey reaches into his coat pocket, retrieves Wildey, takes aim, and fires, blowing a manhole in the Giggler's chest and sending him sprawling like a bloody rag doll in a tumble dryer. As Kersey turns away and walks off, the neighbourhood comes out to triumphant music, and they all begin to celebrate like at the end of *Return of the Jedi*. The Giggler is dead, and there's hope for everyone who likes to dangle expensive cameras over their shoulders.

'They had no business doing that,' Fraker exclaims to his gang regarding the death of his best man, like he's John Major dealing with Tory rebels. The Neo-Kinnocks are mournful, and snort cocaine sadly while talking about how great the Giggler was, how he could run like the wind, and how he had the best laugh in the business. One member identifies Kersey as the killer, and Fraker angrily advises that he obviously isn't a smart man, but says absolutely nothing about what he'll actually do about it.

The Chief arrives at the scene and looks into the gaping hole in the Giggler's chest. A policeman comments that things in the neighbourhood are better, quieter these days, and how he feels more relaxed – so that's nice, thanks, Mr Policeman. They suspect a rifle, and comment that he must have been a good shot as the Chief looks away, probably laughing up his sleeve, knowing his elderly Batman is doing well.

Kersey arrives at Kathryn's apartment for dinner, brandishing a bottle of the finest wine and the sly smile of a man who's just blown up a mugger. She's made chicken, and confesses it's the only thing she knows how to make, which is good news for Kersey. He loves chicken. And this small talk is just bubbling with erotic thunder. After eating all the chicken, they settle down for some brandy and chat about themselves. She asks if he's married or has any children, and Kersey tells her his tragic story: how his wife died, and his daughter, and everyone he's ever spoken to or looked at, and she should really just get in a panic room right now and hide until he is dead. However, she is intrigued by our crime-fighting goblin, and wonders if he's scared to be close to anyone again. She tells him what a mess the city is in – it's full of creeps, and someone has to fight back, which is music to his shrivelled ears. But before the evening can get too out of control with conversation, he tells her he has to go. She asks to see him again, and as he makes it to the door, they kiss, in a very weird, close-up way.

Back at Fraker's happening HQ, he's feeding Cuban (Ricco Ross – Frost from *Aliens*) lots and lots of speed and proudly telling the room that he'll kill tonight. His target will be Paul Kersey, the Saga Robin Hood, and they celebrate and jump around the room like their mum's gone to Iceland. The hunt is on, and Kersey takes the bait of Fraker looking at him from the street. He's soon ambushed, and they chase him down alleyways and fire machine guns as he lollops away behind bins. Dodging bullets, he drops Wildey in the dark and has to seek refuge on a rooftop. Cuban runs to finish him off, but is whacked with an iron bar and thrown off the building, landing on a car below, which cements the fact that even speed doesn't help them from being a very shit street gang. As Kersey returns to the scene and picks up Wildey, Fraker is left shaking a fist, trying to think of another drug that he can give to someone in his gang so that they can fail miserably – and it may as well be Disprin.

'Let's talk,' the Chief tells Kersey as he enters his apartment. He's just come from the scene of Cuban's death, and he asks Kersey if he can take it easy for a bit: it's getting a bit hard to explain all these dead bodies. Luckily, he spies another cockroach on Kersey's wall that he can kill, and you do have to wonder if he's bringing them with him in order to seem tough and sexy. Kersey tells him his work isn't finished and, much like cockroaches, you have to kill them all with a big gun. After the Chief leaves, Kersey is disturbed while cooking his baked beans by another call from Fraker, telling him that he's got him really mad and another old lady has been murdered. Bennett and Kersey have another one of their old-man chats about how this time the punks have gone too far, and so Bennett shows Kersey the secret Charlie was keeping hidden: a massive Browning machine gun and a box full of ammo. Kersey shakes his head and tells him that a lot of people could get hurt, and the walls of irony shatter as they can't take any more pressure. Kersey tells Bennett that it's him Fraker's after; maybe if he leaves, it may all calm down and no one else would get hurt. Before he leaves, he tells Bennett not to use the machine gun and asks for a day to get Fraker.

At Kathryn's place, she drops the bombshell that she's leaving the city and going to stay with her sister for a couple of weeks – obviously aware that if she stays around, she will die an awful death. She just wanted to see him one last time before she goes, and, with that, they make love. As he gets dressed, he busts out his awesome pillow talk about how his wife and daughter were murdered and he never caught who did it, and you can see Kathryn's soul leave her body as he does. She tells him he should leave with her and forget about death and murder for ever, which sounds lovely, and I, for one, can't wait to see how happy they will both be. They decide to head out to a restaurant for a bite to eat, but as they drive away from her apartment, Fraker and his boys are following. While Paul stops to check his PO box – for what? – Kathryn is knocked out and killed after the car's handbrake is taken off and it rolls down the hill and explodes on impact. Kersey arrives to see the flaming inferno that just twenty minutes ago he was having sex with, and walks away with that familiar, resigned look on his face. The Chief arrives at Kathryn's place to tell Kersey that he was seen when the Giggler was murdered and he should lay low, so he places him in protective custody – and he should probably prepare for all his men to die of seemingly innocent-looking accidents.

The next day, Bennett is held back by the police as his cab-repair company building blows up. He races to Kersey's apartment to tell him, but finds he is not there, so has to gallop like an old horse back to his apartment, just in time to find a brick flying through his window. He's had enough and, forgetting everything Kersey said, heads to the cupboard, brings out the machine gun, and wanders out to brandish it at the punks. Regrettably, he can't make it work, and the punks stream up the fire escape like they've heard there are auditions for *A Chorus Line* and chuck him over the side.

The Chief races into the jail cell and tells Kersey that Bennett has been beaten up and is in hospital, but has told police he will identify who did it, if he can speak to Kersey. They race there immediately. Bennett tells him he's sorry he screwed up, but there's another machine gun in the cupboard that he can have, so blow the scum away, and Kersey seems to be into the idea this time. The Chief comes in to see how the chat is going, obviously expecting to find them both in a bathtub going downhill, only to find Kersey has exited via the window.

Kersey stops at his PO box again and picks up a couple of parcels, which he opens back at his apartment. He's bought himself an anti-tank missile-launcher and a few rockets, which is obviously par for the course, and after grabbing the machine gun and ammo from Bennett's place, and loading Wildey, he's ready to commit mass murder. Rodriguez stops by to tell Kersey he wants to help. He drops a hint that all he has is a zip gun, obviously hoping Kersey will lend him a proper weapon, but Kersey ignores him and straps on a bulletproof vest. Sorry, Rodriguez, you're on your own, you mug.

Meanwhile, Fraker gets on the phone, presumably to some sort of performing arts agent, and asks for more guys in order to fight one small, old man, and they arrive in great numbers, riding motorcycles around with menace, throwing sticks, and hassling old people as they walk past. So, Kersey rolls out his own welcoming committee and appears at Bennett's doomed fire escape brandishing his Browning machine gun – only this time it works, and he mows them down in a hail of gunfire. I hope the Chief likes paperwork.

Kersey and Rodriguez then stalk the streets, with Rodriguez helpfully carrying the ammo box, murdering everyone they see and inspiring the good folk of Little Lambeth to lean out their windows and take pot shots as they run away. Don't you just love it when a community comes together like this? It's like when Gareth Malone gets people in hard-up areas to sing operas, but with bullets and death. After running out of machine-gun ammo, Kersey dumps the gun and brings out Wildey, and now the Chief arrives to lend a hand. Together they run along the street shooting stuntmen out of windows and blowing holes in any punk that so much as looks at them. I'm no lawyer, but I think this may also be a case of the Chief violating rights. When Kersey runs out of bullets, he decides to head back to his apartment to get more, only to find Fraker waiting in hiding for him, just like the real Kinnock did with John Major in 1992 – and much like Kinnock in 1992, his ploy fails. He emerges from a back room to find Kersey loading his gun, and is about to shoot when the Chief bursts in and fires a round into him. Fraker fires back and hits the Chief, but is riddled with Kersey's bullets as he does so, and falls down in a heap in the corner. The Chief reassures Kersey that he's only been nicked, and as he takes a seat to recover, Kersey tells him he'll call an ambulance. As he reaches for the phone, Fraker's eyes flicker open, and he jumps to his feet brandishing his gun.

'Bulletproof, asshole,' he proclaims, while showing off his vest. The Chief tells him he can't kill both of them, and as Fraker points the gun at him to boast that he can, Kersey reaches for his anti-tank rocket launcher and blows Fraker, and the front of his apartment, to smithereens.

Miraculously, Kersey and the Chief are totally unhurt by the vast explosion, and as they look out of the massive hole in the wall into the burning pile of rubble in the street, it's clear that this war is over. The punks run screaming for the hills, as it appears that Fraker was their droid control mothership, and the community rejoices as the motorcycles fire into life and the dancers run with them.

The Chief tells Kersey he'd better go as 'They'll be after you', which begs the question as to how on earth he'll explain this away to his other officers.

'Hey, guys, yeah, Compo from *Last of the Summer Wine* accidentally murdered an entire street gang while trying to win the affections of Nora Batty. Put out an APB for a man in fingerless gloves with a rocket launcher.'

'So why did you help him, Chief?'

'I got carried away, sorry about that.'

He mentions that he'll buy Kersey a few minutes in order for him to escape (and I think we all know he'll need considerably more than a few minutes), and Kersey gives a knowing smile before leaving with his luggage and wandering into the street as the sirens wail, knowing full well that, having just murdered at least ninety people with various guns and rockets, he'll be public enemy number one. His mission of revenge would have two further chapters of horror before he could rest and get his final wish to be actually dead. Thanks for your service, Paul Kersey.

SEVEN

1986

UP THERE WITH THE BEST OF THE BEST.

THERE'S A CERTAIN DICHOTOMY at work as Harold Faltermeyer's laid-back Bontempi rhythms ease us into a world of heightened, razor-sharp machismo. Our keyboard maestro wants us to lie back, chill out and prepare to spend a couple of hours in the company of all the lads who kick sand in your face while you eat cake at the beach.

We are presented with a paragraph of text explaining that there is an elite school set up by the US Navy to train the art of aerial combat, and those who graduate are considered the best of the best. The Navy gives it a very unsexy handle of 'Fighter Weapons School', but the flyers call it 'Top Gun', and, honestly, I'm not sure which is lamer. After some moody shots of planes being readied on an aircraft carrier, we say goodbye to Harold's soft, sensual fingering and welcome in the crash-pop stylings of Kenny Loggins, with his adrenaline-pumping number 'Danger Zone'. We watch sexy planes taking off and landing as the rising sun washes the sky and waves with vibrant orange hues. This is a world where men are men, and even the men who carry out basic flight preparations are sexy as fuck. They dance around the flight deck with ear muffs on, and seem to actually orgasm when each basic function is carried out. Tony Scott knew exactly what he was making here. This is soft-core porn for men who like their men to be men, and it shows in every second of this film, with every man, in every shot, sweating like he's just been doing press-ups in a sauna with a moped on his back.

The aircraft carrier is stationed in the Indian Ocean, and there's a situation in the sky, with an unknown aircraft sniffing about. The Commander (James Tolkan) is asking who they have up there to help, and when he's told it's Cougar (John Stockwell), Merlin (Tim Robbins), Maverick (Tom Cruise) and Goose (Anthony Edwards), the last two don't exactly fill him with excitement or pride. In the cockpit, Maverick asks Goose to talk to him – not about his moustache-grooming tips, but about the 'bogies' in the sky – and he gives the details, but with weird language mentioning 'cleaning and frying' and 'bugging out', which may sound fun in the officers' mess, but to the layman just sounds like bollocks, guys.

The bogies turn out to be two MiG-28s, and Maverick decides to scare one of them off by getting him with a missile lock, which works and sends him packing, but Cougar and Merlin have a missile locked on them. The Commander tells them not to fire unless they are fired upon. So Maverick steps in and declares that, as he can't shoot this fighter, he'll instead have fun with him, which involves going upside-down and flipping the MiG the bird while Goose takes a Polaroid photo. This works, amazingly, and the enemy fighter leaves the scene, but the stress is too much for Cougar, and he freezes and panics in mid-air, possibly even flying to Dundee in his bare feet. Merlin tells him their fuel is very low, but he won't listen, and everyone can hear on the radio that he's in trouble, so with Maverick being the, well, maverick that he is, he decides to abort his landing and go back to help Cougar, presumably utilising some sort of elaborate tow-cable. This does not go down well with management, but our Maverick helps a shaken, hyperventilating Cougar back down to the carrier with soothing words and kindness, much like one gets from a binge-watch of *Repair Shop*.

Back on the carrier, Cougar goes to see the Commander and says he wants out as he lost it up there, much like the Commander has with his own hair. He tries to talk him round, but Cougar says he's not cut out for this elite flying lark, he's going home to his wife and child, and he's thinking of opening a carvery somewhere near a busy shopping street to ensure maximum footfall. As he leaves, Goose and Maverick are summoned in to explain themselves, and while the Commander notes what Maverick did was brave, he also mentions that it was stupid, and tells him that his 'ego is writing cheques his body can't cash' – and with an ego like Maverick's, there must be lots of dud cheques floating around out there, with service often refused. The Commander then lists his full badass service history, for no one's real benefit but ours, and essentially tells him to stop being such a, well, maverick. He's also told that, although his father's name is famous, he needs to be better than him, and with all of this in mind, the Commander tells the pair of them that he's going to send them to Top Gun, to fly with the best fighter pilots in the world, and they can walk away with a *Blankety Blank* chequebook and pen.

Miramar, California, Fightertown USA. Population: some arseholes. With the fat sun blotting out the early sky behind him, Maverick arrives at speed on his gnarly motorbike, which he rides alongside the runway, watching planes take off while punching the air and grinning like a cat in a cream factory.

Jester (Michael Ironside) is the instructor of the Top Gun School of Witchcraft and Wizardry, and he's giving a briefing to the class of sexy flying aces. He explains that Top Gun was created to teach 'ACM', which means 'air combat manoeuvring', or 'dog fights' to you and me. As he explains this, one student leans into another to tell him he has a hard-on, although we can't be sure if it's related; maybe he's just wandered into the wrong classroom and thinks this is 'advanced air dogging'. Jester then brings in the commanding officer of Top Gun, the first man to win the coveted Top Gun trophy: a man who goes by the name 'Viper' (Tom Skerritt), and is essentially Dumbledore with flying goggles. Viper tells them all that, although they are the elite and the best of the best, the Top Gun programme will make them better. They will be given many exercises and training scenarios, and by the end of the process, they will be able to fly their planes really well. As he marches through the room talking about flying, Maverick catches the eye of another recruit, who returns his gaze with smugness. It's Iceman (Val Kilmer), and he looks like every jock in every film you've ever seen, every inch of him concisely poured via concrete mixer into one uniform. It's clear that he immediately senses Maverick is a fellow cock, and it's confirmed when our hero tells Viper that he will be the best – a boast that Viper says he likes in a pilot, much to Iceman's irritation.

It's the evening, so our aces head over to 'Animal Night' at the base's watering hole, which is like the Mos Eisley Cantina, but somehow more scummy and villainy. Maverick and Goose arrive at the bar, dressed in their pretty white uniforms, and talk about how easy it will be to get laid in this 'target-rich environment'. Goose begins to tell Maverick all about Iceman, and how he truly is the best pilot in the galaxy and was taking names while he was bulls-eyeing womp rats in his T-16 back home. He's ice-cold and makes no mistakes, apparently, and as Goose is working as his PR man, the Iceman does cometh over. He tells Maverick that he knows he likes to work alone, and asks him if he needs any help, and you have to wonder if he's actually talking about flying here or what. After making sure he knows who the big rooster is, Iceman heads off with a smile on his face so big you could land a plane on it. Goose makes a bet with Maverick that he needs to have 'carnal knowledge' of someone within the bar, and as Maverick scans the room for a potential victim – and, make no mistake, I do mean victim – he spots a lovely lady, Charlie Blackwood (Kelly McGillis). He instantly decides that it's time to approach her, armed with a microphone, while she's surrounded by about

300 leering men. He asks for her attention and then, before even getting an answer, launches into an a capella rendition of 'You've Lost That Loving Feeling', directly into her face via a whining PA system. She smiles and listens politely, with a faint exterior of enjoyment, but there's the very real sense that behind those eyes she's slowly dying inside from the rampant arseholery, especially when a chorus of other arseholes join in, all murdering a classic song right in her face, when she just wanted to go out and have a nice time with friends.

After the excruciating show is over, Maverick basks in the glory of Charlie telling him she loves that song, and tells her this is only the second time he's tried this move; the first time didn't go so well – but he'll let her know how this one does in the morning . . . And I was sick. They introduce themselves, and obviously he tells her his name is Maverick, like that would impress her, and she tells him her friend has arrived, and it's a man, so it's another crash and burn. Before she leaves him to wallow in failure, she tells him she hopes he's a good pilot, as he's shit at singing. As she walks away to get on with her nice evening, Maverick decides that it's probably a really good idea to follow her into the ladies' toilet and propose sex on the sink. She tells him she's not interested, she has work early in the morning, thus putting a lovely full stop to his evening of sex pesting.

This entire sequence should be shown to all men, everywhere, with an accompanying audio commentary from anthropologists and academics that explains why all this behaviour is just really, really not cool and underlines how it serves as a very good metaphor for the female experience in general.

The next morning, the Top Gunners assemble for a lecture from a civilian instructor who has a PhD in astrophysics and is an expert on enemy aircraft performance, and much to Maverick's shock and awe, it's Charlie. She's going on about the limitations of MiGs, when Maverick chips in to correct her. He mentions that he witnessed the enemy aircraft perform a '4G negative dive' – or something like that, God knows – a manoeuvre that she, and the Pentagon, think it would be unable to achieve. He also throws in that he witnessed it while inverted – the ultimate humblebrag. As they leave the lecture, Charlie approaches Maverick and tells him she would love to hear more about the MiG, and he plays hard to get.

The first exercise, or 'hop', begins, with Maverick and Goose having to face off against Jester in a smaller, MiG-like aircraft, on their tail, closing in and coming hard (stop it). Within moments, Jester has them nearly at lock, but Maverick slams on the brakes and gets behind him, turning the tables and engaging in a rapid pursuit. Goose offers words of encouragement and support, saying things like 'Do some of that pilot shit' and 'We're going ballistic, man, go get him', which leads you to wonder what exactly his role is in this plane. Is he just some sort of flying Bez? After a few seconds of frenetic whizzing around the sky, Maverick gets a lock and announces that Jester is dead, with the aforementioned corpse telling them both to get back to base immediately. As they approach the base, Maverick requests a 'fly-by', which is rejected, but he does it anyway, causing a senior officer to spill hot coffee all over himself and his medals, and Goose to suggest that it wasn't a very good idea.

Back in the locker room, Iceman and Slider arrive to tell the other men that they beat Jester, but mention to Maverick and Goose that their win didn't count, as they were below the 'hard deck', though what their patio has to do with anything is anyone's guess. Iceman tells Maverick he doesn't like him: he's dangerous and he will get everyone killed; and they briefly engage in some weird stares and biting motions, but before it can get to naked wrestling, Jester tells him and Goose to get to Viper's office immediately. As they stand outside the office, knowing they're in trouble, the senior officer who got covered in coffee is inside shouting at Viper, laying out all the details regarding the unauthorised fly-by, before leaving and declaring he 'wants some butts', and you have to admire him for it.

Viper tells the boys that they broke the rules of engagement by flying below the threshold, and then scolds them for the fly-by, warning them that they need to play by the rules or they're history, like a teacher with elbow pads. After they've left the office, Viper remarks to Jester that he flew with Maverick's old man (for the avoidance of doubt, he means his dad), and he seems to be saying, without saying it, that he was a great pilot. He then asks Jester if he'd trust Maverick in a battle situation, and the pilot confesses he just doesn't know.

Goose pops in to see Maverick in the middle of the night. Neither can sleep, they're both still very sweaty, and both are worried about graduating, with Goose confessing that he needs to do this, as he has a wife and child to think of. Maverick concedes that the fly-by was a terrible idea, and even though it's not easy with the burden of his dad's legend resting on his shoulders, he promises to stop being such a, well, maverick and not to let Goose down. He's the only family he's got. Sniff.

The next day during class, Charlie has a further chat with Maverick about perhaps toning down his aggressive flying, so he imbibes this information and then immediately asks her out for dinner. Once again, she politely refuses, saying that she doesn't date students, but then she passes him a note with her address and what time he should come over and to be sharp, and someone needs to have a word with her at this point. Never, ever give out your home address to men who follow you into toilets, please. That stuff should remain classified.

It's the moment everyone has been waiting for: the volleyball game. A scene with no purpose other than to show some buff guys with no tops on jumping around and whooping while Kenny Loggins sings about 'Playing With The Boys', the subtext not so much screaming, as roaring. Maverick checks his watch the whole time, so as to not miss his 5.30 sharp date with the teacher, and eventually bails out on Goose while Iceman and Slider high five in tiny shorts.

He's late for the date, and wanders into Charlie's home asking if he can take a quick shower, as he's just come from erotic volleyball. She's been eating crisps for the last half-hour so says no, dinner is ready. So, as they sit and chat about life, he probably smells like Lewis Hamilton's balls. She confesses that she asked him round to talk about the MiG; he's the only pilot who's been up against a MiG-28, and she needs the information to get a promotion. As they dig some Otis Redding, drink wine, and make eyes at each other, it's clear that she has more than enemy undercarriages on her mind. She asks what happened to his dad, and he explains that it's a big mystery; he disappeared in 1965 while flying a plane and it's all classified. And I think Fox Mulder should step in now, he'd be very interested in this story. He then announces that he's going for a shower after all and, playing hard to get again, zooms off on his sexy motorbike to the mournful tones of Giorgio Moroder's 'Take My Breath Away'.

At class the next day, the room evaluates Maverick's MiG manoeuvres, with some being very impressed, and others writing it off as cocky. Charlie even uses it as an example of what not to do, classifying it as a dangerous gamble, causing our hero to slope off in a huff after class on his bike. But wait, Charlie's chasing him down in her car and telling him that she thinks he's the bravest pilot in class and she has to hide it, as she doesn't want anyone to know she's fallen for him. So, they kiss with tongues, and then materialise in her bedroom to have it off via the medium of mood lighting, wafting lace curtains and that Berlin song again.

Time for 'Hop 19', which isn't a craft beer you buy from a lock-up in Dalston, but actually another training exercise with multiple bogies, and we're told that Iceman is firmly in the top spot for the trophy, with Maverick only just behind. The twist this time is that they'll be joined in the air by Viper, who will be doing some hands-on testing today. Unfortunately, Maverick soon reverts to his hot-headed ways. He breaks from his wingman, Hollywood, to chase down Viper himself, which leads to him falling right into a trap, with Jester appearing to get a lock on him.

Back in the locker room, Jester tells a sulking Maverick that that was some of the best flying he's ever seen, but he should never leave his wingman – that's why he was killed. Iceman chips in to say his attitude is dangerous and foolish, questioning which side he's on, and all the while Maverick strikes the oddest pose in cinema: bent over, one foot up on a bench, arse in a prone position. He knows he did wrong, and he promises Goose it will never happen again – again. He broods in his room, steeped in his own misery, and studies the vintage photo of his dad, taken just before he was abducted by aliens and anally probed.

Singing. More singing. Goose is at a piano with his small son perched on the top, belting out 'Great Balls Of Fire', while his wife Carole (Meg Ryan) chats to Charlie about what a slag Maverick is, though she does add the caveat that he's a lovely man, really, once you get to know him, and if you ignore everything that's wrong with him, and he has *definitely* fallen for her. Aww. It's a happy scene, if you know nothing about these people.

Time for 'Hop 31' (a German-style Pilsner with a clean, crisp biscuit finish), with everything up for grabs, and this time it's Iceman against Maverick, with multiple bogies again, like wiping a toddler's nose. The Top Gun trophy is still up for grabs, and the exercise begins. Iceman is taking too long to take down his target, so Maverick takes control, but in doing so he gets caught in 'jet wash', which isn't a comprehensive deep clean, but in actual fact wake turbulence that causes their engines to 'flame out'. The plane goes into a wild spin, but as luck would have it, all planes are fitted with equipment for such eventualities, and they both activate the ejector seats. Tragically, Goose is cooked, as he is fired head-first into the ascending canopy and killed instantly. Maverick parachutes into the sea, where he cradles the bloodied remains of his compadre, and between roars of grief and the noise of the approaching Coast Guard helicopter, he can at least console himself with the fact that he'll never have to hear 'Great Balls Of Fire' ever again.

Viper arrives in the bathroom to find Maverick shaving in tight white underpants, looking solemnly at himself in the mirror. Obviously, he's a bit sad about his mate dying and all that, but he still takes the time to keep up on his personal hygiene. Viper has words of wisdom for him: if you fly long enough, it happens, and in 'nam he saw many men die, and people will always die, so just let him go. Thanks, Viper, do you slow down for car crashes?

Carole and Goose's boy are sitting alone and grief-stricken in a waiting area as plaintive music tugs at the heart strings. Maverick inspects his pal's things, reflects on his many photos and personal effects, before handing them over to his widow, who tells him he loved flying with him, and as they share a snotty, tearful moment, she leaves him with the sentiment that Goose would have hated flying without him and is probably up in heaven now, playing volleyball with Liberace and some of the Village People.

The good news is that the official inquest finds that Maverick was not responsible for the incident. It was a technical fault that induced the spin, and that's enough for Viper, who stands firm and tells Jester to get him up flying as soon as possible. With grief coursing through his veins like a bad sausage working its way through a barbecue guest, Maverick is back in the cockpit on another hop, but he pulls out of the exercise, much to the disappointment of his colleagues. Jester doesn't seem to want to give him another chance, but Viper sees something in him. Iceman offers some words of consolation in the locker room afterwards, but Maverick feels like he's lost it, and he quits.

Charlie finds him at the bar in a local watering hole, head in hands, supping on a glass of regret with a failure chaser. She tries to make him feel better about Goose's death, telling him he's one of the best pilots she's ever seen, that he has to go on, and she once saw the Red Arrows do a fly-past, but Maverick doesn't want to hear it. He tells her it's over and that he doesn't want to be a pilot any more, because he really wants to be a lumberjack, leaping from log to log as they float down the mighty rivers of British Columbia.

Before leaving for good, Maverick heads over to Viper's house for a chat, a house decked from top to bottom with photos of planes, 'nam memorabilia, hats with 'Top Gun' written on them, and more photos of planes, making him very much the

Jed Maxwell of aviation. He reveals that he flew with Maverick's old man, and he's a lot like him, but even better at the planes. He then reveals some classified information: his dad didn't just disappear or get abducted and anally probed by aliens. He died a bloody hero, throwing himself on a missile to save his platoon, or something. He then tells Maverick he has enough points to graduate, and he should, or he could just quit. He's got a confidence problem after Goose's death, and he needs to learn from it – it's his choice.

This seems to work, and after a short period of driving around on his bike and looking at sunsets, Maverick turns up to graduate. He congratulates Iceman on winning Top Gun, but before they can break out the volleyball and short shorts, there's news of a crisis in the Indian Ocean. A ship has accidentally drifted into enemy waters, and they're needed to provide air support while a rescue is carried out, and Viper basically tells our Maverick that if he can't find a buddy, he'll gladly fly with him.

On board the carrier, the Commander gives the briefing. The sky will be full of MiG fighters, so no Polaroids and bird-flipping. Maverick is handed Merlin as his new partner, and as they ready up, Iceman offers a note of caution about Maverick being involved, which the Commander quickly dismisses, even though he's perfectly within his rights to suggest that sharing the air on a combat mission with a man who looks like he's constantly leading a funeral procession might be a bad idea.

In the air, they immediately encounter multiple bogies at twelve o'clock, i.e. loads of MiGs, and Hollywood, Iceman's wingman, is shot down, leaving Iceman exposed, like a pigeon among a herd of cats. Maverick quickly takes off to assist him, joining him just as he becomes utterly outnumbered – dodging missiles and machine gunfire like a drunk, naked man who's somehow ended up inside a coconut shy. Maverick almost immediately flies through another jet wash and loses control, much to the chagrin of his colleagues, but thanks to a spiritual reconnection with the ghost of Goose via his dog tags (think

Obi-Wan Kenobi meets *Antiques Roadshow*), he re-engages with the battle like a man possessed, picking off MiG fighters like a lad at an arcade downing Sunny Delight. After witnessing all their pals getting blown to pieces by the best dang pilot in the world, the remaining two MiGs pull up their skirts and run away, like the big girls they are. The lads in the carrier control room whoop and cheer as order is restored in the Indian Ocean once again, and assorted Ewoks sneak in to jump about and bang their rudimentary drums.

As Maverick touches down, his plane becomes surrounded by celebration, and as he soaks up the acclaim, the Iceman cometh. He shouts, 'You!', points in his face, and tells him he's still dangerous, but, with a smile that nearly cracks his entire face, he tells Maverick he can be his wingman any time. They share a *very* manly hug – all tight squeeze and clenched fists – and the entire carrier bursts into jollification, and everyone pumps the sky as our heroes walk through the crowd.

In a quiet moment of reflection, Maverick, who for once isn't covered in layers of sweat, stares over the calm sea from the carrier deck. He holds Goose's dog tags – a symbol of hope and fraternity, a tiny trophy imbued with love, affection and images of self-betterment – and then tosses them over the railing. It's what Goose would have wanted, wouldn't he?

Later, the Commander congratulates him, and tells him he's been given a choice of duty. He can go anywhere and do anything he wants, and he's interested in knowing just what he will do. Maverick thinks for a moment, before telling him he'd like to be an instructor on the Top Gun programme, at which the Commander laughs heartily, which is probably the right reaction, on balance.

Back at Fightertown USA, Maverick is reading at the bar, soaking in his new life with a beer, when the jukebox in the corner fires into action and begins playing 'You've Lost That Loving Feeling'. This causes a smile to ripple across his face. Charlie appears, and as they lovingly embrace and agree it's 'going to be complicated', she must be kicking herself that she didn't bring 300 drunken women to sing the song loudly right into his bemused face. As we're treated to another example of a Croft and Perry 'You Have Been Watching . . .' ending, we're left to reflect on what exactly it is we have just experienced as an audience, other than a lengthy Levi's 501 advert, and as the gorgeous shot lingers on a couple of planes dancing around the sumptuous orange sky, there can be no doubt that it was all sort of worth it.

EIGHT

COBRA

1986

CRIME IS A DISEASE.
MEET THE CURE.

WELCOME TO 'SOCIETY ACCORDING to Mr Cobra'. Please pull up a chair while our eponymous hero rattles off crime statistics like he's a rogue vidi-printer on a dystopian edition of *Grandstand*. The gist of the husky monologue is that America is a rather violent place, and to prove it he shows us his monogrammed pistols, with pretty pictures of cobras on them, before unloading a bullet into our faces (confirming he is totally part of the problem).

Meanwhile, in a red dawn-hazed Yuletide Los Angeles, a man ominously drives his motorcycle as images of axe-wielding maniacs are piped in via editing – controversial at the time to witness a Conservative party political broadcast, but the eighties were all about pushing cultural boundaries. And scaring the bejesus out of us.

The scary, pockmarked man parks his 'hog' in a 'handicapped' space (aw aw), and makes his way into a crowded supermarket, presumably to bulk-buy more axes for the lads. However, he quickly proves he's not on a little shop for basics when he guns down some innocent people, a trolley, and some fresh produce. A SWAT team quickly assembles, and the police are in place to offer the obligatory calming words over a megaphone. (Phil Collins-style drums batter away threateningly in the background.) But the armed man is not really listening to the soothing instructions; instead he shoots another innocent shopper. So, rather than sending in the SWAT team or carrying on with the negotiations, Captain Sears (Art LaFleur) tells his men to 'call the Cobra', which these days would mean a high-level meeting in London where the Prime Minster doesn't bother turning up, but in 1986 meant calling in THE Cobra, direct from the Zombie Squad (which is in fact a special unit that do all the dirty jobs, and not BBC Radio 3).

Cobra (Sylvester Stallone) duly arrives in his sleek Hot Rod (a customised 1950 Mercury Monterey Coupe), with the licence plate 'AWSOM 50', making him very much the Alan Partridge of crime-fighting. He emerges from the car in his very tight jeans, leather gloves, fairly impressive stubble, mirrored shades and a mouth packed with a matchstick, looking every millimetre like a man whose wife left him for a gym instructor who drinks that stuff in yellow tins. Detective Monte (Andrew Robinson – Scorpio from *Dirty Harry*, fact fans) tells him that he didn't agree to the Captain calling him in and wants him to know it – the pass-agg is large with this one – and he will thus be filed under 'Business Suit who Stands in the Way of Righteous and Murderous Justice'. Cobra is briefed that a lone, armed madman has taken hostages, and he is apparently the only man who can sort the situation out, which begs the question as to why the SWAT team are even there, as all they're doing is lying on the roof holding their guns.

Cobra makes his way into the supermarket, and it's quiet, perhaps too quiet, but I suppose that's tense hostage situations for you. He dodges around the aisles and keeps tabs on the gunman through CCTV and gaps in poorly stocked shelves, before hiding behind a giant Pepsi advert and taking time out to open a nice, cool can of Coors. This agitates the gunman, who begins to mouth off about being part of the 'new world' and claiming to have a bomb (which could possibly be the script to *Rocky V*). Having heard quite enough, Cobra heads down the freezer aisle, which is spewing acres of dry ice out of the open doors. He grabs the PA system and tells the gunman that he's a lousy shot, and he doesn't like lousy shots. He then carries on his in-store radio show by announcing that he shouldn't have killed those people and that coming up after the news at the top of the hour will be his murder. As the gunman checks each aisle for his quarry, Cobra bursts out from a freezer and points his gun. 'I'll blow this whole place up,' the gunman announces, to which Cobra retorts that he's not bothered as he doesn't shop there. He tells him he doesn't deal with psychos, he puts them away, before then announcing that the gunman is a disease, and he's the cure. But he looks NOTHING like Robert Smith.

Anyway, Cobra shoots him dead, before flipping the gun in his hand and placing it back in his belt, giving us a nice close-up of his appallingly naff, angry-snake-monogrammed gun handle. The siege has ended, and are the public grateful that a one-man police force walked in and murdered a violent killer? No, they are not. They criticise his methods, like a bunch of camera-wielding hippies. Cobra shows them a dead body and sensitively points out that death is bad, yeah? Makes you think.

After a tough morning of murder, it's time for Cobra to head home to his beachside condo for some well-earned R&R. However, he instantly has further problems to deal with in the shape of a parking space. Some local lads are having a party in their car, and Cobra wants them to move up slightly so he can park his awesome ride, but they won't budge, so he decides to nudge them along a bit in order to get his crime-mobile parked. The disrespectful dudes take issue with this and decide to confront him, not knowing of course who they are dealing with. The conflict doesn't last too long, unsurprisingly, as the ringleader is quickly humiliated in front of his mates when Cobra removes his cigarette, rips apart his T-shirt and tells him to clean up his act, a bit like when your mum tells you to tidy your cesspit of a bedroom. The kid then wanders away looking like a bewildered tiny deer that's been dressed up as *Faith*-era George Michael in order to appear on a *Stars in Their Eyes* woodland special.

Ensconced in his cool condo (sponsored by a massive Pepsi ad), it is revealed that, although he is a very tough psycho-killer, he is also a humble minimalist, with a simple telescope pointing out his back window (I really do not want to know what he uses that for), football trophies on the sideboard, and a top-of-the-range computer desk, littered with mugshots and red-hot data. He brings an egg box and some leftover pizza to his 'crime station', and, in the most horrific scene of the entire movie, uses some scissors to cut up his leftover pizza. If you thought there were eggs inside the egg box, then you are as big a fool as society. That egg box that he keeps in the freezer in fact contains gun-cleaning tools, and this guy, we're being told, is not a psycho.

Satisfied with his crimes, he points his remote control at the TV in a way that only a real man would – with extreme prejudice. The news is all about the 'Night Slasher'. The presenter states: 'Tonight, the man known as the Night Slasher has apparently struck for the sixteenth time, in just over a month's time', which sounds like a tongue-twister developed by a six-year-old – and seeing as this film was written by Sylvester Stallone himself, sort of tells you a lot. She goes on to say that the Night Slasher strikes seemingly at random, and that his victims have included 'businessmen, Asian immigrants, the elderly, and in one case a sexually assaulted child', the latter part of that statement, of course, making it sound much worse than it sounds. Cobra is rightly disgusted, and we can tell this because he removes his sunglasses with his gloved hands, revealing his pained, droopy eyeballs – the kind of eyes that seem to have JUSTICE written all over them in felt pen. Will anyone ever catch this awful killer who attacks sexually assaulted children? Cobra contemplates this as he manfully toys with his now-clean gun via an arty reflection.

It's night, it's dark, obviously, and a dirty old van is crawling down an empty, rain-sodden street. The occupants are all wearing tights on their head, so have clearly just ram-raided M&S, which opens up the very real prospect that they could return the items for a refund, even though they didn't actually purchase them. Is there no limit to their criminality? A woman is finishing her shift for the night. She locks up her store and gets into her car, but before she can remember if she turned off the gas, she's attacked by hammer-wielding tights men. Another poor victim of the Night Slasher, and that brings the count to seventeen.

'Maybe there's more than one killer,' muses Cobra in the morgue while fiddling with sterile medical equipment. Detective Monte tells him to stay out of it, it isn't his area of expertise, but our man reassures him that he doesn't want to be a hero, he just wants to be 'involved' – a touching sentiment at the best of times. Monte is dead against it. As is by now patently obvious, he's not Cobra's greatest fan, and he says it's just asking for trouble, like letting Boris Johnson mind your dog or lending your Ming vase to Frank Spencer. He says Cobra should stay on the Zombie Squad, but Cobra announces that as long as they play by these 'bullshit' rules, and the killer doesn't, they will lose, thereby showing a fundamental misunderstanding of the basic principles of policing. He receives the requisite dirty looks that you would expect and then exits his boss's office, telling his partner Gonzales that there's nothing they can do until the Slasher strikes again and wandering into the firing range – directly opposite the office for some reason – to fire off a few rounds into a perfect bullseye. Captain Sears might want to have a word with the men upstairs about possibly moving the firing range elsewhere. Can you imagine doing staff appraisals or the monthly budgets with bolshy cops blasting away at cardboard all day long?

It isn't too long before the Slasher and his fellow van people strike again, by bumping into a lone woman's car. As she's chastising them for being bad drivers and suggesting that they might be drunk, she's attacked. However, before they can really enjoy loading her dead body into the van, they see a jeep approaching. Inside it is Ingrid Knudsen (Brigitte Nielsen), and after taking one look at the Night Slasher's face (Brian Thompson looking like a haunted zoo), she does the right thing and speeds away, but not before they get a note of her licence plate: 2CON654 if my memory serves me right. This is very bad news as the Slasher's personal murder assistant, Nancy, is a police officer, and she looks it up on the computer. They now know where she lives, how tall she is, and if she fancies small Italian men.

Captain Sears has seen enough killing, so he convenes a clandestine car park meeting with Cobra and Gonzales. They're given the green light to shake down every sicko in the city and find the Slasher. 'And if I find him?' Cobra asks. 'Do what you do best,' replies Sears, which presumably means he wants him to ponce about in a long coat while chomping matchsticks. After Montes reminds him to 'kill the right guy', Cobra and Gonzales depart. Cobra berates his sidekick for eating too much sugar. 'Try prunes, raisins . . . something natural.' OK, he's a health freak too.

As this is a Sylvester Stallone film from the eighties, it would be remiss of it to not include a montage, and this one speaks to the beauty and the ugliness of Los Angeles. On the one hand, there's Ingrid, a glamorous top model, doing a photoshoot with robots (Stallone loved robots), and on the other, Cobra and his partner walking the filth-ridden streets looking for information from neon-lit lowlifes while 'Angel Of The City' by Robert Tepper burps out of the speakers. Ingrid's joy in posing with sexy robots is short-lived. When she reaches the car park with her photographer Dan (a massively underused David Rasche), he tells her she could be doing bigger photoshoots if only she would sleep with him, but as she puts up a resigned defence, they're attacked by the Night Slashers and their shiny axes. Luckily for her, she is the only one not murdered, and she manages to escape when sirens are heard approaching.

After a time of extreme stress and trauma, there's only one man you want at your bedside: Cobra. Gonzales tells her they're a pair of really nice guys who are here to ask her a lot of hard questions. She says they don't look like policemen, and she isn't kidding. Gonzales looks like he's on the way to a pharmacy for his methadone, and Cobra looks like a mass-shooter preparing for a tour of potential venues. They ask if she knows who would attack her, and if she's been around drugs or drug dealers. She says she hasn't, which Gonzales suggests is 'nice'. He then asks if she's had any threatening calls or letters, and she mentions that a man scared her earlier, which makes Cobra wake up from chewing his matchstick and ask who it was. Obviously she doesn't know, but she confirms that there were three of them. He asks if she'd recognise him if she saw him again, and, after thinking for a moment about his deeply harrowing and terrifying face, says yes.

Back at HQ, the Night Slasher is unwinding. Whereas Sherlock Holmes would often puff away on three pipes in a silk smoking jacket when considering a problem, our man worryingly sharpens massive knives on a block and sweats heavily in a grubby vest. Nancy arrives to disturb his contemplations with good and bad news. The bad news comes first: Ingrid knows his face. The good news is that she knows who and where she is, and that there's a Christmas sale on at Knives R Us. Slasher slices his finger in celebration, and tells Nancy that 'she's mine' and there's some fish fingers and chips heating in the oven if she wants.

Cobra shows Ingrid the police sketch of the man she saw, and it's basically a two-year-old's drawing of He-Man six months into his crack addiction. Instead of laughing, she mournfully confirms that this looks a bit like the man who looked at her a bit funny in the underpass earlier. He tells her that she'll stay in the hospital tonight, and tomorrow they'll move her to 'a place called the safe house', which makes it sound like a pub. Cobra and Gonzales then bust out some comedy bits, where they argue over what Ingrid is having for dinner, with the joke being that Gonzales is a junk-food addict and Cobra likes salad and healthy food. It's like an episode of *Seinfeld* written by an alien.

Cobra returns home after a tough day of prancing around to find the same street punk in his parking spot, wearing a fresh, whole T-shirt, only this time he moves his car, and in the words of

Henry Hill, he did it out of respect. Cobra praises him for being a good citizen and heads on up to his apartment-cum-crime centre, presumably to chew over thousands upon thousands of mugshots that will never, ever match that nightmarish police drawing. Meanwhile, the Slasher, with freshly dyed black hair, gets into the hospital, murders a bespectacled cleaner to take his place on his mopping rounds, and begins to wander the wards with all the charm and confidence of a cabinet minister during the pandemic.

Cobra gets a call from Gonzales telling him he's in his office, having received a message to meet him there. Cobra didn't make that call and senses danger. He tells him to get back to the hospital and leaps to his five feet to run to the door, but he's quickly attacked by two Night Slashers with axes. He swiftly despatches them, in a moment that feels like it was hastily added to give us some form of action/entertainment while we recover from the LOL-fest that was the salad gag bit.

After killing a nurse who gets in the way, the Night Slasher moves in on his target, only to utterly fuck it up as she's in the toilet when he arrives, like when someone delivers your Amazon parcel. She locks the door and hides inside as he, hopelessly, tries to stab it open, but luckily for Ingrid there's another door, so she runs out into an apparently entirely unmanned hospital ward and pulls the fire alarm, causing Mr Slasher to skulk away like the bumbling tool he is.

Chief Halliwell is really upset with Cobra's 'methods' of having a woman who needed hospital treatment put in a hospital (I can sort of see what Cobra means about his employers now) and wants answers. Cobra tells him that he's sure there's someone on the inside helping Slasher, but he can in no way prove it, which sounds promising. He has a plan, though, and it's time to put it into place, so he picks up Ingrid from the hospital and informs her it's time to get to the safe house. Joining them on their vacation will be Gonzales and Officer Stalk, who is . . . *dun-dun-dar!* . . . Slasher's murder assistant, Nancy. (Nancy Stalk is a hell of a name, by the way: pure, undiluted nominative determinism.)

Cobra places Ingrid in his Mr Men Batmobile, and they head out on the open road, but if there's one thing the Night Slasher and his boys love, it's roads, and they take out Gonzales's car and speed after Cobra, taking shots at him as a bewilderingly edited car chase begins. Luckily, Cobra can do really fast J-turns and has a machine gun in his glovebox, so he can gun down his pursuers. He has also seen *Mad Max*, so has a natty Nitrous button he can flick, which makes him go at a very high speed to keep up with his attackers. Ultimately, though, it all comes to nothing, as Cobra's car ramp-jumps into a discarded boat, doing multiple flips, bumps, and rolls that would have definitely killed him and his passenger. The Slasher escapes, leaving Cobra and Ingrid to stagger from the wreckage coughing like all the baddies from *The A-Team*.

Back in Chief Halliwell's office, he sounds off about how things have gotten so far out of control he doesn't know where to start. Cobra angrily argues that it isn't just one man, it's an army of killers, but no one believes him. Monte leads the chorus of disapproval by saying that all they have is the testimony of one scared woman, which should really be enough, to be fair. He then questions the logic of taking her to a safe house, as she'd probably be safer at the police station where all the police are, but Cobra argues that they're dealing with fanatics who will do anything to waste her, so it's best to take her to a small house in the middle of nowhere, with very little protection.

Monte has heard enough and stands up to give a speech, telling the room that this poor woman is just another piece of live bait so the extremely violent and unhinged Cobra can kill some more people, adding that he's let too many people die and should let Ingrid live, which incenses our hero so much he goes for Monte with extreme violence, once again sort of proving his point. As Cobra storms out of the office, the top brass basically all agree that he'll be followed by the Night Slashers, so it's probably best to just let him go and take them all with him. Perhaps he could do a tour of the nation and give LA a break for a while?

So, the Cobra gang head out on their road trip, with the help of a montage scored by the soothing sounds of Jean Beauvoir's 'Feel The Heat'. Ingrid, wearing a jaunty flat cap nestled on her big wavy hair that makes her look like a pet lion from *Peaky Blinders*, asks Cobra how he can be so sure that they won't get to her. He tells her she has to have faith. Hmmm. She asks him why the police can't just put crazy people away and keep them there, to which Cobra responds that she'll need to tell it to the judge as they keep letting them out. Sounds like an idea for a great board game for Christmas: Tell It to the Judge with Cobra and Ingrid.

They stop for a break, and it seems like a good time for Gonzales and Ingrid to have a chat about just what a bloody enigma Cobra is. Yes, he looks like a fugitive from the fifties but he sure is great at catching psychos. He then asks her if she wants to know something fun, and that it's personal. Sadly, it isn't that he has problems downstairs or that he likes to put Gummy Bears in his mouth and drink Diet Coke, it's that Cobra's real name is Marion Cobretti. Armed with this new revelation, she approaches Cobra and tells him his name, and he nearly cracks a smile from behind that ridiculous tooth pick. She tells him she likes it and that it's a great name (lying through her teeth). He laments that it was tough growing up with the name 'Marion' – he'd have preferred Alice – and that to counter the bullying, he got into some serious matchstick addiction to get over it.

In a diner later, he woos her by showing her a giant plastic hamburger he finds on a nearby counter, and then chastises her for eating too much ketchup with her fries. He really is a man for all seasons. She asks him if he's ever had a girlfriend, and he says no one would put up with the way he lives – and I think he's referring to snipping up pizzas and eating the pieces with gloved hands here. Ingrid reassures him that maybe, and I think she's talking about herself, there's a woman out there who would like that, and he says that this woman, and it could be her, would have to be a little crazy. Well, that's that compliment dead in the water. Cheers, Marion. As the flirting continues, Cobra notices Nancy making a phone call while looking highly furtive, but once again he's distracted by Ingrid drowning her fries with more ketchup, which seems to enrage him more than any street punk ever could.

As we see images of the Night Slashers arming themselves to the teeth and climbing aboard motorcycles and pick-up trucks, Cobra goes for a night-time stroll, only to find Nancy once again emerging from a phone box. He asks her where Gonzales is, and she tells him he's asleep, and that she was checking on things at home. She can't use the phone in her room as it's out of order, much like Gonzales's snoring and violent burger sweats. She tells Cobra she thinks he's doing a great job, which he takes with a pinch of salt and returns the compliment, but he knows something is up, so he returns to his room and begins to unpack his machine guns and grenades, and, as it's 1986, you can be sure he has a laser sight. The constant sound of guns being loaded, primed and slapped into place, along with grenades slamming on the counter, wakes Ingrid up, so Cobra asks her if she's having trouble sleeping. Yes, just a bit, you gun nut. The flirting then continues, with Ingrid eventually asking him to join her on the bed. She says she wants to see him more, after this is all over, and brings him in for a kiss, a moment that reminds me of one of the Lollipop Guild being seduced by Dorothy.

The next morning, as they're getting ready to head somewhere else isolated and vulnerable to attack, Gonzales emerges and tells them that Nancy's gone, but before they can compute what has happened, the Night Slashers arrive and begin to mobilise, with Nancy being among them. 'Never liked that bitch,' Gonzales mumbles, like the misogynist he is. They go back inside the motel, and Cobra throws off his long coat to reveal that he's armed to the teeth. As the shots rain in through the windows, he leans out through the broken glass and picks off bikers with wild abandon. They make a break for it, but Gonzales is clipped in the leg and has a lie down while Cobra chucks grenades and jumps into the back of a pick-up truck that Ingrid commandeers. We are then treated to more *Mad Max*-inspired camera work (and I'm being generous) as the bikers and followers are gunned down via his machine-gun fever. After writing off the pick-up by driving through a blockade, Cobra takes Ingrid to a nearby steel mill (what is it with steel mills in the eighties?), where the fight of the decade can commence. A bloody, vicious battle, he goes from man to man slaughtering them, while Nancy and the Slasher try to find Ingrid to kill her, because she's seen his face, even though by now it feels utterly irrelevant. Cobra gets to use his matchstick, at last, to burn a man covered in petrol to death (Chekhov's matchstick), and after shooting Nancy to death, he comes face to face with the Slasher himself. 'You wanna go to hell with me?' the Slasher screams. 'We are the future.' But Cobra has rehearsed his comeback a lot, and he retorts with: 'No, you're history.' However, instead of shooting him dead, Cobra decides it's probably best if they have a manly fist fight, after the Slasher goads him by saying that he'll just say he's insane and get a nice, easy prison stretch. So, they go at it, with the Slasher occasionally trying to stab Cobra with his fancy knife and Cobra punching and pushing him away, eventually culminating in the Slasher being lifted up and impaled onto a giant hook that then transports him into a massive fire. And I hope he writes up that scenario word for word in his police report.

Outside, the press and police have arrived to try to make sense of the bodies and motorbikes littering the area, and Gonzales is stretchered off, asking for Gummy Bears. Captain Sears arrives and tells Cobra that he can leave the Zombie Squad anytime he likes and that he did a 'hell of a job' murdering about forty people and then impaling a man on a spike and burning him to death. Cobra asks if they'll replace his car for him, but they tell him there's nothing in the budget to fix giant shoe cars. As the Captain leaves, Monte tells Cobra that he kind of overdid it and that he would have looked for a more subtle solution. This observation earns him a firm handshake followed by a punch in the chops, which every superior officer around seems to think is fine.

Cobra then steals a random motorbike (which is presumably evidence at this point) and heads off into the great unknown with Ingrid (still calling him Marion) hugging his waist as 'Voice Of America' by John Cafferty and the Beaver Brown Band plays out, soundtracking a chance of new hope for all the decent people of Los Angeles – and a sequel (it never materialised). Still, Marion Cobretti is out there, and if you're up to no good, he'll pounce out of the darkness and snip up your pizza.

NINE

ALIENS

1986

THIS TIME IT'S WAR.

SPACE. THE VAST UNKNOWN, an endless black abyss of dead stars, shattered nebulas, and black holes. Lieutenant Ellen Ripley (Sigourney Weaver) is floating in the *Nostromo* escape pod, fast asleep, and somehow not eaten by her cat. The silence is harshly broken when her drifting pod is located by Adam Klaus from *Jonathan Creek*. The salvage team enter and find Ripley alive and well, and bring her back to civilisation, or at least what's left of it, though if I were her, staying in suspended animation for all eternity would have been the wiser choice.

Her next stop is Gateway Station – essentially a branch of BUPA orbiting the Earth – where she is tended to by nurses and checked over after her 57-year sleep – a service I would have dearly loved as a student waking up after a weekend on the lash. However, her recuperation is soon interrupted by a visit from the venal Carter Burke (Paul Reiser), transporting Jones the cat in a kind of Dr Evil way. Burke is a walking embodiment of corporate eighties America: he wears smiles while dead inside, he tells lies wrapped in truths, and he clearly has a tailor who loves *Miami Vice*. He tells

Ripley that although he works for The Company, he's really a nice guy and he's glad she's feeling better, yet there is a glint in his eye that suggests he's buried a man alive and enjoyed every minute. He tells her she was in hypersleep for almost 60 years, which is a bit of a shock for Ripley, as she had loads of really good things recorded on Video Plus and her tape will have run out. What she doesn't know is that her VHS is now in a hipster coffee bar in Brooklyn, next to a washing machine, and they're both serving as makeshift tables in a booth made from bicycles. He tries his best to explain how she was out there for so long and how she was very lucky to be found at all. His pitch doesn't last long, though; Ripley soon begins convulsing and grappling at objects in slow motion while her stomach begins to bulge and crack, until, eventually, she wakes up in a pool of sweat in the hospital bed. Just another bad dream.

It's inquest time, and Ripley is forced to explain her actions to a room of execs, all of whom have suit jackets with upturned collars, beautifully displaying that eighties view of the future: that if you change something marginally, it makes it believably futuristic – like removing doors from a car or putting pointy bits on a hairdryer. Ripley doesn't waste time. She admits that she blew up the ship because a giant killer monster was onboard and it was trying to kill everyone. The suits are more concerned about the cost of such an action, seeing as the ship is valued at $42 million, adjusted for inflation, of course. She reiterates that it all started when they set down on LV-426 and found a ship full of thousands of eggs, one of which infected a crew member and unleashed a giant right-wing alien. But the suits are sceptical, one so much so that he's furtively doing *The Times* cryptic crossword under the table. They explain that they found no trace of any creature on her space lifeboat and the planet itself is a rock, devoid of life, so it would seem in their eyes that Ripley obviously just got fed up and detonated a spaceship for no reason. She tries, once again, to explain that these eggs are bad news and could potentially wipe out humanity, and she's, once again, met with a wall of cynicism, aptly showing that even in the progressive future, where vertical suit collars are given prominence, it's still hard for a woman to be taken seriously. Finally, she asks why they haven't sent anyone to investigate, only to be told that they don't need to, as around 60 families of colonists have been living there for 20 years, and they've had no complaints whatsoever – I suppose it's tough to complain with an alien clinging to your face.

Ripley burns down a cigarette in her tiny apartment and reflects on how awful the modern world has become, with a hefty caveat that it's not as bad as 2020. She's just about to remember the sea shanty period and cringe, when there's a knock at her door. It's Burke, but this time he's brought a friend, Lieutenant Gorman of the Colonial Marine Corps. It would appear that they've lost contact with the colonists on LV-426, and they may need her help. Credit must go to Ripley here, as it must take every molecule in her being to not shout 'I told you so, you pricks, fuck right off'. Instead, she makes them a hot beverage and listens to their story. They want her to go, as an adviser, with a troop of Marines to check what's happened to the colony. It may well just be a downed transmitter, but if it's something else (maybe a prank?), she is best placed in terms of knowing what they could be up against. Burke tells her they can guarantee her safety and reassures her, while dusting off his Trump dictionary, that these Marines are 'tough hombres'. She is understandably not very keen, as this is basically like asking one of those Chilean miners if they fancy a spot of potholing, so Burke dangles the carrot in front of her that he can get her out of working at the docks and reinstated as a flight officer, but her mind is made up. She's not going back there, and even if she did, she wouldn't be much use. However, after another awful dream, she calls Burke and asks for reassurance that if they do find more of these things, they will destroy them – and definitely *not* bring them back. When he tells her that's the plan, she agrees to it, and we all know nothing will go wrong.

The *Sulaco* drifts gracefully through open space, half-raygun, half-four-point plug. Inside, there's an eerie silence, until a computer boots into life and begins waking up the sleeping pods neatly packed in a row (they only made four for the film but check the clever deployment of mirrors). People begin to emerge from their future-beds, and we get to meet our badass starship troopers. First up is Apone (Al Matthews), who wanders around with a fat cigar in his mouth talking about how being in the army is like a day on the farm, presumably meaning bouts of cider drinking interspersed with leaning on gates. Ripley staggers to her locker, past many a muscled person, including the mighty Vasquez (Jenette Goldstein). She has jumped, Joe Wicks-style, into her punishing morning ritual of doing chin-ups on a metal bar, stopping only to ask who Ripley is; she's told that she's some kind of a consultant who saw an alien once, making her sound like she was abducted in a cornfield along with her brother, Bobby Joe.

Hudson (Bill Paxton), the pan-galactic ambassador for lovable jock assholes, collects his breakfast and joins the gang at the table for a spot of light space banter, whereupon he finds out from Apone that it's a rescue mission and it'll be a right old laugh, and they may even get to have sex, though not with each other, obviously. Hudson then spots Bishop (Lance Henriksen) walking past and asks him to do his parlour trick: stabbing a knife really fast around a splayed hand – the one all eighties schoolkids did at their desks with pencils and still have the scars to prove it. Bishop eventually agrees, but unbeknownst to Hudson, this time his hand will be sitting under Bishop's while he does it. The knife begins dodging fingers, but then quickly begins to move at an incredibly fast pace, almost too fast for a human, causing Hudson to scream like he's on a rollercoaster being piloted by Stevie Wonder. Once the game is over and the wild celebrations die down, Bishop notices he's nicked a finger. The very ominous sign of seeping, white, milk-like blood is obviously not a good sight for Ripley to behold. She wants to know why no one told her an android would be aboard, and with good reason, seeing as the last one stuck a newspaper in her mouth and tried to feed her milk. After some initial embarrassment on Burke's behalf,

Bishop tries to explain that the new models of synthetic humans are much better and wouldn't even know how to put a newspaper in someone's mouth, never mind feed them milk, but Ripley isn't having it, and tells him in no uncertain terms to stay away from her and to keep his creepy milk-blood to himself.

It's briefing time in the hangar, and Gorman assembles the team to tell them all about their next excursion. He isn't exactly the commanding commander one would want in a situation such as this, and the feedback from the troops isn't exactly glowing. The message is simple: there's still no contact with the colony, and a Xenomorph may be involved. Gorman hands over to Ripley, who gives an impassioned précis of what occurred on her last mission, at times becoming very emotional, but it's all sadly wasted on a largely unimpressed audience, and she may as well be reading from a Jeffrey Archer novel. She leaves behind one last important nugget, though: if one of these aliens wiped out her entire crew, thousands of them will be very bad news indeed.

One of the many drawbacks of long-distance space travel is the amount of downtime. The Marines counteract this with tasks and chores in the loading bay, preparing for the forthcoming mission, but Ripley is bored. She's obviously read all the *Grazias* in the waiting area and smashed that sudoku book, so is in need of something to do to pass the time. She heads down to the loading bay and asks if she can help out, as she has experience from her brief day job with a power loader. Apone says she's welcome to join in, and he and Hicks (Michael Biehn) watch on with increasingly impressed faces as she brings out the loader and asks where she should put the load. What a shining example of a happy workplace environment.

It's time to make the drop down to the planet, and as the military drums ring out, the Marines are suiting up and firing out laser-sharp banter while shouting and whooping 'Get it on!', like they're going paintballing for Phil's 40th. Hudson makes final checks of the troops and begins to tell Ripley that he and his team of 'badasses' will protect her, and she gives him the very look any woman on the internet would if that arrived in her DMs. As the drop commences, and there's a massive amount of turbulence, Gorman begins to look like someone's put a food mixer up his rectum. He admits that all his experience of combat drops is from simulations. As the team look at each other in disbelief, it's fun to see that Hicks is happily asleep.

They finally reach the planet, and as they circle slowly over the complex, it's immediately clear that the power is still on and everything looks normal, so they can be sure it's not a surprise birthday party gone horribly wrong. The dropship begins its descent, like a model-maker's porn dream, and opens its undercarriage to reveal a highly erotic M577 Armoured Personnel Carrier, which was converted from a Hunslet air-towing tractor bought from an airport. The bastard behemoth zooms out and begins the journey over rough terrain to the colony, drawing up outside, and releasing the Colonial Marines as the rain pours down like Ridley Scott's in charge of the weather.

Once Hudson cracks the door and gets them inside, it's pretty clear that the place is as empty as Boris Johnson's imagination – and there's not even a painted cardboard bus. Something strange has definitely happened: the place is trashed, and there are signs of barricades, half-eaten wet doughnuts, and hasty exits – like the last eerie days of Blobby Land. Gorman, Burke and Ripley watch through the Marines' camera headsets as the search continues for life, but there's nothing to be found. Ripley, though, sees something all too familiar: a big sweaty melted hole in the floor. That can only mean one of two things: either it's the remnants of a dead Xenomorph with battery acid for blood or Geoff Capes has been doing *Riverdance* again.

For reasons that will only ever be known to him, Gorman, even after seeing these visuals, is happy to announce that the area is secured and wants to come in, bringing a very reluctant Ripley with him. They wander around and take note of the carnage: the terrible welding work, the flappy bits of plastic, and the signs of explosives and gunfire. Eventually, they enter the lab and find the very last thing Ripley wanted to see (apart from Geoff Capes in Spandex): facehuggers in jars, two of which are very much still alive. Bishop checks the records and explains that the subjects died when the facehuggers were being removed, which, although bad for the subjects, was good for the guy in the next bed who wanted his slippers.

Just when this all looks to be a pointless rescue operation, suddenly the motion tracker fires into life and begins beeping and humming. Something is in the building with them, and it's on the move. They slowly stalk the glowing image as it pops around their scanner like Pac-Man on a pub crawl. The nearer they get, the higher the frequency becomes, and just as the tension is as high as Richard Pryor in 1983, a shape runs out in front of them and darts into an air duct. Thankfully, it's not a scary alien with acid for blood; it's a grubby little girl called Rebecca with really, really messy hair, who has spent a long time alone in this living hell, like everyone who voted Remain post-2016. She resists being rescued, but Ripley manages to coax her out with her calming, maternal ways, and they bring her back to the control centre. She's not very communicative with Gorman, who it's fair to say isn't exactly Supernanny, but when Ripley brings her a hot chocolate and a face wipe, she reveals that everyone calls her 'Newt', her entire family are dead, and that it's not been very nice living here. And, for good measure, all the soldiers in the world won't make any difference in terms of protection.

Meanwhile, Hudson and the lads are using the computer to check for Personal Data Transmitters, something every colonist had surgically implanted, so if there are any left alive, still playing hide-and-seek or something, they will be able to locate them. Within a few moments, Hudson announces that it's time to 'stop your grinnin' and drop your linen' (a line from an AC/DC song, fact fans) as he's found them – and it looks like all of them – at the processing station under the main cooling towers. Gorman orders the team to 'saddle up' and perform a good old-fashioned 20th-century rescue, so they jump in the battle bus, and head over to the town meeting.

The Marines stride into the complex, in formation, led by Vasquez and Drake with their M56 Smartguns – a beautiful piece of production design based on Kawasaki motorcycle handlebars and an MG-42 machine gun (a creation every kid in the eighties wanted to have). Gorman and Ripley are back in the battle bus watching the video feeds as the grunts explore the hot, sweaty caverns, which become more ominous and Giger-like, the deeper they go. It's here that Ripley has a thought: mightn't it be a bad thing if the Marines fired their big guns underneath the cooling towers? What with them being big fusion reactors and all? A fact that Burke quickly confirms to be true, so Gorman has to make the difficult call to his team and inform them that they can't fire any explosive rounds, only harsh language and flamethrowers, which is a big shame, as that's pretty much all they have. The order goes down as well as Jacob Rees-Mogg at a Momentum cookout, but Apone does his job and collects the ammo.

It's not too long before they come across the colonists, and they're not doing that well. They look very, very dead in their drippy cocoons, and they're surrounded by hatched alien eggs and skeletal facehuggers. Amazingly, one is still alive, though looking a bit peaky. She doesn't get many words out, though, and has to be torched when an angry little alien bursts from her chest. This brings back traumatic memories for Ripley, and also sets the walls inside the processing station hissing, moving, and literally slithering to life. Before anyone can realise what is happening, the Marines begin to get picked off one by one, with Gorman watching on gormlessly as his video screens lose signal after signal. Ripley demands he take charge and get them out of there, but he freezes, so she races to the front of the battle bus before driving it right into the war zone, sadly (or happily, depending on your point of view) knocking Gorman out with falling debris as she does. The stragglers stumble aboard, shocked and terrified by what they've just encountered, and as Ripley speeds away, bursting through the doors and into the wilderness, Hicks calms her down and gets her to stop the vehicle. Of what was once a vast crew of badasses, only Hicks, Hudson and Vasquez remain. So much for a rescue mission.

Hudson notes that the screens show that some of the team are still alive, but Ripley rightly points out that they're as good as dead – news that Hudson takes very calmly, as you can imagine. Vasquez suggests that they pump in nerve gas to take out the nest, but Hicks isn't sure that it will work, so Ripley brings up her much better idea: take off and nuke the site. It's the only way to be sure. This plan is a winner, and everyone is on board, but, predictably, bean counter Burke objects, pointing out that the installation has a 'substantial dollar value'. He is, rightly, told to fuck off. So, they ready up and call the waiting dropship to pick them up and get them out of there.

There's a well-known, and oft discussed, problem with the outcome of best-laid plans, whether it be mouse, men, or aliens. As the ship begins its final preparations to depart, the wonderfully named Spunkmeyer notices some of his namesake on the docking bay and mentions it to pilot Ferro, but she rushes him on board so they can take off. Big mistake. The door opens in the cockpit, and Ferro's about to admonish him for taking his sweet time, only to be met with an alien that swiftly fires its second mouth into her face, which in turn causes the dropship to crash and burn in front of the sad eyes of the remaining Marines. 'Game over, man,' wails Hudson, like a coward's mantra. Newt calmly suggests they get back inside, as they 'mostly come at night, mostly', like she's doing a live link for *Wish You Were Here*.

They salvage the remaining gear from the wreck – very little ammo, some grenades, a flamethrower, and some tea bags – and there's more good news: they can't expect a rescue for seventeen days. Hudson takes this news badly, but Ripley quietly points out that Newt has survived for longer than that on her own, so all hope is not lost. It's just massively fucking misplaced. She asks Hudson to gather as many complex maps and plans as he can, so they can be sure on all the access points and draw up some sort of plan, while also telling him to relax, which is like asking The Hulk to do a huge house of cards in two minutes. After taking a small break, and probably crying more than any man every has, Hudson returns with the plans, revealing that a long service tunnel between both buildings must be the preferred method of entry and route that the aliens are using to zip back and forth. So, if they repair some barricades and weld the doors shut, that should keep them back for a while.

It's bedtime, so Ripley takes Newt to a room with a bed and tells her to have a nap, whereupon Newt mentions that she doesn't fancy it, as she has scary dreams, for some reason. Ripley promises Newt that she'll never leave her and that she'll always be there for her, a lovely scene that has added weight when watching the Special Edition, in which we find out that Ripley's own daughter died without ever seeing her again while she was floating in space for 57 years. She leaves Newt to sleep and heads to see Bishop for a chat about just what makes these aliens tick. What's their favourite music? Who does their nails? And if there's hundreds of eggs for each colonist, who's laying them? Bishop concludes that it must be something they haven't seen yet, which is comforting, and also mentions that Burke gave sneaky instructions that the facehuggers were to be preserved and taken back to Earth, which goes down like a balloon full of acid.

Ripley goes to see Burke armed with receipts. She knows about the facehuggers and that he sent the colonists to that ship to check it out, and she's going to tell everyone when they get back. He'll lose his 'exclusive rights' to these creatures, and she'll make sure they nail him to the wall for this. As she storms off, Burke is left to visualise his bank balance going back into overdraft.

Bishop calls a meeting of the survivors. He has further news, and it's another doozy. The crashed ship damaged one of the cooling towers, and in about four hours it will explode, with a blast radius of 30km, so a good time to top up your tan. There's only one way to get round this nightmare, and that's for someone to go out and remotely pilot another dropship down from the

Sulaco, which is an assignment low on uptake, bringing to mind doing a push-start of a Ford Capri in a war zone. But Bishop chips in and says he'll do it. This makes him a double hero, as it involves getting in the smallest imaginable pipe and crawling in the darkness for hours, like Andy Dufresne if he'd eaten only pork pies for the six months prior to his escape.

While Bishop takes to the tube, Hicks gives Ripley an up-close-and-personal demonstration of the M-41A pulse rifles that the Marines use, including the grenade launcher, just in case she needs to use it – and the chances of that happening are pretty much sky-high. She also makes him promise that if anything happens, he mustn't let her become like the others, a credo every goth has lived by for 40 years. After the weapons demo, Ripley heads back to Newt's room to get some well-earned rest, and as she lies down with her little friend, everything seems fine . . . Until she notices a facehugger tank, empty and dripping on the floor. As she rouses Newt and tells her they may be in trouble, the creature strikes, and although they manage to repel it, the lab doors are locked, and a watching Burke switches off the monitor while twirling his moustache of corporate evil.

They're all alone in there, and attempts to break the glass also fail. Thinking fast, Ripley holds a lighter to the sprinkler and sets off the alarm, causing Hicks and his guys to mobilise. When they arrive, they find Ripley with a facehugger around her neck, dangerously nearing her face, and Newt barely holding one back. Hicks dives head first through the window and soon both creatures are history. As the smoke clears, Ripley gasps that it was Burke.

'I say we grease this ratfuck son of a bitch right now,' Hudson yells as he pushes his rifle into Burke's neck, and so rests the prosecution. Burke protests that they're all crazy and paranoid as Ripley reveals his obvious plan of getting the aliens back to Earth via impregnation of her and Newt – eeeuugh – then jettisoning the sleeping bodies of the remaining Marines and making up any damn story he fancied. There's a nanosecond of deliberation on what to do next before the jury returns with a verdict of Just Killing

Him. However, before sentence can be carried out, the lights all ominously shut down. Hicks orders everyone to arm up and bring out the trackers, and a now-awake Gorman keeps an eye on Burke. Hudson has a worrying reading: they're inside the complex and inside the barricade. They all rush back to operations and seal the door, with the readings on the motion tracker becoming more alarming by the second. Ripley concludes that it must be something they missed – Bishop got there first, just saying – but Hicks disagrees; they covered every square inch in their planning. Except maybe one – as they all instantly look up at the ceiling and gulp in fear. Hicks slowly hauls himself up and lifts a ceiling tile while pointing a light, only to find that their worst fears are coming towards them at high speed and in big numbers.

A manic, visceral firefight begins, bathed in deep red hues, with some very coarse language from Hudson. He goes out like a hero as he's pulled through the floor shooting wildly at anything that will listen. Burke uses this distraction, if you can really call it that, to make a break for it and shut all the doors behind him but is soon met with some instant karma. Unable to get the doors open, Newt takes the guys through the air ducts that she knows only too well, and as they scuttle inside, a group of Xenomorphs aren't far behind. Vasquez and Gorman bring up the rear, but with the former injured via acid splashes, Gorman brings out a pulse grenade as the aliens approach, and in a moment of beautiful poetry in a scene of chaos, they both hold the trigger and set it off. The explosion is felt all the way through the tunnels (think Eric Pickles after bad eggs), unfortunately sending Newt plummeting down a duct with Ripley and Hicks unable to reach her. But she's wearing Ripley's motion detector, and when they find her in the water below a walkway, they begin to cut a hole to get her out. Sadly, they have to witness Newt being carried away by an alien that emerges from the depths behind her – a genuine shocker of a scene that induced nightmares in every kid I knew.

Hicks and Ripley have to get to Bishop's waiting dropship, but they know that Newt is still alive. Surely, they'll think of something to get her back? But before they can fire up the grey matter, a rogue alien pokes its head into their elevator, and as Hicks blasts away, he's covered in a barrage of acid. They finally make it to the ship, and Ripley informs Bishop that they're NOT LEAVING, in the most certain of no uncertain terms ever. As Hicks rests, hand on forehead, Ripley gathers extensive weaponry, tapes a pulse rifle and flamethrower together, and pockets handfuls of grenades. She'll get Newt – of that there is no doubt – and then come back, and they'll be out of there before the complex evaporates in nineteen minutes.

As the strobe lighting flickers, Ripley boards a downward elevator and tools up. She studies the motion tracker and calmly lays out flares as she makes her way deeper into the aliens' den. Rounding corner after corner, until her beeping monitor becomes more urgent by the second, she finally locates the wrist beacon, but it's lying dormant on the floor. She takes a moment to mourn, but it's disturbed when she hears the sound of Newt screaming from within a sticky cocoon as an egg begins to hatch in front of her. Ripley wastes the facehugger, along with a few marauding aliens, while scooping up Newt to make an escape, but she gets the strangest feeling that something vast, drooling and menacing is behind her, which one supposes must have been akin to working for Trump. Ripley turns to see the answer to the egg riddle, and it's not Wilf Lunn, but a monstrous, egg-laying queen alien – a beautifully designed feat of creature work. She pokes her head out of her vast hood, revealing a mile of sharp teeth and gallons of drool. There's an unspoken negotiation as Ripley threatens the eggs with a flamethrower if the Queen doesn't withdraw her troops. The Queen nods and the workers begin to stand back – a moment that cries out for a David Attenborough voiceover. However, the Queen didn't get to where she is without breaking a promise or two, and some eggs begin to slowly open as Ripley passes, causing her to unleash hell with everything she's got: a flamethrower, grenade launcher, machine gun, and seriously stern looks. As the Queen looks around and rues this inferno as her 'annus horribilis', Newt and Ripley leg it back to the elevator before she can reach them.

They reach the landing pad, only to find that the dropship is nowhere to be seen and the other elevator has been activated (clever girl). The tension mounts as the structure begins to explode and fall apart around them, and then Her Majesty emerges from the opening elevator door. But luckily, at the best possible second, the dropship rises behind them and picks them up just in time. As James Horner's beautiful score plays out a countdown, the complex roars into hellfire, and as they depart into the atmosphere, it explodes in a giant white flash of closure. They made it.

The dropship arrives back on the *Sulaco*, and with Hicks out cold on board, Ripley, Newt and Bishop head out, with the android apologising for scaring her, but, you know, he had to circle round a bit as thing were getting hairy. As Ripley compliments him on his great work, everything seems like it's going to be fine. But then a spot of acid blood drips beside him and a giant alien tail rips through him, tearing him in half like a used love doll. As Bishop's leaking torso (great name for a band) is sent spinning across the hangar, Ripley looks up and sees the Queen, looking down from the inside of the ship. Newt runs off to hide in the ducts while Ripley locks herself away behind a giant steel door. After a short game of space Marco Polo with Newt, the Queen nearly has her in its grasp, only for Ripley to open the door and reveal that she's now inside a giant power loader and is ready to kick some alien ass – thus giving birth to one of the most satisfying and awesome boss battles in movie history, all contained within a jar marked 'Get away from her, you BITCH'.

The fight is fairly even, with the power loader able to contain the tail whips and toothy attacks, but with it becoming slightly boring, Ripley hits upon the idea of grabbing the Queen and dumping her down the airlock, a plan that works perfectly until she too is dragged down with her quarry. With the Queen trapped under the heavy loader, Ripley jumps out and pulls the switch, and after a short struggle – the sci-fi equivalent of getting ketchup out of a bottle – the screaming Queen is blasted into space, and we're also given the hilarious spectacle of a half-Bishop whizzing across the floor in the vacuum.

At last, Ripley closes the airlock, to be greeted by a heart-wrenching 'Mommy' from Newt, which gets me every time. 'Not bad for a human,' remarks Bishop as he lies there looking like the last love doll in Saigon.

Hair freshly blow-dried, Ripley tucks up Hicks in his space pod, pours what's left of Bishop into a vacuum pack, then sets up the next pod for Newt, who asks if she can have dreams, to which Ripley lovingly replies that they both can.

As the ship passes into darkness, we see one last shot of Ripley and Newt fast asleep, little knowing that the movie gods have something awful in store for both of them, but until then, they can both dream about how Burke may well have been alive when his beautiful, substantial dollar-valued complex was decimated before his evil corporate eyes.

TEN

1987

CHRISTMAS IS TRADITIONALLY A joyous time of year. It's the season for miracles, gifts, too much chocolate and booze, and the *Only Fools and Horses* festive special. However, for Amanda Hunsaker, who will never, ever see *Only Fools and Horses*, it's a time for taking too many drugs, wearing as little as possible, and jumping off the balcony of a high-storey apartment building to her death.

Sergeant Roger Murtaugh (Danny Glover) is indulging in one of the few pleasures granted to middle-aged people: a nice quiet bath. Once you reach a certain age, and especially if you have children, there's nothing quite like a quiet soak to regroup mentally and build up the courage to admit that your life is over. He's probably just about to calculate how many dumps he's had in his life when his fragile peace is shattered by a family invasion. Today is his fiftieth birthday, and his three kids and wife charge in to shout 'Surprise'. He sits up in his bath in shock, as you would, as a cake is thrust into his face and his wife Trish (Darlene Love) lovingly lays a flannel over his meat and two veg. He blows out his candles and wallows in the love that he has in his life, probably thinking that he has it all, before the bubble is well and truly popped by his daughter Rianne (Traci Wolfe), who tells him his beard is too grey, it makes him look old, but she still loves him, so that's OK. As the family depart, he slumps in the lukewarm tub and, as a melancholy saxophone blares out, looks at himself in the mirror, knowing full well that he looks old as fuck.

On a lonely beach somewhere in Los Angeles, a trailer sits among others on the seafront, looking as lost and beaten as the man who wakes up inside it. That man is Sergeant Martin Riggs (Mel Gibson), and as he bumbles around with a fag in his mouth, arse hanging out, the TV blares and his dog Sam looks at him with sadness in his eyes. He goes to the fridge and cracks open a beer, and burps, looking for all the world like he's two weeks into the third lockdown. There's no family for him (if you don't count Sam) and no joy in his life, unless the wee he has directly afterwards is a really good one.

A freshly shaved Murtaugh, now just wearing a moustache, comes down the stairs to greet Trish and grab some freshly cooked bacon. As he pours himself an orange juice, she asks him if he knows a Michael Hunsaker – he's been trying to reach him via his office for three days. Murtaugh takes a moment, probably still thinking about his ancient face in the mirror, and then remembers the name. They haven't spoken in twelve years, not since they were buddies in Vietnam together. As he contemplates the passage of time, he heads off to work, still mumbling about things as he goes.

His first call is to the scene of Amanda's death. The attending officers wish him a happy birthday, as is the tradition while standing at a death scene, and present him with their only witness, Dixie. She's a sex worker who was walking by and saw the whole thing. Murtaugh kindly suggests that as they have what they want from her, they should send her home, which is music to her ears, only then he spoils the mood by making an inappropriate joke about her giving blowjobs for a living. When an officer tells him the victim's surname is 'Hunsaker', it sends a ripple through Murtaugh. As he mournfully goes through Amanda's apartment, he finds a photo of her and Michael in happier times, and then calls home to Trish for that phone number.

Across town, Riggs is sitting in a Christmas-tree lot with three dealers straight out of Drug Dealer Central Casting. He's digging through a bag of cocaine with a pocket knife, checking its potency by eating it like sherbet. The sellers (one of whom is Blackie Dammett, Red Hot Chili Pepper Anthony Kiedis's dad) want his verdict, and, like the Man from Del Monte, he say yes. They're over the moon that he'll take all their stash and tell him it's his for a hundred – and they'll throw in a big Christmas tree for free. Riggs flinches at first, but accepts their offer and begins laying down the cash to make up $100. This causes consternation. The sellers stop his count and tell him it's $100k, but Riggs laughs at this outlandish price and gives them a counter offer: he'll take it all for free and they'll go to jail. He lays down his LAPD badge. They tell him he's crazy, and to prove it he begins acting like Curly from the Three Stooges, then pulls a gun. Thus begins a shootout, which ends with the remaining living dealer's gun pointed to Riggs's head. As other police officers move in from behind various Christmas trees, Riggs begins to bark, with an alarming level of authenticity, that he wants the dealer to shoot him. The dealer is rightly terrified, and this gives Riggs the opportunity to head-butt him and hand him over to his colleagues, after which he stands and reflects on what just happened, growling like a dog, blinking rapidly, and looking a wee bit unhinged.

Later that night, he sits in his trailer, drinking alone and gripping a photo of his late wife. Bugs Bunny cartoons play in the background. Tears pool in his eyes as he reaches for his gun and slowly slips a single bullet inside. This is a special bullet he's kept for this exact scenario (legend has it that Zeffirelli cast Gibson as Hamlet based on this scene alone), one that will do the most damage possible. He takes off the safety catch, and after giving it a quick polish, cocks the pistol and points it directly into his face. But then he changes his mind and pushes it into his mouth. He stays like that for a moment, eyes shut, before eventually pulling it out and cursing himself for not being able to go through with it. While Eric Clapton plucks some mournful strings, he holds the photo to his face and tells his wife that he misses her, before painfully discarding it and telling her he'll see her '*much* later'.

At the police station, as an amateur choir practise a rendition of 'Silent Night' that only dogs could hear, Captain Murphy (Steve Kahan) is chatting with LAPD shrink Stephanie Woods (Mary Ellen Trainor) about how he thinks Riggs is pretending to be mad to get a pay-off but he'll soon come around. She reminds him that he recently lost his wife of eleven years in a car crash, is very much on the edge, and should be removed from active duty. He may very well be psychotic. Murphy scoffs that this is 'psych bullshit' and Riggs is a tough bastard, adding that if he does off himself, he'll know he was right – the beneficent leader at work.

Murtaugh sits in his office and listens to a colleague telling him he's way behind the times. This guy cries in bed because he's alone and wants to get laid, which means he's a sensitive eighties man. Luckily for Murtaugh, he isn't a nineties man, or he'd be going on about Kylie and spraying Murtaugh with shit beer while surfing on his desk. After his sad colleague leaves, Detective Dan Boyette (Grand L. Bush) enters with news of the Hunsaker case. It appears that someone was with her before she died and that her pills were doctored, so even if she hadn't jumped, she would have died anyway. This is now a murder case. Murtaugh, though, is distracted by a man skulking around outside his office; decked in casual attire and a baseball cap, he looks very much like a Manson Family member on holiday. Boyette then informs him he has more exciting news: he's to have a new partner on this case, and it's some burnout case from the drugs squad who's on the 'ragged edge', which isn't exactly music to Murtaugh's crinkly old ears, and neither is the sight of the scruffy guy outside his office pulling a gun out of his trousers. Murtaugh races out of his room, shouting, 'Gun!' as he picks up speed. He's then tackled and flipped to the floor by the gunman, with the weapon thrust purposefully in his face. As the dust settles, Boyette introduces Murtaugh to his new partner, Martin Riggs. Murtaugh shakes his head and sighs deeply, giving us the birth of a catchphrase that will go on to decorate this saga like tired tinsel on a Christmas tree: 'I'm too old for this shit.'

Riggs and Murtaugh have a getting-to-know-you chat as they make their way through the car park. Turns out Murtaugh has been doing some digging in the files, and for our benefit will explain Riggs's background. It turns out he was in the 'Phoenix Project' in Vietnam, which could have been a working men's club he opened with Brian Potter, but turns out to have been a crack team who carried out top-level assassinations. Helpfully, Murtaugh reminds Riggs that the war is over and then compliments Riggs on his 9mm Beretta. He mentions that his file says he's also heavily into martial arts, suggesting that they register Riggs as a 'lethal weapon'. Riggs has heard enough. He says that they both know why he was transferred: some think he's suicidal and don't want to work with him, and some think he's putting it on to get a psych pension and don't want to work with him. Either way he's fucked. Murtaugh heartily agrees, and as they get into the car, you sense this is the start of a beautiful friendship.

Mr Mendez (Ed O'Ross), a shady drug baron, arrives for his meeting at a happening nightclub on Hollywood Boulevard. While a hair-metal band rehearses, to mixed reviews from the Cowell-esque promoter, he's shown in by Mr Joshua (Gary Busey), and then begins his meeting with Peter McAllister (Mitchell Ryan). To say he's unimpressed with the set-up is an understatement. Mendez is none too pleased that McAllister uses mercenaries and is worried about going into business with an employer of Psychos R Us goons with big guns. McAllister tries to soothe his worries by pointing out that his men are highly loyal and will do what they are told, and he illustrates this by holding a lighter to Joshua's arm for a prolonged period of time. Joshua takes the pain with only a mild grimace, thus proving himself worthy and leaving the audience to lament the lost Roger Hargreaves book, *Mr Joshua Has a Lighter Held to His Arm to Prove His Loyalty*. Mendez is suitably freaked out, and agrees to do business and make a purchase, despite reservations that they all seem as mad as a dog in a blender. McAllister tells him that he'll have his heroin on Friday night and says he has to leave; he's just remembered that it's Christmas and he's left his son Kevin at home with two weird burglars.

Murtaugh takes a melancholic reading of a black-and-white photo of himself and Michael Hunsaker in Vietnam, happily arm wrestling and smiling. Happy days indeed, when they could get blown up in the jungle without a care in the world. He puts it down and turns to Hunsaker (the always brilliant Tom Atkins) to deliver further bad news about his daughter. She was murdered because of the poisoned drugs she'd taken. Murtaugh asks him why he'd been trying to call before, and Hunsaker makes up a story about how maybe Murtaugh could have helped to get Amanda out of the business she'd found herself in. He goes on to explain that she was making 'video tapes', and I am sure a lot of parents these days would like someone like Murtaugh to help stop their kids making TikTok videos about their shoes. Hunsaker then reminds Murtaugh that he 'owes him', obviously harking back to that incident in Vietnam when he saved him from getting VD – or maybe it was a bayonet in the lung. He wants Murtaugh to find whoever is responsible for his daughter's death and kill them. His friend reminds him that he's a police officer and doesn't really make a habit of going on killing sprees – at least not until the sequel.

It's unclear exactly why Mr McCleary didn't have the best office party. Perhaps the punch was bad, the sausages on sticks were off, or someone put on a William Shatner album, but whatever the reason, he's decided to go up to the roof and threaten to jump. Riggs and Murtaugh arrive at the scene to the news that the designated officer is stuck in traffic, so Riggs announces that he'll do it; he's done it before. He wanders upstairs to the roof and joins McCleary on the ledge, wishing him a merry Christmas. He tries to calm him by telling him he's equally as terrified as he is, while also mentioning that his boss is down on the ground and he doesn't want to look bad. McCleary isn't having it at first, but Riggs does well, not referring to him as 'sugartits' once. He offers McCleary a cigarette, and as he brings up the lighter, he whacks on a set of handcuffs, presenting him with the fact that, now cuffed together, if he jumps it will be murder, as he'll be taking him with him. Which begs the question why McCleary doesn't ask how the fuck they could charge him with murder when he would also be dead? While protesting this mildly shitty move, McCleary pushes Riggs's buttons and refers to him as a 'psycho', which Riggs takes umbrage with. Before McCleary can protest, try to get away, or even ask if this is in the rules, they both leap from the building and hurtle all the way down into the giant inflatable crash mat on the ground.

Riggs giggles as he disentangles himself from the traumatised man, and they both roll out of the crash mat. Murtaugh is not best pleased, pulling him to one side to give him a bollocking. He wants to know, in no uncertain terms, if Riggs really does want to kill himself, and after a few verbal tennis shots, Riggs finally admits that he does, and he even has a special hollow-point bullet set aside for that very occasion, like when your mum gets out the best crockery for visitors. Murtaugh doesn't believe him at first, but decides to draw upon his years of management training by offering Riggs his own gun with which to do it, which seems like a sound idea. They stare sweatily at one another as Riggs puts the gun under his chin and slowly presses the trigger, until Murtaugh has to intervene and stop the pin from activating. He looks on in disbelief as he realises that Riggs isn't doing this for a psych pension; he really does have mental health issues. As he contemplates what to do next, Riggs announces he's going to get some lunch and wanders away. Oh, to be back in that bath with the beard.

'There's something eating away at this guy . . . I think he has a death wish' is Dr Woods's professional opinion. She thinks Riggs is on the edge, and that it won't take much to push him over. Murtaugh is thankful for this insightful prognosis from Los Angeles' answer to Dr Gillian McKeith, and laments the fact that he's been on the force for twenty years and there's not a scratch on him. While he's moaning about his lot in life (in the presence of a man who's lost everything he ever loved), he and Riggs begin to chat properly and get to know one another. In between smiles and laughs, Murtaugh announces that they're on their way to Beverly Hills to speak to Amanda's pimp, so Riggs promises that he'll let Murtaugh do all the talking and he won't damage or kill anyone.

Inside the luxurious compound – the sort of place you'd imagine would give Robin Leach a hard-on – all is not what it seems. A quick peer into the window reveals two ladies divvying up piles of cocaine, and while they smile at first at their two visitors, those smiles quickly turn upside-down when Riggs and Murtaugh reveal their police badges. The girls dash away from their distribution duties, but before our heroes can see where they're going, the peace and quiet is shattered by shotgun blasts from Amanda's pimp as he comes racing out of the pool house with all the malice and fury of a *Daily Mail* commenter. Murtaugh puts one in his knee, and then boasts to Riggs about how they can now question him. However, things go quickly awry. The pimp has a hidden pistol that he pulls out in Murtaugh's direction, and before he can bust out another catchphrase, Riggs puts a few more into him, killing him instantly. As the dust settles and they dry their clothes, tender classical guitar notes waft in the air like plump cherubs, and Murtaugh takes a moment to apologise for what he said earlier and to thank Riggs for saving his life.

It's dinner time *chez* Murtaugh, and the kids flood through the door to welcome Dad home, but he's not alone. He's decided to bring Riggs to meet the family, obviously praying that he doesn't ju-jitsu any of them. As he roams his lovely house, showing off, introducing his new partner to everyone, the warm flow of family life washes over Riggs. After avoiding the frankly admiring eyes of daughter Rianne, our two heroes grab a beer outside. They sit on Murtaugh's fishing boat to discuss just how 'neat' the Hunsaker case is. While on the surface it would appear that Amanda's pimp must have killed her, Riggs isn't happy with this theory. It's too easy. However, Murtaugh is. As Riggs calls it a night, after a brief chat with Rianne that may or may not lead to her continued use of illegal drugs, he congratulates his partner on having a helluva nice family, before asking him if he trusts him. Murtaugh thinks about it, and tells him that if he gets through the next 24 hours without killing anyone, he will. Riggs uses this moment of gentle reflection to tell Murtaugh that he's the best at killing, and that in Laos he was really good at shooting people from long distances. It turns out that, apart from drinking, smoking and carrying off that wild-eyed look, killing is the only thing Riggs is any good at. As he gets in his truck and drives away, Murtaugh is left standing in his driveway, worrying about just what will happen next – and why no one likes his wife's cooking.

While enjoying a quiet midnight beer, Murtaugh checks the mail that's been left for him on the kitchen counter. Among birthday cards and cute presents from his kids, he finds a jiffy bag stuffed with Amanda's high-school yearbook and a VHS tape ominously entitled 'Amanda and Her Friends'. He sits back in his armchair and presses play, only to find that rather than being Amanda hanging out with her great chums, it is in fact a dirty movie, and enough to make his glasses steam up. As he watches the naked ladies cavort and laugh in a shower while flipping through the book full of schoolgirl pictures, he must be thanking God that Trish doesn't come downstairs, or he'd have some serious explaining to do.

While indulging in some target prowess-based dick-waving at the firing range, Murtaugh and Riggs go over the details of the Hunsaker case again. This time they focus on witness Dixie and speculate as to whether she was involved. Perhaps she spiked Amanda's drugs with drain cleaner, then had to run when she jumped? Seems like a good idea to go and speak to her about what exactly happened; however, as they saunter over the road to Dixie's house, it explodes. Luckily for them, some cute kids got a good look at the scary, blond-haired visitor she had earlier that day, and he had exactly the same 'Never Quit' Special Forces tattoo as Riggs. This isn't good news, as along with this information and the highly distinctive nature of the device that caused the explosion, Riggs informs Murtaugh that whoever did this must be a serious professional – rather than a silly one.

With Amanda's funeral just having taken place and grief hanging in the air at Hunsaker's fancy clifftop villa, Murtaugh decides it's a good time to go and see exactly what his old buddy's involved in, and he's not in the mood for any bullshit. Hunsaker plays it cool at first, well, as cool as you can play it when your daughter has just been murdered by terrifying mercenaries, but Murtaugh reminds him that he called *before* Amanda was killed and was clearly trying to blow the whistle on something. Hunsaker eventually caves in and confesses that it all goes back to the war and his involvement in Shadow Company, a team of mercenaries who stopped the flow of heroin during the Vietnam conflict. They've now reformed – and not to back Cliff Richard on his next tour – and they're using those same sources from Laos to bring heroin into America. He was having second thoughts about the whole enterprise. They couldn't kill him because his bank is the perfect front for their operations, so instead they killed Amanda to keep him quiet. He reminds Murtaugh that it's big business, and very much like a Dragon from the Den, Murtaugh says he's out. He wants to close this operation down once and for all. But Hunsaker has another daughter who must be protected, and so, regretfully, he can't give Murtaugh the information he wants. This is made all the harder when, seconds later, a helicopter arrives from nowhere carrying Joshua, who then proceeds to fire a hail of bullets into Hunsaker from mid-air. That's quite the wake Amanda is having there. Looks like the band will soon be playing to no one and they'll have to ask for their money really awkwardly. As the helicopter flies off into the distance, Joshua calls McAllister to tell him Hunsaker spoke to the police and they may have a problem, but in the plus column, the buffet looked amazing.

It's late, and the streets of LA are awash with falling rain, broken dreams and soggy sex workers. Riggs and Murtaugh are wandering around the Strip, asking questions of women on corners – not about tariffs but about Dixie and her pimp. Riggs is reassuring a lady that he won't arrest her when a car screeches past. As he turns to see what's happening, Joshua pokes his mad head out the window. He's brandishing a shotgun, and gives Riggs both barrels, which sends him flying through a shop window. As the car hurtles away, Murtaugh races to the broken glass, only to find that Riggs was wearing his bullet-proof vest, is very much alive, and is now 'really pissed'. He tells Murtaugh that the man who shot him is the same blond guy who killed Hunsaker. As Murtaugh asks if he's sure, Riggs says yes and that they now have an advantage – the bad guys think he's dead – though what advantage that truly gives them is questionable. While they celebrate their newfound 'advantage', a message comes over the radio that prompts them to speed off to Murtaugh's house.

There, they find a note confirming that Rianne has been kidnapped (you should always leave a collection note), and while Murtaugh tries to style this out with Trish by pretending nothing is wrong, she can obviously sense that he's lying, and we're spared a sitcom where a husband has to pretend his daughter hasn't been kidnapped, with hilarious consequences.

In a quiet moment of contemplation while waiting for the baddies to call, Riggs tells Murtaugh that he will need to trust him and do things his way. Things will get bloody, messy and, at times, after a few drinks, anti-Semitic, but it's the only way to ensure that they get Rianne back alive. As Murtaugh reflects on whether he should trust his partner's more cavalier approach to policing, the phone rings into life, and he is told that they don't want his daughter, they just want to know what Hunsaker told him. He's instructed to meet them at El Mirage Lake at sunrise, and I, for one, believe that everything will probably be fine.

With a trail of desert dust in his wake, Murtaugh speeds his way to the rendezvous, but it doesn't go well. After threatening Joshua and his boys with a grenade, and Riggs firing some sniper shots from a hill, they're quickly captured to the sound of a slow trombone, to join a traumatised Rianne, who made a very decent and brave attempt at escape, but had to give in when being threatened by a helicopter. As Riggs is frogmarched out of his sniper nest by the General, he reveals that he knows exactly who McAllister is and then throws in for good measure that everyone in Shadow Company was a twat.

'Why don't you save your strength? You're going to need it,' taunts Joshua as Riggs hangs from the ceiling with water pouring on him like he's performing in the North Korean remake of 'Singin' In The Rain'. He then introduces his friend Endo (Al Leong), who will be his torturer today, and explains that Endo has forgotten more about dispensing pain than he will ever know, which sort of suggests he has a problematic short-term memory. Joshua goes on to explain that they want to know all the information the police have about their large heroin shipment that's coming in, and as they don't really need Riggs alive, he promises him a quick death if he tells all. Riggs tells him that they don't know anything, they killed Hunsaker before he could tell them, but Joshua just doesn't believe him, so he calls on Endo to bring forth his torture sponge that's wired up to a car battery. After a few hits from the electrocuted sponge, Joshua requests the information he needs again, but Riggs is a bit cross by now, and informs them both that he will kill them.

In another room, Murtaugh is tied to a chair and being tortured via fists, with the occasional application of literal salt into his wounds. When it's clear he won't talk, they bring in Rianne and give him one last chance to tell them what he knows about the shipment.

Meanwhile, as Riggs hangs limp in the torture-fall, Endo informs Joshua that he must be telling the truth: no one could take that amount of pain and keep quiet. Joshua agrees – Riggs is one badass soldier – but as he leaves, he tells Endo to keep at it. Once again, Endo picks up the torture sponge and approaches Riggs to give him another few thousand volts, but he doesn't count on Riggs's ability to murder him using only his legs.

Timing is something you just can't buy – ask any comedian. It's something innate and fused within the very DNA of those who possess it. As well as being able to murder people with any part of his body, Riggs is also blessed with the gift of timing, and proves it as he storms Murtaugh's torture room just as McAllister is monologuing about how there are no heroes left. As Riggs throws Endo's corpse from his shoulders like a javelin, there must be a part of McAllister wishing he'd just opened a sandwich shop instead of entering the tiresome world of drug trafficking. As the bad guy makes a break for it, Riggs unties Murtaugh and proves that he's feeling good about life by cracking a joke as they gather some weapons: 'Let's do what one shepherd said to the other shepherd, let's get the flock out of here.' Murtaugh just doesn't have the time or energy to point out how truly awful this joke is. But he should have.

They race through the club with Rianne, shooting wildly at miscellaneous goons, and bump into Joshua, who seems to have abandoned any pretence of being even remotely aware of health and safety practices in the workplace by firing blindly with an assault rifle into the room as he runs away. Riggs gives chase as Joshua steals a car and drives away from the Strip, still shooting randomly out of his window like a paperboy selling bullets. After Murtaugh tells Riggs that Joshua is heading for the freeway and advises on the best way to get ahead of him, Murtaugh then composes himself and utters those powerful words: 'General McAllister, time to die.'

Murtaugh heads back to the club, just in time to find the General and his driver manoeuvring out of the rear garage with bags of cocaine, grenades and a tartan rug in the backseat, obviously planning some sort of explosive picnic. As they spot him, then speed towards him with lethal intent, Murtaugh puts a bullet in the driver's face before getting out of the way as they career into traffic and crash into a bus. McAllister struggles to free himself from the vehicle as flames lick around him, and is clearly regretting bringing all those explosives as he stretches his broken arms to reach them. To do what exactly we shall never know. Murtaugh arrives just in time to watch the car explode into a ball of flames, and no one would think any less of him if he decided to piss on the burning wreckage.

With Joshua having escaped, Riggs and Murtaugh race back to the house, knowing that that's exactly where he'll be heading next, though why he doesn't just get on a plane to Mexico is anyone's guess.

Not one to disappoint, Joshua duly arrives and begins wandering around Murtaugh's living room, shooting his gun and mumbling to himself. He finds a note telling him that there's no one there except 'the good guys', and as he's reading it, a police car drives through the living-room wall, which seems entirely reasonable at this point. As Joshua tries to comprehend why someone would wilfully drive a car into his own house, Riggs appears with a gun pointing at his face. Within minutes, they have him out on the lawn and disarmed, but rather than arresting him and taking him to prison for multiple counts of murder and drug trafficking – and probably other stuff we don't even know about – Riggs decides this is a good opportunity to have a karate tournament in his partner's front garden. As the two white men leap about and occasionally kick and punch each other, all under a broken fire hydrant – more water to soak Riggs in pain and regret – other policemen gather to watch, with even Murtaugh occasionally shouting, 'Come on, Riggs! Break his fucking neck.' (An indicator of how it will all work from now on, with every arrest a gladiatorial trial by combat.) Eventually, Riggs gets Joshua in a powerful thigh-lock and chokes him into submission, leaving him to be arrested by normal policemen in the normal manner. However, as he's taken away, everything goes into slow motion, and Joshua manages to grab a gun from one of them and point it at Riggs and Murtaugh. They turn and fire at the same time, sending him down to the ground in a flash of squibs, putting an end once and for all to an international drugs syndicate, and this novelty episode of Celebrity Wrestling.

It's raining again. Riggs, a little bruised and battered, visits his late wife Victoria's grave. He lays some flowers, wishes her a merry Christmas, and wanders away. His next stop is Murtaugh's house, where he hands his customised bullet, gift-wrapped, to Rianne, and tells her to tell her dad he won't be needing it any more. She asks if he'd like to come in, and, probably realising that the bullet gift is a bit weird now that he comes to think about it, he declines, saying that he has to go. As he walks away, possibly to have the best wank he's had in years, Murtaugh comes running out of his house and tells him that after everything they've been through, he can't leave him to eat a lousy Christmas dinner on his own. They have a brief, warm chat about how Riggs isn't really crazy and how everything is great, despite them both standing on the spot where they beat and murdered a man the night before, in front of the fractured house that they drove a car through, but it's best not to focus on the negatives. Riggs happily accepts the invite, and brings his dog Sam in with him, an act that causes further internal strife as Murtaugh's cat smashes up the place in terror. 'I'm too old for this,' says Murtaugh with a sigh, adjusting a lone faulty Christmas light and, as the credits roll, contemplating ten more years of this shit.

Dystopian One Man (Mel Gibson) and his Dog
vs the Post-Nuclear Chicken Run (Vernon Wells). *Alamy*

The T-800 (Arnold Schwarzenegger) practices at Laser Quest (L), while Kyle Reese (Michael
Biehn) and Sarah Conner (Linda Hamilton) prepare to blow him up (R). *Alamy*

'What mean "expendable"?' *Alamy*

John Rambo (Sylvester Stallone) flaunts his curves as he heads out for a spot of light mass-murder, before taking in a show. *Alamy*

Matt Hunter (Chuck Norris) dares you to question his double denim life. *Alamy*

John and Chenny, together again. *Alamy*

John Matrix (Arnold Schwarzenegger) asks you to remember to leave quietly, as this is a residential area. *Alamy*

An American weary wolf in London.
Alamy

Shoot out to help out. *Alamy*

Maverick (Tom Cruise) offers Iceman (Val Kilmer) a bunch of fives, but this gesture is obviously taken out of context by the rest of the men. *Alamy*

'Yes, Tom, keep your mouth closed, your teeth aren't ready yet.' *Alamy*

Mr and Mrs Cobra. *Alamy*

The Cobra-mobile, complete with the worst personalised number plates. *Alamy*

Mother and child reunion. *Alamy*

Ripley's survive it or not. *Alamy*

Riggs (Mel Gibson) and Murtaugh (Danny Glover) show off their guns in the shop window of Harrods in 1987. *Alamy*

Riggs and a friend celebrate their perfect A-Level results. *Alamy*

Axel Foley (Eddie Murphy) goes deep undercover to play a millionaire who's heart just isn't in the current project. *Alamy*

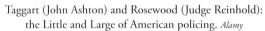

Taggart (John Ashton) and Rosewood (Judge Reinhold): the Little and Large of American policing. *Alamy*

A crack team of mercenaries pose for photos before heading to their eventual deaths. *Alamy*

Dutch (Arnold Schwarzenegger) comes face to face with a Predator (Kevin Peter Hall), who demands to know his beauty regime immediately. *Alamy*

Part man, part machine, all recyclable. *Alamy*

'You're fired.' *Alamy*

The Butcher of Bakersfield. *Alamy*

All hail and praise the Weathers man. *Alamy*

East meets West, and wears a tent. *Alamy*

Going to tell my kids this was Rod, Jane and Freddy. *Alamy*

'DIPLOMATIC IMMUNITY!' *Alamy*

The magic is back, and the mullet is bigger. *Alamy*

Blind Date was becoming more violent, and was therefore axed from the schedules. *Alamy*

Getting some Cash out, before heading into town. *Alamy*

ELEVEN

1987

 AXEL FOLEY IS BACK.
BACK WHERE HE DOESN'T BELONG.

A LIMOUSINE GLIDES SERENELY out of the Beverly Hills traffic and draws to a halt at Adriano's jewellery boutique – a fancy establishment that looks like it reeks of hairspray and furniture polish. The doorman opens the car door, from which emerge the six-feet-long legs of Karla Fry (hello, Brigitte Nielsen), an eighties glamazon in sophisticated, head-to-toe white, with very cool metallic sunglasses. As she strides towards the entrance, she drops her purse, and as the kindly doorman stoops to retrieve it for her, she pulls a gun. This is a fancy yuppie stick-up. Karla tells everyone to 'eat the floor', and a group of robbers run in and demolish the display cabinets while she acts as time-keeper, counting down from two minutes. After they smash up the joint and for some reason Karla shoots the chandelier, she announces it's time to go. She leaves a highly unnecessary calling card on the back of the cowering manager – an act that, while on the surface may seem cool and fun, in reality would surely only lead to their immediate arrest. One can only imagine that the staff of Adriano's must have thought this was an episode of *Candid Camera* rather than the highly organised heist it's supposed to be.

Back in Detroit, Michigan, Axel Foley (Eddie Murphy) is readying himself for another day, walking around his apartment and weirdly dropping a slice of bread in his fish tank, like some sort of psychopath. As Bob Seger belts out 'Shakedown', Foley dresses himself in a fine suit and fastens on a gold Patek Philippe watch, in a moment of art very much imitating life, with Murphy's situation changing considerably since he first walked the beat in Beverly Hills. As he roars out his catchphrase throaty laugh, he jumps into his Ferrari and heads out to work his elaborate sting operation, posing as a very rich, and dodgy, businessman looking to get hold of some credit cards. An operation that no senior police officer would green-light in a million years.

Vinnie (Robert Pastorelli) is sitting at the bar with his girlfriend, and calls Foley over as he walks through the door. He introduces his companion to Foley by boasting about how good she is at oral sex, which he should really save for the wedding-day speech. Foley isn't interested in this casual misogyny, though; he's here to acquire some more credit cards for his highly elaborate sting operation, and he then goes off on a comedy riff about being a businessman with a giant bag of money and how he's got things to do, which goes over like 11th hour improv. Vinnie tells him to meet him in three hours; he'll have the cards for him.

Back in Beverly Hills, police captain Andrew Bogomil (Ronny Cox) is out for his morning run through an oil field backdropped by a trademark Tony Scott hazy sunrise. He stops to catch his breath, and it's clear that he's being watched by a suited gent standing by a limousine. When he gets home, he puts in a call to Foley to tell him he'll have to cancel their upcoming fishing trip, as it seems since the events of the first film, Bogomil and his boys have become so friendly with Foley that they go on fishing trips and take photos of each other posing with a large catch to prove it. After Foley talks about how his daughter is so pretty that, if her dad didn't have a gun, something awful would have happened to her, Bogomil tells him that something big has come up and he'll call him in a week to tell him how it's going, while somehow skating over what Foley just said about his daughter.

At the police station Bogomil takes a meeting with John Taggart (John Ashton) and Billy Rosewood (Judge Reinhold), and they go over the letters that the Alphabet robbers have sent to the paper. They agree that these guys seem to know what they're doing, and when Rosewood suggests speaking to someone about it, Bogomil asks him why he's involved. He's already assigned to an extortion case, which begs the question as to why he's showing them anything to do with this case if he doesn't want them to be involved. But before we can get any answers, Chief Lutz (Allen Garfield) tells him to bring his men into his office for a dressing down. It turns out Rosewood asked the FBI for help on the Alphabet case, and Lutz is as pleased with this as someone who's just found out their food has been cooked by a rat under a chef's hat. While he's reading everyone the riot act, Bogomil stands up for Rosewood, saying that he was just following a hunch, so Lutz suspends him immediately, and sends Taggart and Rosewood to work traffic duty.

Bogomil leaves the police station and heads home. He notices a very tall woman with car trouble, so naturally he stops to help, but it turns out to be Karla Fry in disguise, like you can actually disguise yourself when you're 11 feet tall. As he's rooting around in her engine, she hands him an envelope with the letter 'B' stuck on it and uses his name. Naturally, he looks confused and asks who she is, but, sadly, he never gets an answer, as a car drives by and shoots him. When he stumbles towards Karla like he's about to bite her, she fires another shot into him before jumping in her car and driving away, leaving Bogomil on the verge, twitching, in a pool of blood.

Back in Detroit, Foley is all set to meet Vinnie at a bodyshop. However, when he gets inside, he's the only one there. He takes a seat in the office and flicks through a copy of *Playboy*, the TV chattering in the background. Within moments, the news has a breaking story about Bogomil being gunned down in broad daylight, so he uses the office phone (which seems sensible given he's mid-sting operation at the villain's premises) to call the Beverly Hills police department. He's transferred to the hospital, and he speaks to Jan Bogomil (Alice Adair), who tells him her father has been operated on and that she thinks he'll be OK. Rosewood gets on the phone and tells Foley that it was the Alphabet bandit (definitely should've been a character on *Sesame Street*) and he can't investigate it. Before Foley can take up more time on a criminal's phone talking to policemen, Vinnie and his contact show up for the deal. Only this time there's a slight snag: Carlotta, the contact that Vinnie has invited Foley to meet, is one of the men arrested at the start of the first film, and he instantly tells Vinnie that Foley is a cop. Foley styles it out by accusing Carlotta of also being a cop, as he got busted after the cigarette-truck chase. Vinnie hilariously says that he can't be a policeman because he's his nephew, despite being about twenty years older than him, but Foley sticks to his guns and storms out of the credit-card deal after doing a Muslim-related comedy scene and Harold Faltermeyer's theme bursting out for no discernible reason.

Back at Detroit Police HQ, Foley finds Jeffrey (Paul Reiser) and asks him to drive the Ferrari around while he's out of town for a few days, so no one knows he's gone, even though he's just ruined his own credit-card sting and will never be able to wind up the case. Jeffrey happily agrees and takes the key as Foley goes off to speak to Inspector Todd (Gil Hill, who in real life headed up Detroit's Homicide Division, fact fans). Todd is very displeased with how Foley's sting operation is panning out, owing to the department having paid out for flash money, a $2,000 suit and a $50,000 Ferrari, all just to stop some guys dealing in credit cards. He asks when he'll be making any arrests, and Foley doesn't really have any answers, so Todd tells him to get some results in three days or he'll grind his ass into dogmeat, which seems fair enough. Foley agrees and tells him that, in order to get results, he'll need to go 'deep undercover', and then he mentions something about not shitting in his Ferrari and leaves.

Foley arrives in Beverly Hills and meets with Taggart and Rosewood standing vigil at Bogomil's bedside. He tells them he wants to see the Alphabet letters, and for some reason they agree to show them to him, even though they've never actually worked on the case and have just got in trouble for trying to.

After a brief montage of Foley once again driving around affluent Beverly Hills and laughing while looking at rich people, dogs having sex and the bottoms of ladies in Lycra leisurewear, he notices a house that is being renovated by construction workers. He decides to pull over and bother them. It appears the owners are in Hawaii for a week while the building work is going on, so Foley decides to pretend to be a building inspector. He tells everyone to stop working, demands to see the plans from the foreman, and informs him that they're doing it all wrong: the owners want to live in a 'house with no right angles' and changed the plans before they went to Hawaii. He then sends everyone home to have a week off, thus causing them all to be sued and fired by the property owners when this film is over, with the building company easily losing thousands of dollars and possibly going out of business, just so Foley can have a wank in a pool.

Taggart and Rosewood show Foley the letters, and tell him that Lutz thinks it's the work of a serial robber, but Taggart thinks it's a nutcase, even though the very fact that the same bandits are leaving the same letters at every scene seems to back up Lutz's theory. Rosewood then hands over a bag of shell casings, which Foley is able to determine are .44 auto mags, a very distinctive bullet that they don't make any more as they are cut down from a .308 rifle and too expensive. This leads Foley to believe that whoever did this knew what they were doing – or, to interpret it in a different way, it's just more traceable fucking idiocy from the Alphabet crew, to go with leaving a letter at each scene. Foley's detective work is interrupted by Lutz storming in and, rightly, asking what they're all doing. Foley seizes the moment to do a little performance pretending to be a psychic from the Island of St Croix, who goes by the name of 'Johnny Wishbone' and is there to help the police department solve some cases. Lutz buys it. Foley meets up with Taggart and Rosewood outside and tells them they need to solve the case together. No one else can do it, and, more importantly, they have to do it, because Bogomil put his job on the line for Foley in the last film, so they all need to do this for him now, even though, if he were conscious, he'd tell Foley to go home immediately.

Our intrepid trio head to the Beverly Hills Shooting Club to speak with a ballistics expert, which gives Foley another chance to try out some more wacky improv. This time, he pretends to be a man dropping off a bag of 'plutonium-nitrate, multi-explosive, sound-seeking projectiles', and he manages to get into the gun club by pretending that they'll go off if anyone does even a tiny fart. What is Axel Foley, if not a failed improv who's ended up being a reasonably clever policeman? At this point he's essentially Sherlock Holmes meets Tony Slattery.

The gun range looks more like something in the Tyrell Corporation HQ in *Blade Runner* than a normal gun club. It's bathed in neon and UV lights, the kind of place where you can shoot a gun while also answering questions about tortoises. Foley walks up to Russ Fielding, the gunsmith, who is helping someone fire a weapon, and begins to ask about the bullet he stole from evidence. Fielding naturally asks where he got it, and Foley explains that Charles Bronson gave it to him for Christmas, as he's a close personal friend. Before Fielding can ask what the fuck he is talking about, Karla enters to ask if she can speak to Fielding for a minute, which leads to Foley standing on tip-toes to try to be as tall as she is, something he obviously learned from Sylvester Stallone. Foley ignores the laser-sighted practice guns that are on offer and fires a few rounds off from his own pistol in the range, blowing three holes in the target and doing his laugh as he puts his gun away, to stunned silence.

Maxwell Dent (Jürgen Prochnow) is the suave and sexy owner of the gun club, and, more importantly, the 'mastermind' behind the Alphabet jobs. Pure Tony Scott here . . . he sits, a silhouette enveloped in cigarette smoke, amidst the shadows in his office, emanating evil cool as he calls in club manager Chip Cain (Dean Stockwell), to tell him that he wants the next job to be perfect – unlike Adriano's. When Cain points out that Adriano's *was* perfect, Dent fixes him with a pitying look and informs him it was 'executed with Neolithic incompetence'; the choice of ammo has brought a man to the club asking questions about them. Dent senses that Foley is a cop and tells Cain to kill him as soon as possible, maybe leaving a note to say who did it. Luckily, they have Foley's address, as he gave it to them when they asked for it for a club membership application form, which is excellent policing.

Talking of excellent policing, Foley then pops over to Bogomil's house to dig around in his files. He comes across everything the captain has on the Alphabet bandits, which seems to consist of nothing but a slim manila folder with an advert for a club called '385 North' and some newspaper clippings – he was so close. After some dogged detecting of a muddy pair of trainers, he heads to his stolen house to chill in the pool. There, he receives a friendly visit from Rosewood and Taggart, the latter falling hilariously into the pool and then having to steal some amusingly natty gear from the real owner.

Following their only lead, they head to 385 North and blag their way in by pretending that Taggart is President Gerald Ford without his make-up. The lap-dancing club fulfils the eighties quota of having lots of boobs waggling in front of our heroes, who gawp and laugh like desperate hyenas waiting for the lion to sod off. While wandering around giggling, Foley spots Nikos Thomopolis having a nice time, and finds out from Taggart that he's the biggest arms dealer on the West Coast. This, after knocking back a couple of complimentary drinks, is their cue to leave and be shot at and nearly run over by the worst hitmen in California, who utterly fail in their mission and end up abandoning their car and running away. As the police arrive en masse, Foley retrieves a matchbook from the wreckage before facing down the wrath of Chief Lutz. He demands to know who Foley is, given there's no record of a

'Johnny Wishbone'. Foley tells him Wishbone is his codename, he's part of a multi-jurisdictional federal task force investigating organised crime, and Inspector Todd will provide all the info if he calls Detroit the next day, which, amazingly, Lutz swallows.

Back at Rosewood's apartment, which looks like it has David Bellamy living in it, with wall-to-wall greenery and low lighting, Foley sets out to do some basic forensic science with the found matchbook, by putting it in Big Al the turtle's tank (a turtle he demeans by looking for his penis) and covering it in superglue. While he waits for the glue to take effect, he pops into the bedroom to make a call, and sees that Rosewood now has an arsenal of weapons on his bedroom door, which is obviously supposed to be a joke about how Rosewood now thinks he's Rambo, but seen through the prism of the intervening years, only makes one conclude that Rosewood will one day perpetrate an atrocity.

Within minutes, the glue causes fingerprints to appear, and Foley explains that the fumes from the glue attach themselves to the prints on the card, making them visible, which causes Rosewood and Taggart to behave like they've just witnessed the discovery of fire.

They decide to head downtown and check the prints against the police database, and the fancy computer brings up a match: one Charles Cain, the manager of the gun club. Taggart suggests they put out an APB, which Foley dismisses outright, as a fingerprint is not enough evidence, thus educating Taggart on what it is he's supposed to do for a job. Foley's not convinced about Cain, however; he says he's a weasel, not a criminal mastermind, and wouldn't be clever enough to have anything to do with Bogomil's shooting – like only clever people shoot people now. Foley then decides that, despite just telling Taggart about what policemen can and can't do, it would be a great idea to break into the Beverly Hills gun club at 11 o'clock at night and snoop around, and, as luck would have it, in Cain's office they find map coordinates.

The following morning, Jeffrey, who looks like he's been up for days inhaling sweet, hot crack, sends Inspector Todd out on a spurious errand and sneaks into his office to intercept the call from Lutz to corroborate Foley's federal task force bullshit story. Thus, the web of lies continues to be weaved.

The coordinates found in Cain's office turn out to be those of the City Deposit – the federal reserve where banks send all their money – and that just happens to be the next destination for the Alphabet bandits. After a further highly elaborate heist arranged by men in shirts with no collars who drink Perrier occurs, Foley and Rosewood give chase in a wacky cement truck, hotly pursued by many squad cars, and eventually track down their quarry to, of all places, the Playboy mansion, because the screenwriters clearly haven't had enough boners as yet. After leaving the truck with a very young Chris Rock, they storm into the mansion, and Foley pretends that he's there to clean the pool because someone has had 'an accident' in it (another 11th hour idea, there). The ruse works, and within moments our heroes are wandering around the grounds looking at some bored-looking women in swimwear playing volleyball on the lawn while some bland music drearily topples out of the speakers. If this is the level of entertainment at the Playboy mansion, no wonder Hugh Hefner always looked so tired. It's not too long before Foley spots Karla Fry, Maxwell Dent and Nikos Thomopolis hanging out in a gazebo, so he strolls over and, after some playful banter, loudly announces that Max kills cops for a living, which alerts Hef to arrive on the scene and tell them that they're ruining his incredibly boring party, which has caused him to not have an erection for the first time in 40 years, and ask them all to leave. Dent ominously tells Karla that the plan will still go ahead. Little does he know. Foley has a new lead; he managed to lift Dent's wallet, and he now has the details of his accountant.

Sidney Bernstein (Gilbert Gottfried) is sitting behind his desk, talking like a machine gun into his phone and permanently squinting like he's got a corner office next to the sun. The door swings open, and in walk Foley and the lads, with a story about 25 unpaid parking tickets. Bernstein points out that it's his wife's car and picks up a phone to scream 'Bitch!'. This latest subterfuge (and a $200 bribe) gains Foley access to Bernstein's computer, so he can do some further digging on Dent. He finds out that his businesses are in trouble, he intends to leave the country for Costa Rica, and deduces that the next robbery will be at his own heavily insured racetrack. On the way to the track, Foley announces out of nowhere that he's cracked the Alphabet bandit code, like he's doing a sudoku puzzle, and that all signs point to Charles Cain being the ringleader. But he's suspicious. This code was too easy to break, and he thinks whoever did it wants everyone to know that Cain is in charge.

The next elaborate robbery occurs, and as the bandits are scooping up bundles of money to sexy keyboard music, Karla does her human-alarm-clock thing again, then murders Cain and his men. She joins Dent back at his trackside dinner table and they make their escape. Lutz calls a press conference to tell the world that the Alphabetti Spaghetti crowd will not strike again, as Cain is now dead, and then brags about how his men cracked the code, which seems presumptuous at best, and gives off huge George W. Bush 'Mission Accomplished' energy.

Foley's hawk eyes have noticed some familiar red dirt at the racetrack stables, though, and it's the same dirt he found on Bogomil's trainers earlier. He traces the mud to Dent's oilfield, near where the horses are sent to graze, so this must be where Dent has gone . . . apparently. The great criminal mastermind has gone to his own oilfield.

Foley, Taggart and Rosewood find lots of trucks, and Foley surmises that, together with Thomopolis, Dent must be selling weapons. While they scope out the area, Rosewood races to the boot of his car and retrieves a duster jacket and two shotguns. This is the moment he's been waiting for! He'll get his chance to murder lots of people with his toys. His excitement doesn't end there. They find a truck full of grenades and bazookas, and Rosewood pockets a few, with a smile on his face like he's arrived back at the Playboy mansion and it's full of sexy guns as well as volleyball ladies. Before too long, a shootout commences, and Rosewood gets to use his bazooka to blow up an escaping truck. After telling him that they need to talk and asking if he's 'nuts' about 300 times, Taggart now exclaims, 'Fuck Rambo,' which if anything is pure uncut enablement. As the police arrive and the majority of the bad guys give themselves up, Foley sneaks inside the main building to find Dent. As this is a Tony Scott film, he's standing in a perfume ad, with shadows, shards of light, flapping birds and whirring fans filling the room. After shooting at each other for a bit, Dent decides to just drive through Foley, which doesn't work out well when Foley puts a bullet in his head as he motors towards him, causing the car to career down a hill and explode. Before Foley can do his laugh or say anything amusing, Karla appears with a gun to say goodbye to Foley. But she's shot multiple times by Taggart, who appears from the sidelines, looks down at her corpse and simply says 'Women!' – all of which earns him a Foley laugh and a job on LBC.

Lutz arrives at the war zone, apoplectic with rage and demanding to know why they have been shooting people, blowing stuff up, and still investigating the Alphabet crimes that he personally solved at the racetrack. When Rosewood tries to explain, Lutz tells him to shut up, causing Rosewood to shout at him that the Alphabet case has always been about guns and the robberies were merely a means to fund the purchase of weapons from Thomopolis. If they hadn't arrived to stop them, Dent would be on the way to Costa Rica now. Lutz has had it; he tells all three of them they're fired, which visiting Mayor Egan (Robert Ridgely) takes issue with. He now tells Lutz that's he's had enough of the abusive way he speaks to people and that he's actually fired, and that Foley, Rosewood and Taggart are heroes for solving the case, and other such platitudes that wander into this film with an awkward gait.

The next day, Bogomil is back at police HQ in a wheelchair, presumably more machine than man now, and the new chief of police. However, there's no time to celebrate or give him the bumps, as Mayor Egan is on the phone to Inspector Todd to congratulate him on his expert tutelage of such a fine officer. Todd asks to speak to Foley and isn't best pleased; it turns out Jeffrey's crashed the Ferrari and he's now in his own wheelchair with a leg in plaster. Foley promises he'll come back immediately and get to work on that credit-card scam that's now so dead in the water it might as well be Robert Maxwell.

As he packs his bags away and leaves his stolen house, Foley tells Rosewood and Taggart that he loves them and that they should come visit him one day, while doing a few of his familiar laughs and joking about the size of Taggart's penis. As he drives away, the real owners arrive home, with the man, who looks like Michael McDonald if you pumped him full of jam, asking what exactly is going on, leaving Foley to look back from the driver's seat and smile in freeze-frame. Somehow, I don't think that will cut it in court.

TWELVE

PREDATOR

1987

IT HUNTS FOR SPORT.
IT KILLS FOR PLEASURE.
THIS TIME IT'S PICKED THE WRONG MAN.

FROM WITHIN THE BLACK depths of space, an alien craft rockets into view and speeds past the stars, sending a capsule hurtling out and down to our Earth. Could this be a kindly alien here to bring peace and goodwill to all men? Given it's the eighties, highly unlikely.

On Earth, as Alan Silvestri's tub-thumper blasts out, a helicopter full of giant men lands at a beachside base. They all stride out like bouncers at a fight convention, rippled with muscles and enough machismo to fuel a GI Joe factory, but there is a clear leader: Major Alan Dutch (Arnold Schwarzenegger), the only man in action-movie history to carry off the name 'Alan' with a genuine swagger. No one calls him 'Alan' to his face, of course; he goes by 'Dutch', as well he should. He's come to the base for a briefing from General Phillips (E.G. Marshall). A helicopter carrying a cabinet minister and his aide has crashed in a South American jungle and will need a rescue, pronto. They have a fix on their position, and it would seem they strayed off course and have fallen into guerrilla hands. Dutch asks why he and his elite band of brothers have been tasked with such a normal rescue mission, but before Phillips can explain, a voice cries out from the back of the room explaining that they needed the best. It's Dutch's old friend Dillon (Carl Weathers) – a big, handsome suitcase of a man. They embrace in the only way two men with muscles the size of mountains can: by calling each other names and grasping hands while flexing their guns with maximum pressure. This opening scene really is an anthropologist's dream. What made men of this era behave like this is worthy of its own study. After the mano a mano palaver, Dillon tells Dutch that some good people are about to get squeezed by baddies, and they can't let that happen, and he's coming with them. They need to drop in, grab the minister and his aide, and get out before anyone knows they were there. Dutch doesn't like the idea of CIA man Dillon tagging along, despite him being a pal, but he's told by Phillips that Dillon will be commanding the mission.

As Little Richard's 'Long Tall Sally' toots out of a ghetto blaster, we get to know Dutch's team. They're all aboard a helicopter making its way to their drop-off point. There's Mac (Bill Duke), who really likes dry shaving, Blain (Jesse Ventura), who loves chewing tobacco and being a man, Poncho (Richard Chaves, who is just a guy, Billy (Sonny Landham), the eighties answer to Drax the Destroyer, and Hawkins (Shane Black), the plucky comic relief, who may as well be wearing a red Starfleet uniform. There's excellent banter as we get to know our rugged team of heroes, with jokes about big vaginas, offers of chewing tobacco and ball catching, but the light-hearted mood comes to a swift end as the green light flashes in the chopper. It's time to descend the ropes, gear up, and enter the jungle.

It's not too long before Dutch and his squad come across the missing helicopter. It's dangling from a tree, looking very much like a Tracey Emin installation, and as Poncho climbs up to investigate, he comes face to face with a scene of devastation. The whirly bird has been blown out of the sky by a heat-seeking missile, and in Poncho's experienced view, this looks more like a surveillance chopper rather than a governmental one. Dutch suggests to Dillon that a heat-seeking weapon seems quite advanced for a bunch of guerrillas. Billy has news, too: it seems there were twelve guerrillas, and they took two men from the helicopter – and that's not all, there were also six men wearing US Army boots who came in from the north, and followed behind. Dillon suggests it could be a rebel patrol – they operate in the area – but Dutch doesn't look convinced by this answer. When Billy stops for a water break and scans the trees above him, something catches his eye. As he climbs up to see what it is, he's confronted by a gory scene: three men hang upside down from the trees, skinned and eviscerated, like Frank from *Hellraiser* decided to go bungee jumping with a couple of his mates and got stuck. Tucked inside the guts beneath them is a dog tag, which Mac locates and throws to Dutch. It's General Hopper's. Dutch knows this team; they were Green Berets from Fort Bragg, and he wants to know why they were here. But Dillon has no answers, concluding that they shouldn't have been here at all, and certainly not with all their skin missing.

Billy examines the evidence at the scene, and reports to Dutch that there was a fire fight, but not a normal one, as they were firing randomly in all directions, like wallies. Dutch can't believe Hopper and his men would have walked into an ambush, and Billy doesn't think they did, as he can't find a single track from anyone else. The squad are shaken, but they decide to follow the guerrilla trail and rescue the hostages, as per the mission. Mac turns to Blain and recommends it's time he brings out 'Old Painless', which of course is a reference to his fucking ginormous mini-gun, which must have been in a ginormous pocket this whole time. Blain straps it to his arm, cocks it, and announces that it's payback time. As they move out, it becomes very clear that they are not alone. Up in the trees, shrouded in greenery, something is watching them – something with heat vision and something that is invisible to the naked eye. While it's not exactly clear who or what it is, one thing is for sure: it's not what you'd normally find in the trees in a jungle at this time of day, unless of course it's Bill Oddie in a hide.

They spot an enemy encampment and slowly crawl along the crest of a hill to peer at it through binoculars. It's your bog-standard enemy camp, with guards stationed in sand-bagged platforms, men in high towers, old cars lying around the entrance – just an overall *Deer Hunter* aesthetic that really ties the place together. Dutch, however, sees something through his goggles that turns his stomach: a man, presumably an American soldier, is executed at point-blank range by a guerrilla. This causes him to deflate and sigh, and momentarily curse the brutality of war, before he indicates to his men that it's time to get into position and murder hundreds of people. He kicks it off by lifting up a stationary truck and planting a bomb on it, before releasing it into the camp. And when it explodes, all hell breaks loose. Dutch's men rampage through the camp, shooting, stabbing, exploding and murdering everyone and everything. After telling Poncho that he doesn't have time to bleed (and you think your schedule is tough?), Blain takes great pleasure in using 'Old Painless' to decimate an entire generation of guards. As the smoke clears, the bodies cook, and the dust settles, Dutch finds some paperwork that casts a bit of a gloom over the outing. It would seem that the entire mission wasn't about rescuing a cabinet minister at all; instead it was an intelligence-gathering operation. Dillon confirms it and, unwisely, also tells Dutch that his men are expendable assets that he needed to get the job done, which doesn't go down well. He then reveals that his men went down in the helicopter, and Hopper and his team were sent to rescue him, but instead ended up as kebabs. Dutch is about to get very cross, but he's interrupted by Hawkins, who tells him that air surveillance say a load more guerrillas are on the way, and they have thirty minutes to get out. Dillon wants to bring Anna (Elpidia Carrillo), a female insurgent found among the carnage, but Dutch doesn't like the idea, going on to declare that she's baggage, which seems a bit harsh seeing as they've only just met. As they plan the best way out of the devastation they have just created, they are once again being watched by heat-vision eyes, and listened to intently. As they set off on their planned route, it's not long before Billy has to stop and look into the trees. He's spooked, and his keen tracking skills and powerful nose are sensing that something isn't right. Dutch comes alongside him and asks what's up, and Billy tells him that there's something in the trees, and he's pretty sure that it isn't Bill Oddie this time, either.

Anna is not greatly happy about being abducted by a flock of wardrobes and dragged through the hot jungle, so she makes her feelings known by thumping Poncho with a log and making a run for it. Hawkins gives chase and catches up with her, reassuring her that although his friends all look like big-rig trucks in khaki, they are in fact lovely, but before he can explain how much they give to charity, a transparent, highly camouflaged figure rips through the undergrowth and whisks Hawkins away in a swift wave of blood, leaving Anna to ponder exactly what just happened. I mean, no way would Bill Oddie do that.

As Dutch and his men arrive on the scene they find blood trails, Hawkins's stuff and a pile of guts, but no body. 'The jungle came and took him,' Anna says in her Spanish voice, as Poncho translates, but Dillon isn't buying it. He thinks she's crazy and some men took Hawkins, but Dutch quite rightly points out that if it was guerrillas, why didn't they take his radio or weapon? And why didn't Anna escape? Dillon then remembers that the same thing happened to Hopper, so they decide to try to find Hawkins's body, for some reason, so they double back and retrace their steps.

Blain steps through the trees with his giant mini-gun in his hand, chewing his tobacco as usual, and probably planning what he'll do when he gets home. Maybe he'll give up this whole soldiering lark and open a sweet shop, or buy a cool car and drive to Denver, but before he can even contemplate sourcing suppliers for sherbet dips, a bright light leaps from the trees and shoots through his chest, leaving a hole the size of Texas. Mac races to the scene of his best friend's body, and sees a camouflaged figure standing yards away. It's eyes light up before it turns and runs into the undergrowth, so Mac opens fire and begins to call it names; however, he quickly runs out of ammo, so picks up 'Old Painless' and carries on shooting. Dutch and his team arrive at the scene as Mac is energetically strafing everything in sight, and being the level-headed commander that he is, Dutch decides to join in, and the team, as one, spend what seems like hours filling the empty jungle with enough bullets to build a rocket to the moon.

After the third hour, Dutch orders a ceasefire and sends Poncho to go and see what they hit, but he swiftly returns to advise that apart from a ruined barbecue in Madagascar, where some stray bullets decimated a beanbag, they hit nothing. Dutch inspects Blain's body, and notes that there are no powder burns or any kind of shrapnel, and the wound is cauterised. He then asks Mac what he saw, which he probably should have asked before his team destroyed an entire rainforest, but Mac says he doesn't know. Dutch orders Dillon to get on the radio, and tells Mac to snap out of it and arm the area with every tripwire, explosive and flare they have. As the team race off to get organised, Anna touches a patch of neon-green blood on a leaf and brushes it off on her trousers.

Across the jungle, our camouflaged villain sits down on a log and deactivates the disguise. That same green ooze is running down its leg, and a clawed hand opens a battlefield medi-kit to retrieve some tools. There's an open wound in the thigh and as it presses it, an implement slips and it roars in pain. Anna and Billy hear it, and look suitably worried, but the rest of the team are listening to Dillon, who is being informed that extraction from their current location is impossible: the area is still compromised, and so they'll need to move to a safe zone. Dillon once again tries to get some sense out of Mac, but he still can't describe what happened, just that he let it have 200 rounds. Anna chips in that it 'came out of the jungle'. Billy tells the team he's scared and whatever is hunting them ain't no man. Just as the team try to come to terms with Billy's alarming announcement, he then decides to cheer them up by telling them that they're all going to die. It must be like going on holiday with Thom Yorke.

Nightfall arrives and the team hunker down to catch some rest. Mac is on first watch, sitting by Blain's body and toasting him with his flask of booze. He regales the corpse with stories of their many adventures and battles through the years, and how he still owes him twenty quid, but before he can go into what happened to his favourite Toby jug, the tripwire sensors burst into life and the sky is lit up by chaos. Mac jumps on the intruder and rolls around in the dark, stabbing wildly at it and calling it offensive names. As the others' torch beams highlight him in the darkness, it's immediately clear he's wrestling with a wild boar, which Poncho thinks is hilarious. As the team relax in the light relief of pig slaughter, Billy notices that Blain's body has vanished.

The next day, the team inspect their traps. Nothing. Poncho is confused about how something could come in and take the body without leaving a trace, and it's then that Dutch realises that, whatever the thing is, it's hunting them one by one. He grabs Anna, and asks what it was, and she speaks perfect English this time, telling them that it changed colours like a chameleon, which Dillon dismisses immediately, thinking that she means an actual lizard did it. This suggests he's not taking this seriously, especially after all that's just happened. Dutch cuts Anna free as he wants everyone on hand for what they need to do, which annoys Dillon as he wants to get to the rendezvous point, but Dutch tells him they need to make a stand or there'll be no one left to get there.

There then follows a sequence where our heavily muscled men take off their tops and bring down the very trees, ripping up roots in unison, like some sort of jungle-based episode of *Challenge Anneka*, but rather than building an orphanage for kiddies, they're constructing a no-man's-land of tripwires, claymores and nets in order to snag their hunter. Once they've finished with their death trap, they sit back in the foliage and wait for the thing to appear. Anna then entertains the team with happy stories about how this isn't the first time this hunter has appeared in her neck of the woods, and how it comes when it's hot, and how they would often find men without skin. In fact, he's such a regular visitor that he's earned a nickname from her village, 'the demon who makes trophies of men' – which needs a rethink from the marketing department, as it really doesn't trip off the tongue.

The silence is deafening, and after a long wait, it's clear that nothing is coming. Dillon suggests using cheese as bait, but Dutch decides to use himself. He heads out into the clearing in order to tempt the hunter. As he steps over wires, strings and bombs tucked in the ground, the tension is high – a bit like waiting for the Tesco delivery when it's coming to the end of the one-hour slot – but it soon becomes clear nothing will happen, so he turns to walk back to camp. As he does so, a trap is triggered and the hunter is caught in a giant, comedy net. As it flails and screams, blasts fly out aimlessly, with Poncho falling victim to a random swinging log. As Dillon composes himself and looks up, he sees the glowing eyes of what's been hunting them all this time: the Predator. A masked creature, covered in body armour and with flowing dreadlocks, it looks like Eddy Grant if he'd turned into a crazed survivalist. It skims the trees and swings away into the jungle, whereupon Mac breaks away from the squad and gives chase, much to Dutch's chagrin. He's about to go after his clearly unhinged friend, when Dillon tells him he'll go, and to hold the chopper, and to smoke him some kippers, he'll be back for breakfast.

Mac blunders through the jungle, belting out 'Long Tall Sally' like a drunk at three in the morning. Dillon, meanwhile, follows the trail of dumped equipment that he's left behind, and is just about to run on further when Mac grabs him and pulls him into some bushes. He has a good fix on the Predator; he can see it sitting on a branch, bending the light with its unique, rippling camouflage as it looks around. As he points it out to Dillon, he suggests that they flush it out front and back, and work as a team to bring it down, and Dillon agrees. When Mac crawls under some logs to get a better shot, he is distracted by a strange, red laser pattern that rests on his arm, so he decides it would be a good idea to look directly into that light, only to have his head blown clean off. On hearing the noise, Dillon stops in his tracks and turns back, racing through the jungle to see if Mac is OK. He soon finds out that he most certainly is not, and let's just say Mac won't be attending that hat convention in July. Dillon scans the trees, looking for the hunter, and there, standing on a branch nearby, those same eyes glow once again, and as he raises his gun to shoot, a laser fires out, severing his arm as his weapon begins to fire, and as if that isn't bad enough (that was his wanking arm), the creature leaps down from the trees, bringing out a mounted arm knife, and races towards our one-armed hero. As Dillon tries in vain to shift another weapon to his one remaining good arm, it's all too little, too late. The creature plunges the spike into him, lifting his body up in the air as he does so (and keen-eyed viewers will note that Carl Weathers is clearly lifted on a wooden springboard during this scene), causing him to scream out in agony.

Bill hears his anguished cries echoing through the trees, and as Dutch, Anna and Poncho head across a log over a river, he decides he will take a stand. He promptly begins to dump his gear into the stream, like an overworked Christmas postie. While Dutch doesn't agree with Billy's decision, he respects it, and let's be honest, Billy is a bit weird and very, very scary, so it's best not to ever argue with him. As they head on to the rendezvous point, Billy unsheathes his massive knife, and with the maddest of mad looks in his eyes, carves a wound in his chest, and waits for the Predator to emerge so they can have it out in the ultimate battle of man versus alien, which I'm sure will be a long and incredible spectacle.

However, mere seconds later, a scream is heard, and Dutch and his team stop in their tracks. One can only assume Billy didn't actually last very long against his quarry, and by the sounds of it, received the world's biggest wedgie. Before Dutch can think about what to do next, a laser blast kicks out from the jungle and fires into Poncho's head, killing him instantly. Dutch tries to return fire but is also hit, and as Anna tries to fire back with a gun she found somewhere, Dutch kicks it out of her hand, telling her to keep running and 'get to the chopper'.

As Anna runs for it, Dutch rises to his feet and stumbles the other way through the trees, with the creature giving chase, but he quickly finds himself falling into a mudslide and tumbling over a cliff edge into a large body of water below. As he emerges from the blue and crawls up the muddy riverbank, he must think he is safe from danger. Maybe it's time to give himself some special time out to remember what a great team he had. How Mac just loved dry shaving, how Blain loved chewing his ol' baccy and firing a big gun, how vagina jokes are probably a bit boring once you've heard them thirty times a day, and how he will definitely shit on Dillon's grave. However, his reminiscing is disturbed when the water behind him erupts in a large, invisible splash, so he quickly crawls through the mud and sits up against the bank, with the resigned look of a man who knows his time is up. The Predator emerges from the water like Peter Andre in the 'Mysterious Girl' video, with its cloaking device sparking and malfunctioning as it does so. It turns the device off and begins to walk the bank, seemingly with intense purpose, and seemingly with another body to collect, but as Dutch looks right down the barrel at the creature that's come to kill him, it would seem that something is wrong. It's scanning the area, but it's apparent that it can't see him. The mud has perfectly camouflaged Dutch's position. The Predator quickly gives up, and after kicking a log in a moment of petulance, it heads back towards the jungle, leaving Dutch to realise that the tables have turned: he will now become the hunter.

After a montage of both hunters readying themselves for what comes next – Dutch constructing hundreds of traps from logs, and a bow and arrow from tree branches, the Predator sharpening his wrist knife with a laser while turning Billy's head into an ashtray – night falls over the jungle.

Dutch has covered himself once again in mud, and has prepared a welcoming bonfire for his inevitable visitor. He unleashes a mighty roar, and the Predator approaches. After walking past our hidden hero, it comes down from the trees and walks across the log over the roaring fire. Dutch readies his bow and arrow, and fires an explosive right in front of the creature, causing it to screech in surprise and its cloaking device to once again short-circuit. It fires aimlessly into the trees in response, with one blast sending Dutch falling out of his nest to the ground below. A foot chase begins, with the Predator leaving a trail of fluorescent green blood for Dutch to follow; however, in the chaos, he falls into some water and loses his concealer-mud advantage. The Predator grabs him as he emerges from the wash, and pins him up against a tree, looking him right in the face as he does so. It lets him go, removing all weapons as it does so, clearly signalling that it wants a punch-up. The mask is last to fall, and as it does so, Dutch sees for the first time the face of the creature that's been ruining his day: a lobster-faced, spider-headed man from space, who is clearly livid. After noting that the creature is not the most good-looking of chaps, a brief bout of fisticuffs ensues. The Predator is clearly stronger, better and taller, so Dutch crawls back into his main trap. The creature quickly figures this out and navigates around it, only for Dutch to have the last laugh. He kicks out the drop mechanism, causing a giant log to fall from the trees and crush the creature in one satisfying thud.

Dutch is relieved, and takes a moment to revel in his victory, only then to notice that the log is still moving. He grabs the biggest rock he can find and heads to the body to finish the job, like he's just hit a badger on the M23. He takes a moment to ask the Predator what the hell it is, only for the creature (with Frank Welker's voice) to basically ask him the same question, revealing a philosophical bent. The Predator is now pressing buttons on his little wrist device and laughing maniacally, which in Dutch's world can only mean one thing: a massive explosion is about to happen. He races away as fast as he can and jumps into the air, just as the area behind him is consumed in a vast inferno.

As daylight breaks, with huge plumes of smoke enveloping the scorched earth that was a jungle, Major Phillips, Anna by his side, arrives in the chopper to pick up a battle-scarred and bloodied Dutch. As they head into the horizon (piloted by Kevin Peter-Hall, who played the Predator), Dutch reflects on how war is hell, how men are merely made of clay, and how there's one thing he now knows for sure: this had nothing whatsoever to do with Bill Oddie.

As the credits roll and we see the names of our brave fallen, we can revel in the fact that this is as close as Hollywood ever got to a Croft and Perry 'You Have Been Watching . . .'-style end sequence, and it's to cinema's detriment that it doesn't happen nearly enough for my liking.

THIRTEEN

1987

PART MAN, PART MACHINE, ALL COP

THE (NOT SO) DISTANT future. Detroit. A time of rabid right-wing media, ultra-violence and public services being throttled to the point of strike action. A world that seems almost impossible to visualise as we limp with broken hearts and minds through the landside of shit that is the 21st century, doesn't it?

'This is Media Break. You give us three minutes, and we'll give you the world': a bold claim that many a foolish man has made in his time, but on this occasion happens to be true. With rolling news a few years off, in 1987 people liked to have their news thrown into their eyes like gravel in handy, fist-sized portions. The urbane Casey Wong and Kim Wilde lookalike Jesse Perkins are the faces of the station, and very much the Susanna Reid and Bill Turnbull of the future, serving their viewers hot shit sandwiches of news in an effort to dress up this dystopia of unchecked crime and nuclear escalation – all of it about as effective as putting a cocktail dress on John Merrick.

We learn that not only is the planet fucked but the Detroit police force are talking about going on strike due to gross mismanagement by vast super-corporation Omni Consumer Products (OCP), and if that wasn't enough, there's a violent cop-killing mob boss on the loose – one Clarence Boddicker. A sort of pallid, bespectacled post-Brexit Sven-Göran Eriksson, he's exactly the kind of character you would find in a wasteland, pillaging your meagre allotment before crucifying your family members and chucking the remains in a bin. OCP's Division President doesn't really have a lot of sympathy for the police force losing so many men and essentially calls them all cowards. It's a bold move, and let's see how that turns out.

Alex Murphy (Peter Weller) is an affable family man of admirably chiselled features, and also a good cop, a very good cop – the kind you'd expect to find in a police training video hosted by Paul Coia. He's been transferred to the Metro West precinct, which is, to put it mildly, a bit of a rough one. Police officers are dropping like flies thanks to Clarence and his team of hyper-bastards, and talk of a strike is very real – as is wandering around the locker room with their flabby bits hanging out. There's heightened tension in the air as Fredrickson, the latest policeman attacked, is confirmed dead and his locker emptied. Sgt Reed tells everyone to forget about the strike: they're not plumbers, they're police officers, and police officers *don't* strike. Though it might be an idea to actually wear bulletproof vests rather than the very thin sheets of grey packing foam they seem to go out in when tackling homicidal criminals. Just a thought.

However, there is one cop who is very much 'on the job': Officer Anne Lewis (Nancy Allen). Murphy quickly discovers that she kicks vast amounts of ass and takes names later when he witnesses her beating up a suspect in the station, and he considers it 'pretty neat', showing him to be a hip and pragmatic dude. The Captain declares that they are now to be partners, and Murphy cements this by announcing to Lewis that he always drives when 'breaking in a new partner'. So off they speed, on their first assignment together. I am sure everything will be fine.

Meanwhile, over at OCP, Bob Morton (a permanently enraged

Miguel Ferrer), Johnson (Felton Perry) and Kinney (Kevin Page) are in an elevator heading on up to the high floors to watch Division President Dick Jones (Ronny Cox) give a presentation. Morton fears that Jones has the 209 programme online and wants to show off about it. This is bad news for Morton, as when the 209 programme hit major snags, he was tasked with putting together a back-up plan, and he firmly believes it's a better idea. As the boardroom fills with excited execs, the Old Man (Dan O'Herlihy) starts the meeting, telling everyone he's had a dream for more than a decade, and in six months – cue shot of Styrofoam model – Delta City will be constructed where Old Detroit stands, with job opportunities galore. But before it can begin, they need to address the problems of Old Detroit, namely, crime, and that's where Dick Jones comes in. He's excited about his new scheme to wipe out crime entirely. A 24-hour cop, who doesn't need to eat or sleep, has superior firepower, as well as the reflexes and will to use it. As he approaches the double boardroom doors, he announces 'the future of law enforcement, ED-209'. The doors swing open, and there stands a giant robot chicken wielding massive machine-gun arms. This, supposedly, is the future of crime fighting, and this will stop Old Detroit from eating itself. They activate the beast, and Phil Tippet's wonderful go-motion springs into action, as it stomps into the boardroom and roars like a lion chicken. The boardroom shits itself in unison until Jones brings it to a halt and announces that the Enforcement Droid-209 is currently programmed for urban pacification, but after a tour of duty in the city, it will be the number one hot military weapon of the future – for all those wars that really need the intervention of a giant angry robot chicken.

To demonstrate just how effective the product is, Jones asks for a volunteer to act as an arrest subject, and poor Kinney is picked from the table for a typical disarming simulation. He's handed a large gun and told to point it at ED-209. As he does so, the robot springs into life and informs Kinney that he has to put the gun down and he has twenty seconds to comply. Kinney flings the gun to the floor and stands back, but the droid carries on counting down while panicked technicians faff about in the background, pulling out cables from circuit boards to no avail. As the countdown ends, Kinney is absolutely riddled (depending on which cut you watch) with hundreds of bullets, throwing him back onto the model of Delta City where he spurts blood like a blender at high speed with no lid on. Eventually the ED-209 powers down as Bob Morton belatedly shouts, 'Someone wanna call a goddamn paramedic!' The Old Man looks at Jones with a furrowed brow and announces that he's very disappointed, but Jones attempts to reassure him by declaring that it's only a glitch. The Old Man is not convinced and worries that this setback could cost millions with the delay of the Delta City construction. Sensing the boss's anger, Bob Morton darts into the conversation like the rat he is, telling the Old Man that his RoboCop programme could save the day. They've placed prime candidates in police stations around Detroit according to risk factors and it should all be ready to go in ninety days with a prototype. This is music to the Old Man's ears, and he asks for a presentation in twenty minutes, hopefully complete with a song and dance number with Ashley Banjo doing the robot. As the Old Man walks away, Jones fires Morton with daggers, and Morton smugly departs the boardroom towards the elevator with Johnson. He's so excited about getting one over on Jones that he takes a brief second out of his fun to lament the passing of Kinney with the heartfelt remark that 'that's life in the big city' – not much of a eulogy, it has to be said. Johnson asks exactly when they can start, and Morton replies, 'As soon as some poor schmuck volunteers.'

Across town, Lewis and Murphy have stopped for a coffee break. She notices him practising twirling his gun into his holster like a cowboy and compliments him on his skills. Murphy tells her that his son watches a show called *T.J. Laser* and he wants to make his son happy, before confessing he secretly likes doing it. Before Lewis can laugh at Murphy for being uncool, a call comes over the radio about armed suspects in a van escaping from a robbery. This time, he lets her drive.

Clarence Boddicker is examining the money stolen during the robbery. He is a bit miffed with his colleague Bobby that the majority of the notes are burnt, as he was only supposed to blow the bloody doors off. However, before he can get even more angry, he hears that a police car is following them. It's Murphy and Lewis, and Murphy has a plan: he requests back-up, asks for Lewis's gun, and puts his plastic visor down – that'll definitely stop the bullets. As Clarence and his men kick open the van doors, the police car has vanished, but it's all part of Murphy's plan, and as they swing into view alongside the van, he clips Bobby in the leg. So, Clarence, like any good boss, decides to utilise Bobby and let him take one for the team, by throwing him out of the back of the van and onto the police car, causing it to grind to a halt. But that doesn't stop Lewis and Murphy; they quickly locate the van at a steel mill. There is no back-up available, and they are outnumbered, but they decide to head on in and apprehend the suspects. They make the questionable decision to split up, and Lewis is quickly knocked out by laughing Joe while he's having a wee. Murphy, though, has more success, and finds Emil (Paul McCrane) and his buddy watching Bixby Snyder, the Benny Hill of the future. Snyder's TV show is basically him pushing cakes onto women's breasts and proclaiming that he'd 'buy that for a dollar'. People laughed in 1987, but he'd have his own YouTube show now. Murphy interrupts their enjoyment and shoots Leon's buddy. As Leon goes for his gun, Murphy ominously tells him, 'Dead or alive, you're coming with me.' He calls Lewis for some assistance, but she's a long way away, sprawled in a heap on the floor, and only just waking up. As Murphy goes to cuff Leon, he hears the sound of shotguns cocking, and before too long he's surrounded.

There then follows a generation-defining scene of sadistic, horrific body trauma, that I would wager has stayed with every single viewer from the first moment they saw it until now. Murphy is dismantled piece by piece by Clarence and his men, who cackle and taunt their victim as he's blasted full of bullets and shells – losing limbs and gallons of blood, and finally being put to the floor with a bullet to the head from Clarence. As the gang members walk away laughing, Lewis arrives all too late, and, like everyone watching, is permanently traumatised by what she sees. Murphy is rushed to hospital, though at this point he could probably be posted in several small envelopes to save any bother. Images of Murphy's wife and son flash before his eyes as he's given CPR. But it's too late – he's beyond saving.

A screen flickers and flutters, then comes to life. The gawping faces of bespectacled scientists loom into view, and one happily tells Bob Morton that they were able to save the arm; he briefly confers with Johnson and tells them to lose it, and to be fair, he has a point. A robot arm is wheeled into view, and Bob Morton shakes the hand that nearly crushes his, and then excitedly proclaims to Murphy that he is going to be a 'bad motherfucker' – presumably a legitimate technical observation. The LED screen once again flickers to life and it is now covered in a gauzy plastic sheet. Bob tells the assembled room that they will get 'the best of both worlds' and a 'lifetime of on-the-street law enforcement programming'. He then pulls back the sheet and announces the birth of 'RoboCop' to a roomful of maniacally applauding techies.

Back at the precinct, Sgt Reed is dealing with a drunkard at the desk when his attention is diverted by excited OCP execs pouring into the station with machines and boxes on wheels. He demands to know what's going on, Bob tells him to get lost, and before he can complete his riposte, he sees something big and metallic marching past a glass partition. RoboCop is in the building. Within seconds the entire force of Metro West is scurrying in to see what is happening, and there is a lot happening. Robo is seated in a giant chair, and the OCP people are running through his settings and some basic commands. Bob breaks through the crowd and asks Robo for his prime directives. They are:

1. Serve the public trust.
2. Protect the innocent.
3. Uphold the law.

And sitting ominously at the bottom is Directive 4: 'Classified' – which one can only assume is something like 'Don't go to a party and only hang around in the kitchen endlessly talking about bitcoin'. Bob is impressed, very impressed, and tells everyone, in no uncertain terms, that he is a big fan of our new hero. When Robo goes to the firing range and destroys the paper targets with his immense 'Auto-9' gun – a 9mm handgun with a large barrel extension that fires in three-round bursts – the assembled police officers stop to watch in awe. Lewis spots something interesting. When Robo finishes blasting the targets into tiny pieces, he swivels his pistol and hooks it back into his leg holster. It's Murphy.

Robo is handed a set of car keys and told by Bob to 'go get 'em, boy'. As Basil Poledouris's RoboCop theme kicks into gear, Robo fires up his car and speeds away into the night to fight some crime, leaving Lewis to come to terms with what she has just seen.

Robo's first night is an interesting one. He foils a grocery-store stick-up by throwing the criminal into a fridge and then immediately leaves the scene (not sure about the legal repercussions there), stops a violent sexual assault by shooting one of the perps in the penis, and then offers to contact a rape crisis centre for the victim, and, finally, ends a tricky hostage situation by punching an embittered former city councilman, whose demands include a bigger office and a vote recount, through a window. These tactics might not appear in any police handbook, but you can't really argue with the results.

The press are delighted. He appears on the news, surrounded by excited kids in a playground, and Bob tells everyone that there will be an end to crime in the city within 40 days, that there's a new guy in town, and his name's RoboCop. As part of his ongoing good work, Bob is rewarded by the Old Man with a sweet Veep promotion, and he decides to celebrate it by going to the toilet and mouthing off about Dick Jones – 'he's old, we're young, and that's life' – who just happens to be in a nearby cubicle having an Armitage Shanks interface defecation scenario. Dick is not happy. He tells Bob that he's just 'fucked with the wrong guy'. Consider that card well and truly marked.

Back at Metro West, Robo is in his chair having a nap after another exhausting day of shooting and maiming, but then something unusual starts to happen, and he begins to flinch and grimace. The machine readings go crazy. No, they didn't put the wires in the wrong hole; he is in actual fact having a DREAM, and he has very clear and specific memories about his death and the men who caused it. As the OCP guys flail around, shouting, 'Hey, wait a minute!' and waving egghead printouts, Robo leaps to his feet and walks out of the precinct with a sense of purpose. Lewis introduces herself and tells him his name is Murphy, but he tells her he has to go: somewhere there is a crime happening. He gets in his car and speeds away. Bob Morton is livid with Sgt Reed and tells him as much. The OCP guys have a quick confab, and Morton tells them they're not taking RoboCop offline because he had a *dream*, and before he leaves, he tells Reed to stop his people messing about with his product or he'll have his job. Though you can't really see Bob being welcomed into the precinct as the new duty sergeant.

Meanwhile, Emil has to get some petrol for his motorbike. As he threatens the poor college-boy petrol-station attendant, who is busy swotting up on plane geometry, and mocks him for seeking a higher form of education, he fails to notice RoboCop pulling up at the forecourt like Rod Stewart and drawing a gun from his leg. 'Drop it,' Robo loudly announces, and Emil turns. 'Dead or alive, you're coming with me.' Emil's face drops as he hears those familiar words, and he begins to babble that he knows him and, probably more damning, 'We killed you.' Murphy records this on his in-head VCR and lowers his gun as he begins to process what he just heard. This allows Emil to shoot the petrol pumps, toss a lit cigarette into the pools of petrol, and take off on his motorcycle, leaving an exploding petrol station in his wake. However, amidst the flames, Robo shoots the bike out of commission and watches as Emil is thrown from the wreckage. As he picks him up from the ground, he asks who he is, but Emil can only emit strangulated noises, which may be due to Robo standing on his testicles by accident.

Robo strides into the records room, and as Cecil the clerk protests that this is a restricted area, Robo shoots a giant spike from his hand. The appendage serves as a neat method of accessing computer data and a nice flip-the-bird gesture to 'the man'. This, my friends, is proper film-making. He scans all of Boddicker's gang, and then checks his own record, which informs him that he is very much considered DECEASED, which must be awful to see – like Laurence Fox checking his entry on the Equity website.

He drives to his old address in Primrose Lane and wanders around the house. It's empty, hollow and sad, and feels very much like a sort of *Through the Keyhole* for victims of police murder. We see that he had a happy marriage, and a very happy family, and one can't help but get caught up in the tragedy of it all while Basil Poledouris melts the room with his 'Murphy Goes Home' strings. This is all too much for Robo and his new cyborg brain, and as the anger and loss rise in him, he punches the screen out of the virtual estate agent computer, just before it gets to the bit about which room would be best for dead single robot policemen.

At a sexy disco Robo, in ARREST MODE, pushes through the spiky-haired punters, standing out like Pete Waterman in any episode of *The Hitman and Her*. However, instead of looking for hip young people to stand near while he does links to camera, he is very much looking for one man in particular: Leon Nash (Ray Wise). A key member of Clarence's gang, Leon is one of the young guns who ended Robo's life. Robo finds him, grabs him by the hair (spot the Paul Verhoeven cameo as a mad dancer), and tells him he wants to have a chat outside.

Meanwhile, Bob Morton has two women round at his for a bit of cocaine-on-boobs action. Things are certainly going well for Bob. He's the new Vice President of OCP, and he has the world at his feet, and up his nose. The doorbell rings. He assumes it's a nice bottle of 1987-style Deliveroo prosecco to liven up the proceedings. However, it's not. It's Clarence Boddicker with a gun and a message from Dick Jones, a professionally made CD video message, which just goes to show what a pro Dick really is. Clarence plugs Bob's legs full of bullets, places an unpinned grenade on the table, and walks out as Dick's voice informs Bob that he's being taken out of the game. Bob tries to reach for the grenade, but it's all too much with his pulverised chino legs, and he's consumed in a great ball of fire. Bye, Bob, nice knowing you.

At a huge cocaine factory, Clarence is having a meeting with Sal, one of the big coke suppliers, telling him that if he wants to work with him, he'll need a good discount. Sal tells him that he doesn't want to work with him as he kills a lot of policemen, but he does have the muscle and heavy connections. There's some cock waving and gun toting, but before it can get prolonged and strained, the front door begins to thud and heave under pressure. As it falls in a plume of coke dust, Robo strides in from the darkness and orders them all to come quietly or there will be trouble. Sensing they don't want to cooperate (as they begin firing heavy weapons at him), he walks through the lab and assassinates every single one of them with clean, precisely targeted shots – like he's a really amazing cyborg. With Clarence the last man standing, Robo tells him that he is under arrest before throwing him through a series of windows and beginning to strangle the life out of him. Just as the life is draining from his body, Clarence reminds Robo that he's a cop and he shouldn't really kill people, which Robo reluctantly can't really disagree with. Clarence just can't stop blabbing; he tells Robo that he's working for Dick Jones of OCP, which is conveniently captured on video. One *You've Been Framed* fee in the post.

After dropping Clarence at Metro West, Robo drives over to OCP HQ to arrest Jones. However, upon arriving in his office, Robo hits one small snag: the mysterious Directive 4. It turns out that Robo's programming won't allow him to arrest any senior officer of OCP and attempting to do so will cause him to shut down. He hopes that this can be fixed by backing out of the room and coming back in again. As Robo flails and writhes, trying to fight this software issue, Dick opens his big double doors and unleashes ED-209. As the giant roaring chicken stomps into the room, Jones tells Murphy he had to kill Bob Morton because he made a mistake, and now it's time to erase that mistake – hope those words don't come back to bite him later.

After being heavily battered and bruised by the giant chicken, Robo escapes to the staircase, and in doing so, exposes ED-209's greatest weakness: like the Daleks, he can't do stairs. As the sad armoured bird wheezes and screeches, Robo staggers into the car park, only to be ambushed by OCP's armoured police force, who, after some protests that he's a cop, are instructed to fire at will. They obediently riddle him with bullets and then hunt him down as he crawls to the lower level to seek refuge. Luckily, Lewis arrives and bundles him into a car, and together they speed away to safety, probably stopping off at a Kwik-Fit to get him patched up.

Clarence swaggers into Jones's office, sticks his chewing gum on the receptionist's name plate and, after some unreciprocated innuendo, surveys the wreckage of Robo's visit the night before. Jones isn't happy that Clarence spilled his guts to RoboCop and reminds him that the video memory is admissible as evidence. So, he will have to kill RoboCop once and for all. Helpfully, he not only offers Clarence access to OCP's major arsenal of weaponry, but also reminds him that once construction of Delta City begins, he will be first in line to stock it with drugs and sexy sex workers. This appeals to the villain, and they decide to be friends.

At the steel mill where she's hidden Robo, Lewis arrives back from a supply run to Metro West. She's brought him the gun he dropped at OCP, as well as the little drill he asked for so that he can remove his broken helmet (stop sniggering at the back). He tells her she might not like what she's going to see as he removes his helmet, and thankfully it isn't Rick Astley under there. Lewis holds a piece of shiny metal to his face and says it's good to see him again, then she breaks the news that his wife and child moved away and started over again, which doesn't really cheer him up very much. Lewis tries to comfort him, but he asks to be left alone. Sniff. Just wait until he finds out his ex-wife is now shacked up with Clive Sinclair.

But there's no time to dwell on the sadness of the past, because Clarence and his cohorts have located RoboCop at the steel mill. There's explosions, car chases, death, and just when you think you've seen it all, poor Emil crashes his fun-mobile into a tank of toxic waste, emerging as an under-the-counter Garbage Pail Kid. He does what any normal melted goblin would do and seeks help immediately from his friends, but is ultimately rejected, and sadly vaporised when Clarence runs him over. Clarence, obviously shaken after turning Emil into soup, crashes his car, and after shooting Lewis, comes face to face with Murphy in a pond full of debris.

It's not a fair fight, though, as mad bastard Leon, the last remaining member of Clarence's gang, uses a crane to dump girders on Robo. He's so happy about what he just did, he waves cheerily out of the cab to Clarence, before being blown to smithereens by a bullet-riddled Lewis, who's managed to get hold of a bazooka (snagged from Clarence's hands). Clarence storms towards the pile of rubble and drives a metal pole right into Robo's chest, gleefully barking, 'Sayonara, RoboCop.' Hubris can be a funny thing, though, and as Clarence is thinking of all the money he will make from his future life as the best pimp ever in Delta City, Robo produces his hand spike and drives it deep into Clarence's throat, causing him to gush blood like something you'd find in Sam Peckinpah's ornamental garden. Murphy calls out to see if Lewis is OK, and she tells him she's a mess, but he reassures her that she can be fixed, and he should know: he got fixed once before.

Back at OCP, the Old Man is holding another board meeting, and Dick Jones is reassuring the assembled masses that whatever happens next, OCP will meet each new challenge head-on, with conviction. Suddenly, the boardroom doors fly open and Robo strides into the room to announce that Dick is wanted for murder. Dick tries to explain to the room that RoboCop is just a violent, mechanical killing machine and no one should really take him seriously. The Old Man asks Robo if he has any proof to back up these charges, so he fires out his multi-purpose hand spike, still blood-spattered, and plugs it into the TV banks. The whole room listens, agog, to Dick's confession about killing Bob Morton, and about how he did it and that it was great and he'd do it again if he could – the only problem being that Robo's Directive 4 programming won't allow him to act upon any OCP officer. Luckily, Dick takes that problem out of his hands by putting a gun to the Old Man's head and making demands for his escape, which seem to consist of being given a helicopter or 'the old geezer gets it'. Now, if there's one thing that the Old Man will not tolerate, it's ageism in the workplace, so he rightly informs Dick that he is fired, which then allows Robo to fire many, many rounds into Dick's body, causing him to fall from the window, turn into a plasticine vulture, and plummet to his death many floors below. This is how Alan Sugar should end each series of *The Apprentice*.

As the Old Man recovers his composure, he commends RoboCop on his nice shooting and then asks his name. Robo stops, turns, states that his name is Murphy, and walks away proudly, Basil Poledouris's martial theme blaring out. Old Detroit can rest easy.

The future of law enforcement is here, and he's ready to violate your basic human rights in the name of the law. Let's just hope they don't make any more of these.

FOURTEEN

THE RUNNING MAN

1987

THE 'RUNNING MAN' IS A DEADLY
GAME NO ONE HAS EVER SURVIVED.

THERE WERE MANY THINGS that the futurists of the eighties
got wrong – untidy missteps along the way such as flying cars,
robot waiters and hoverboards – but there was one thing that was
right on the money: TV. *Robocop* laughed at a format out of control
in terms of ethics, and *The Running Man* took that ball and kept
running with it. And here we are, in the 21st century, regularly
cheering on actors from *The Bill* eating gonads in a jungle.

It's 2017. The world's economy has collapsed, and a paramilitary
police state controls every facet of life, including television. The
highest-rated show, in fact the most popular show in history, is
The Running Man – a sort of *Big Brother* meets *Jeremy Kyle* meets
Gladiators, but with added sadism and death. While the majority
of people are happy to go along with their copies of the *Radio
Times* written by frothing right-wing mouthpieces, there is an
underground network of resistance, and they will not go quietly
into the night: they will fight, they will endure, and they will
hopefully offer a channel that just shows *'Allo! 'Allo!* repeats and
canal programmes.

Ben Richards (Arnold Schwarzenegger) is a police helicopter pilot. He's flying a team of officers to check out a food riot that has broken out in Bakersfield. He reports back to HQ that the crowd is unarmed and hungry and there are women and children down there, so there's no need for any excessive force, but his superiors give the order to shoot anything that moves. He refuses, what with him being a deeply honourable man, so the men in his chopper commandeer the vehicle, hold Richards down and knock him senseless before proceeding with the slaughter. So much for the right to protest.

Eighteen months later, and Richards, now with a pretend beard for some reason, is working in the Wilshire Detention Zone, a giant refinery full of rubble, smoke and wheelbarrows. It's a hard life, made even harder by the fact that the prisoners all have to wear restraint collars that will blow their heads off if they cross the perimeter. Luckily, this extreme environment gives Ben the chance to expose his vast, muscly arms and show how strong he is as he carries beams of steel around the place. He's not alone in his struggle, though. He has two friends: Laughlin (played by Yaphet Kotto of *Live and Let Die* fame), and computer whizz Weiss (Marvin J. McIntyre). They have a plan to escape, and it all hinges on their working together and using their heads, or at least it would if it wasn't for the fact that Ben prefers to lift men up in the air like heavyweight belts and toss them into the sky. As chaos breaks out, and more men are chucked like used tissues into the mist, Weiss hacks the system by keying in a five-digit passcode again and again and again, which deactivates the explosion fields and allows them to escape.

Their first port of call is to meet the resistance leader, Mic (Mick Fleetwood), who, while helping them to remove their bomb collars, explains that cops like Ben locked up all his friends and burned his songs, which seems to suggest that he is playing Mick Fleetwood in an alternative 2017, one in which Fleetwood Mac are largely irrelevant and unpopular and . . . oh. He explains that the TV network just airs trash all day every day, to numb the brains of the people. Weiss suggests that if they can get to the uplink dish and hack it, they can broadcast 'the truth', which Ben, chomping on a cigar, rightly proclaims hasn't been very popular, leading me to stamp this as an important historical document that should be studied by future generations. Once the collars are off, Ben rejects the opportunity to join the resistance, telling his chums that he's not into politics, he's into survival. He wants to go out on his own and escape to another country – and for God's sake don't go to the UK, Ben, it's much worse.

A shiny red limousine powers towards the entrance of a vast skyscraper that just screams angular eighties chic – like a Lego construct made by Gordon Gekko on bags of gak. Damon Killian (Richard Dawson) gets out of his fancy ride and approaches the entrance, waving to hordes of screaming fans as he makes his way inside. This is the headquarters of ICS, the TV network that broadcasts *The Running Man*, and Killian is the beloved host with the most. But his assistant greets him with news that he doesn't want to hear. The ratings haven't moved in weeks, and she suggests that they may have peaked. This is not music to his media-savvy ears, and as he gets in the lift with his burly minder Sven (Sven-Ole Thorsen), his mood is not on the sunny side.

Dressed as the rejected builder character from the Village People, Ben arrives at his brother's apartment and lets himself in for a shower. It's quickly apparent that his brother no longer lives there, unless he now wears tiny silky pants and bras (and I'm not judging him). The identity of the new tenant is not a mystery for long, though, as Amber Mendez (Maria Conchita Alonso) arrives home and aurally brings her home of the future to life, with shouts of *lights!*, *toast and coffee!* and *ICS!*, before she strips to her undies to do a no-pain-no-gain fitness workout with Captain Freedom (Jesse Ventura). The show is interrupted to bring an urgent newsflash announcing that Ben Richards, the 'Butcher of Bakersfield', has escaped from captivity. While Amber does her sit-ups and thanks her lucky stars she won't run into this giant hulk of a man who is alleged to have massacred a town full of starving people, she is suddenly face to face with him, which is awkward, and she must be pleased she didn't say anything about him out loud. Ben, now free of his pretend beard, asks her why she's in his brother's apartment, and she says she moved in the previous month after the last tenant was taken away for 're-education', which either means the government have whisked him away or he signed up for the Open University. Either way, Ben is not impressed; after a little chase around the apartment he tells Amber he was framed and that if she plays along, he'll be out of there in five minutes.

Back at ICS, Killian and his team are sitting in the production office chewing on complimentary spring rolls and reviewing possible contestants for the next *Running Man* show, and even though one of them is an actual toddler, which would be great TV, no one really fits the bill. But then Killian spots the footage of Ben and his vast physique breaking out of jail. He reckons he'll get ten points on his ratings for Ben's biceps alone and wants him immediately. Even though he's told they can never have military prisoners, he won't listen. Hell, he's the star here. He picks up the phone to speak to the 'Justice Department, Entertainment Division' and then 'the President's Agent' – some properly sharp satire that you only get when the director of your film is Starsky from *Starsky and Hutch*.

Back at Amber's flat, Ben uses her teletext and travel pass to book a flight out to Honolulu as he says he needs to work on his tan – eighteen months' porridge can be hard on the skin. She is resistant at first, but when he lifts the weight bench she is sitting on high in the air, she eventually agrees to join him. At the airport, Ben does his best to blend in, what with him being twice the size of any normal human and wearing a Hawaiian shirt so loud it could headline Donington, but it's only a matter of minutes before he is spotted, and Amber screams for help as he makes a run for it. He's captured in an elaborate comedy net, and he surrenders at gunpoint.

Ben comes to in a darkened cell at ICS, and as he tries to get his bearings, the wall opens up and sitting at the window is

Killian, lighting a cigarette and suggesting that they do a deal. He can have his freedom if he wins *The Running Man*, a deal that on paper sounds excellent but in practice may be hard, like telling a convicted murderer he can walk free if he smashes the Gold Run on *Blockbusters*. Ben isn't keen, and would obviously rather return to the muscle mine than help Killian's ratings, but his mind is soon changed when he sees they have Weiss and Laughlin, and if he doesn't do the show, they will, which is like getting Monkman and Seagull to stand in for The Rock. So, Ben agrees, and before he can ask what the rider will be and if he can meet Noel Edmonds, he's prepped with drugs and 'interphalangic injections', and thrown back in a cell to await his big turn.

Back in her apartment, Amber is relaxing at her futuristic synthesizer when she sees a news report on the capture of Ben Richards at the airport, but the content troubles her deeply. It claims that Richards murdered lots of people during the arrest, which she knows is a big fat lie, as he merely ran away and then comically fell over in a giant net.

It's time. Ben's cell door opens, and in walk some burly guards and his 'court-appointed theatrical agent' (lovely stuff), with his contract, which Ben signs on the agent's back. He then adds a full stop by stabbing him with the pen, which seems fairly heavy-handed to our modern eyes, but in the cut-and-thrust future of 2017 shows you mean business.

The *Running Man* show begins with strobe lights, Spandex, dry ice, some Paula Abdul-choreographed dancers and Harold Faltermeyer pressing shuffle on his keyboard. Outside, the mob scream and love 'the stalkers' as they arrive in luxury. They're the muscle-bound assassins with names dreamed up by toy companies, who will stalk the players as they navigate the zones and try to complete the game. Bets are being taken as to who will win and who will die and when. Amber has also arrived (she works at ICS, writing jingles) with her friend, and as they navigate a vending machine, they watch Ben being led into the zone in his blue jumpsuit. It's all awkward eyes meeting as he passes; she knows she's the reason he's here and she also believes that he probably didn't murder loads of people. As Ben is loaded into the lift, she cries off drinks with her friend, saying that she has some last-minute paperwork to do. She heads back into ICS to do some digging around the files.

Killian takes to the stage to wild applause, basking in the warm, effervescent glow and telling the audience he loves them, before announcing that 'It's SHOWTIME!' As the rapture dies down, he asks the guys in the booth to run the VT on their guest runner for this evening: Ben Richards, the Butcher of Bakersfield. The crowd are told that he slayed many women, men and children, and the tape is edited in such a way that it suggests he did it all himself and ignored orders to not attack – which directs a harsh light on how 2017 works, with fake news becoming real news. Glad that never became a reality. Ben is brought out to boos and wild choruses of disapproval as his blue jumpsuit is removed, and his canary-yellow, skin-tight playsuit is revealed. As Killian lists the prizes in store for Ben, like a trial by jury or even a full pardon, he also reminds us of the only previous winners of the competition – Whitman, Price and Haddad – who are all basking in freedom under the Maori sun, a segment that can't help but remind me of the featured winners in Postcode Lottery adverts, who surely don't really exist either.

As Ben is strapped into his chair to make the short journey down the tube to the gaming zone, Killian has one more surprise for him up his sleeve, and it's not Cilla Black (though she would have made a perfect stalker), but his buddies Laughlin and Weiss. They'll be entering the zone with him after all, thus well and truly breaking the terms of his deal and making Ben a bit more pissed off than he was already. Ben tells Killian, 'I'll be back,' to which the host offers the simple yet cutting riposte, 'Only in a rerun,' before sending his chair down to the zone through an elaborate pipe system – surely reflecting the eighties craze of zooming through pipe tunnels, and if it's good enough for The Goonies, it's good enough for Ben Richards.

They have three hours to get through all four game quadrants, and anything goes, apparently, so you can expect plenty of 'death by vulture up the arse'. As Ben and his friends arrive, the first stalker is chosen, and it's Subzero (real life pro-wrestler Professor Tanaka), a smiley, overweight Oddjob impersonator who really, really likes slicing up his victims into sushi with an ice-hockey stick.

Amber meanwhile has navigated the ICS records room and found files clearly marked with the real Bakersfield footage, which would prove once and for all that Ben is innocent; however, before she can start a blog, she's caught red-handed in the cabinet.

Ben, Laughlin and Weiss stumble into the first zone and are instantly met with low-level mood lighting, which is then sharply interrupted by lights, cameras and action. Before they can declare themselves ready for their close-ups, Subzero bursts from the darkness on his ice-skates and begins knocking them over, like the fat kid who can only play in goal. Back at the studio, the person who chose Subzero is receiving prizes such as a board game and an ICS home video as poor Weiss is dragged around the rink and slid into goal. A goal that is also a prison: this is the harsh reality of the future. Richards, though, has had enough of watching his buddies getting their asses handed to them, so decides to grab a length of barbed wire and throttle the giant stalker to death with it.

The studio falls silent, and you can hear a grenade-pin drop. A stalker is dead, and this has never happened before, even though with Subzero you'd imagine nature would get there sooner or later. Killian is dumbfounded, and while he tries to think of something to say, Richards shouts a message to him – 'Here is Subzero, now plain zero' – which maybe needed a punch-up from Barry Cryer. As Ben walks away, happy with his zinger, he shares a high five with Laughlin, and they set about rescuing poor Weiss from his mini-hockey prison.

After a long commercial break, Killian has audience member Leon join him on stage to choose the next stalker to track down our heroes. The trouble is, he can't decide between Dynamo or

Buzzsaw, so Killian makes it easier for him: why not have both? Even though they barely fit in the same postcode. Looking very much like Ted Bovis from *Hi-de-Hi!* if he joined up with Dog the Bounty Hunter, Buzzsaw enters first, brandishing a chainsaw and displaying his skills by chopping things up with it. As the audience lap up these feats of chainsaw, Killian is given two pieces of good news: the ratings have gone up and Amber has been caught pulling Ben's files. He couldn't be happier.

Dynamo comes out next – basically George Dawes done up as the fat Cenobite from *Hellraiser* after falling into the Blackpool illuminations. He sings opera as he shoots electricity into neon signs asking for applause, which all feels a bit needy, if you ask me. The crowd go wild for it, though, and then go wilder as Amber is brought out in a Spandex jumpsuit and many a lie is told about her personal life in order to whip up the mob. Before she can truly protest about how she didn't have sexual relationships with two, sometimes three, different men in a year, she's clamped into the chair and whizzed into the zone.

Weiss is excited. He's spotted a satellite dish that's pointing into the zone, and not up, which causes him to announce excitedly that the uplink must be in there, which explains why no one ever found it. Ben wants to forget the crazy uplink business and keep moving before they are all killed, but Weiss and Laughlin go running to find that uplink, to see if they can jam the network, and it's only a matter of minutes before they run into Amber, who is very cross about being down there and blames Ben for it. He jokily offers to strangle her for the home audience if she doesn't shut up. Weiss has spotted another dish, so he goes running off to find it, just as Buzzsaw, on a motorbike, and Dynamo, in a teeny-tiny car, arrive to throw many cats among many pigeons. As Weiss and Amber find the uplink interface, and he starts to hack the 'Hexagonal Decode System', which he mentions will take a while, Ben and Laughlin face off against Buzzsaw, who lands a killer blow on the latter, making Ben angry. After being dragged for what seems like many miles at the end of a rope, Ben manages to take down the mad, heavy-bulked bastard and murders him by driving his own chainsaw up his nuts, significantly reducing his chances of parenthood and causing further shock and uproar back at the studio. Weiss, meanwhile, has cracked the code and asks Amber to remember a series of numbers to get to Mic in the resistance, though it could be second-hand news. As they triumphantly set out to leave the uplink, Dynamo shatters Weiss's happiness with a bolt of electricity up his jacksie.

Ben races to the site of Amber's screams to find Dynamo, far and away the weirdest man at Comic Con, wrestling with her and delivering a bolt of energy that lands her unconscious. Ben pulls out further zingers to get the stalker's attention, calling him 'light-head' and 'Christmas tree' – sticks and stones, Ben. Dynamo makes a critical mistake at this point, when he decides to run Ben over in a car, rather than, you know, shooting him with deadly bolts of high-voltage electricity from a safe distance. Ben outwits the butterball by running up a hill, causing Dynamo to topple his little car while in pursuit. As he screams, 'Cut to the commercial!' and begs for help, Ben stands over him, wielding a metal pipe. A lone voice in the audience calls out for Ben to kill him. But Ben is a decent and pure man, and announces that he won't kill a helpless human being, despite the fact that he's just murdered two, and the audience begin to boo him for not murdering another one of their heroes.

Killian tries to put on a brave face about how much of a spectacle this show is, but he's seething, and as he tries to quell the mob, the next stalker, Fireball (ex-NFL running back, Jim Brown), is told to get to wardrobe and prepare to enter the zone.

Ben and Amber return to Laughlin, still suffering after the Buzzsaw attack, but he tells them both it's too late for him, and he's dying, and Ben has to get that code to the resistance, and don't let his death be for nothing, as he doesn't want to be the 'only asshole in heaven', and I can assure you, Laughlin, you won't be. As he passes away, Killian pops up on a screen with a secret broadcast. He offers Ben a job as a stalker, with many perks such as a three-year contract, a credit line, a beachfront condo and, presumably, as many steroids as he can eat. Ben doesn't even take a moment to consider this generous package. He rips the camera off the wall, then tells Killian he'll shove the contract down his throat and break his spine, which seems like a fairly comprehensive no.

As Fireball makes his entrance, using a flamethrower to torch some things, Killian goes out to the audience to speak with Mrs Agnes McArdle, his number one old lady fan, and asks her who she thinks will make the next kill. To the surprise of everyone, she announces that she thinks Ben Richards will be doing the killing, not any of the stalkers, and Killian reminds her that she has to pick a stalker. But Agnes won't have it. Her declaration that Ben is 'one mean motherfucker' incites a moment of audience participation that feels like it fuelled Michael Barrymore's career for many years. The crowds inside and outside the studio begin to root for a player for the first time in the show's history, like when Mr Blobby took our TVs by storm, and as Fireball begins to chase Amber and Ben, there's a real feeling of change in the air.

Amber and Ben become separated while dodging Fireball's fiery blasts, and she comes face to face with three dead bodies. A quick check of their dog tags reveals them to be Whitman, Price and Haddad – last season's 'winners' – thus confirming that the game was always rigged and they never really won the Postcode Lottery. As Fireball enters the room and confirms Amber's fears that they were actually losers, he activates his flamethrower, only to be set upon by Ben and eventually murdered via a gas explosion. Ben declares him a 'hothead', much to the enjoyment of not many.

Captain Freedom and his massive shoulders watch as another comrade in arms is decimated, and then he hears the sad message on the intercom that it's his turn to get to wardrobe and enter the zone. But he's had quite enough. He races into the control room, half dressed as a last-minute Halloween costume of a tin robot, and tells Killian that he won't go in and the theatrics and fancy dress have ruined the sport. It used to mean something:

it was about death and honour, and the code of the gladiators. Essentially, he quits. Killian orders his henchman Sven to remove him at once, asking him when he doesn't reply, 'Do steroids make you deaf?' To which Sven should totally say, 'What?' But he's too professional for that, and merely stares at Captain Freedom as he makes his clanking, ungainly exit. Killian has one last plan up his sleeve, though. His team of computer wizards knock up some 'structurally synthesized' footage of Captain Freedom murdering someone, with Ben's face substituted as the victim.

As the *Running Man* dancers play out a funerary dance number for the fallen stalkers, Ben and Amber locate the resistance and come face to face with Fleetwood Mic and his men, thus confirming that their location wasn't just rumours, after all. They are welcomed by the People's Network, a band of freedom fighters with banks of TV sets and computers, who look more likely to bust out a game of Warcraft than topple a government. But there is hope. Amber tells Mic she has the uplink code, and as they celebrate the news, ICS broadcasts Ben's 'death', causing the audience to go wild. Killian congratulates his team on a sensational show, but Ben is livid. He knows they'll never be allowed to leave the zone alive and will be hunted down like dogs. Mic explains the plan: they will jam the signal, broadcast a message, and go into the studio to take control. Amber offers a further sweetener; she has the original, uncut footage from the Bakersfield massacre that she was, mystifyingly, able to secure about her person all this time. This piques Ben's interest. He'll get to clear his name and righteously kick ten shades of shit out of Killian, so, y'know, win-win.

Ben and the resistance dudes storm the studio and get into place for the uplink to arrive, and arrive it does, just as Killian is delivering his final thoughts to the crowd. These resistance guys may be nerds, but it really works in their favour here. They deliver a tight, wonderfully edited package laying out all the lies ICS have been telling regarding Ben and the previous winners. The audience watch open-mouthed and begin to boo Killian as he watches the betrayal spill out on the screen and a defiant Agnes denounces everything he says as 'bullshit' (they just loved a foul-mouthed granny in the eighties). As Killian tries to calm the storm, Ben and his boys boot down the door and storm in shooting, clearing the studio in panic. As the floor clears and the folks at home watch in disbelief, Ben comes face to face with Killian and takes great pleasure reciting his own catchphrases back to him. Just when it looks like Ben has his man, Sven plods out from the darkness and approaches, looking like a furniture warehouse. Killian laughs and tells Sven to have a word with Ben, but Sven sadly tells him he won't be his friend any more, as 'he's got to score some steroids'. Sven gives Ben a friendly nod as he stomps off, leaving his boss with egg on his face.

As Killian tries to talk his way out of his predicament, giving a monologue on the state of the 2017 television industry and telling Ben he's just giving the audience what they want, Ben is unimpressed. He tells Killian he'll give the audience what they want and duly drops Killian into the chair and sends him hurtling down the tunnel like a turd in a waterslide. After crashing through a poster of himself, he dies in a horrible inferno. Now, that, my friends, is television. The crowd outside roar in approval as their former hero is chargrilled for their pleasure, and we are left to believe that everything will now be fine as Ben and Amber do some sensual necking to the sultry tones of John Parr.

I, for one, am positive that this fascist state will now be toppled, and I'm over the moon that Fleetwood Mac had a hand in it. The people can now break the chain and go their own way.

FIFTEEN

1988

NAME: JERICHO JACKSON
NICKNAME: 'ACTION'
HOME: DETROIT
PROFESSION: COP
EDUCATION: HARVARD LAW
HOBBY: FIGHTING CRIME
WEAPON: YOU'RE LOOKING AT 'EM

IT'S LATE. THE CITY is blanketed in dark skies, and in a lonely office building, union official Frank Stringer (Ed O'Ross) is dictating a letter about the death of a colleague to his secretary (Mary Ellen Trainor – she did get everywhere). They're about to call it a night when some bumps are heard from the floor above. There are many things it could be: Santa, a janitor performing auto-erotic asphyxiation, or a fleet of ninjas who move like shadows but somehow manage to announce their arrival via the medium of loud bumps. Sadly, for our hard-working duo, it's the third thing, and as they swarm in through the windows and murder the secretary, Stringer must have wished that his janitor was a bit more of a kink guy. He scrambles around the office, occasionally receiving the odd punch, kick and knife here and there, before finally being shot with that most popular of eighties weaponry, a grenade launcher. He out the window in a ball of flames and lands in a high-class restaurant, where hopefully someone asked the waiter if they could have what he's having.

After a brief montage containing the delights of Detroit, namely a General Motors car factory and various big buildings and trains, to a bouncy Pointer Sisters track, young wannabe mugger Albert Smith is caught by two policemen after failing to mug a woman much larger and tougher than him. As he rides with them to the station, he's told he'll have to deal with 'Action Jackson', the baddest dude in the world – with some wild tales about him being the mutant offspring of Bigfoot or that he was created in a lab by NASA to walk on the moon without a space suit. Apparently, Jackson is the man to call to re-educate the youth of today, and mind them to change their ways, so they don't become real criminals, or even pretend ones. When they get to the station, Albert takes the opportunity to try to escape, and in the process causes a whole jug of coffee to smash all over the desk of Sergeant Jericho Jackson (Carl Weathers), who stands to his full height, looks down at Albert, and simply utters the words 'mellow out' – all of which causes Albert to faint. It quickly becomes apparent that Jackson is working a desk these days when his colleague Detective Kotterwell mocks him on his superb admin skills and mentions that he fucked up so badly he was demoted.

Jackson goes to see Captain Armbruster (Bill Duke), and they have a chat about how it's been two years since he lost his lieutenant stripes and that the time has been 'uneventful'. Armbruster, after mentioning that Jackson was a top athlete and got an A+ at Harvard in Law, has an actual assignment for him. He wants him to represent the force at the 'Detroit Businessman League's Man of the Year' fundraiser, which Jackson is happy to do, until he finds out the man of the year is Peter Dellaplane, a name that wipes the smile off his face. It turns out Dellaplane's son is a 'sexual psychopath', and that dealing with the family got Jackson demoted (he nearly tore the guy's arm off and brought too much heat on the department). This behaviour lost him his gun permit and, more importantly, his marriage, so all in all, probably a bad idea. The Captain orders him to attend and to make sure his 'Action Jackson' days are far behind him, so that he can win back those lost stripes, and maybe even his wife, who is probably living with a personal trainer now.

At the award show, Peter Dellaplane (Craig T. Nelson) takes the stage and begins to talk about his humble beginnings and how proud he is to be in front of all his peers. Jackson is standing in the wings when a woman approaches and mentions that he won't be able to hear the speech properly, which he indicates is the best part of standing there. His smug grin soon vanishes when he discovers that the woman is Peter's wife, Patrice (Sharon Stone).

During the after-show mingle, Jackson shares a chinwag with a stuffy old posh English chap who asks his opinion on 'the man of the year', to which our hero comments that he thinks he's a 'greedy, conceited, two-faced, back-stabbing asshole', and, refreshingly, despite his buttoned-down appearance, the man readily agrees – and I respect him for that. Dellaplane appears and introduces his wife to Jackson, pretending he can't remember his nickname and running through various synonyms before Jackson reminds him he's very much 'Action'. After a brief, pointed chat about his son, and how he's languishing in jail, Dellaplane mocks our hero's demotion before slinking off with his driver (played by the wonderfully ubiquitous Al Leong from a couple of *Lethal Weapons*, *Die Hard*, *The A-Team*, *24* and *Deadwood*, to name but a few).

Meanwhile, on a yacht moored at the dock, union official Lionel Grantham is enjoying listening to an aria while bragging on the phone about how good his security is, when his boat is infested by ninjas (typical). Within moments, all his guards are dead, a bomb is handcuffed to his arm, and his yacht explodes in a giant fireball, all of which disproves the 'you don't get me, I'm part of the union' song lyric, once and for all.

Jackson hears the news of another dead union official, and decides to hound Kotterwell for what information he has on the case. He's sure the cases are linked, unless two union officials have sadly succumbed to spontaneous combustion in one week – a phenomenon in 1988 where the jury was very much out in terms of its plausibility. Before he can join too many dots, he gets a call from his friend Tony (Robert Davi), who wants him to come over as soon as he can; it's a matter of life and death.

Over at Tony's happening pad, he's not having a great time. He cuts a sorry figure in tracksuit bottoms, white vest and suit jacket, and is frantically throwing things around, muttering about the walls having ears, and generally seeming a bit stressed, looking like he hasn't slept since 1975. When Jackson offers to take him to the hospital, he puts a gun to his own head, which seems a bit worrying – the food isn't *that* bad, Tony. He says he wants Jackson to sit down and listen to what he has to say, and after collecting his thoughts, tells him that he's the last union official standing, and he thinks Dellaplane is behind all the deaths. All well and good, but this witness, who is behaving like a wasp in a pint glass, may crumble under cross-examination.

Over at Joey's Club Elite, Sydney Ash (Vanity) is singing a song about someone having faraway eyes while looking meaningfully at Peter Dellaplane, who watches creepily from a lone table on the dance floor, shrouded in darkness, enjoying a cigar and a bottle of champagne to himself. After the song finishes, he escorts her out of the club and lets slip that he has a boner, which just screams 'class'.

Tony suggests checking out Dellaplane's mistress, Sydney. Jackson promises he'll look into it, and leaves to do some digging, which relieves Tony, who lights his 400th cigarette of the day. But the relief doesn't last long, as he's immediately murdered by an assassin posing as a courier, who's just passed Jackson in the corridor.

Back at Sydney's place, Dellaplane is reminded that he promised he'd get her record deals, money and fame, so that she can go places, but instead he offers her heroin in a box. It's a brave move, but as he slips the needle into her thigh, it seems to be a hit with Sydney.

At the morgue, Jackson is told that Tony was full of speed and would probably have died anyway if he hadn't been shot in the chest, which doesn't exactly sound like it holds water. Talking of which, the official verdict is that he did commit suicide, because he was found with the gun that killed him. Jackson dismisses this outright – smart guy – as he knows Tony had a different gun, and to compound matters even further, it's personal. It turns out he and Tony were on the same track team when they were in high school.

Patrice emerges from a sensual, topless sauna and overhears one of her husband's goons talking about the recent murders and how Jackson may have to be taken care of. She leaves the house to go into town, only to bump into our man, who was just arriving to talk to her, at the front door. He offers her a ride. Over a drink, she tells him exactly what she heard and how another murder is being planned for the coming Sunday, for a man named Oliver O'Rooney, a former employee of Dellaplane. She's keen to tell Jackson that her husband isn't the man he thinks he is, that he's actually a very nice guy, but as they leave, a taxi cab driven by the courier assassin tries to run them both over. This leads to an exciting foot chase, which culminates with one of the most extraordinary sequences in film history, a feat of magical aerodynamics that even Dynamo would struggle to explain. The driver has Jackson in his sights, dead straight in the road, with Jackson egging him on to run him over. So, he hits the gas. But he hadn't counted on his quarry being ACTION MUTHAFUCKIN JACKSON, and as he nears at high speed, our hero performs a forward somersault over the top of the car, causing it to miss him entirely, hit another vehicle, flip, and barrel-roll into a garage. When Jackson reaches the wreckage, the villain has vanished.

Back at Joey's Club Elite, Sydney is on stage to sing another song, with way too much slap bass, and Jackson has joined the packed audience to watch her. He likes what he sees. He's cosy in his big leather blouson jacket, bobbing his head along to the fresh beats, and clicking his fingers in glee, looking every inch the sexual tyrant.

Dellaplane returns home to his luxury mansion to have a word with his wife and find out if she's OK after the minor traffic collision she was nearly involved in. Much to his chagrin, she starts asking a few too many questions about his business affairs and all the men he's had killed. So, rather than asking if she would like a full and frank discussion about how he works, he tells her he loves her, shoots her dead, gives her a weird kiss on the lips, and takes off her wedding ring. And *this* is Detroit Businessman League's Man of the Year?

After the show, Jackson goes backstage, but he bumps into Sydney's massive bouncer, Edd. He's a peaceful Muslim who's just paying his way through medical school, but he's also built like a branch of Dixons, and he takes every punch Jackson throws at him like a fly has landed on his face. However, he, too, forgets who he is dealing with, and before he knows what's happening, Jackson uses his 270lb body to bust a door down and then knocks him out with a table. Sydney is impressed. She's very happy to let Jackson drive her away into the night, although that may be due to the fact that she's just shot up a big load of smack. (Jackson thoughtfully enquires if she's diabetic.) In his chariot, she tries, and fails, to seduce him; he's not just your common or garden man, he's called 'Action' for a reason, and he don't do no dopeheads. His attention is also diverted by the fact that he hears of Patrice's death over the police radio, and is none too impressed by the news: it sounds like he's been framed for the murder, which is enough to dissolve the lead in any pencil.

After nearly being blown up via a bomb at Sydney's apartment, they check into a hotel that's run by ex-boxer Kid Sable, one of Jackson's old cohorts, who sounds like he's been gargling bees. They exchange a brief catchphrase to denote that they are pals: 'The pulse may fade, but the reflex never dies.' Probably something they picked up when they were touring with Duran Duran. Jackson asks for a room on a 'relatively unoccupied floor', and as they settle down for the evening, he lectures Sydney on her drug use. She asks him if he fancies some sex, but, once again, he turns her down. He is a real gentleman.

The next day, Jackson takes Sydney to a pool hall to see an old informant of his, Papa Doc, who he thinks might be of some help. After asking around and meeting basically every actor that's ever been in a Joel Silver-produced film, he's shown to a back room and asked to look inside a cupboard. There's a jar with some testicles in it, which he's told used to be Papa Doc's. While he's taking in this information – that his previous informant is now just a tiny jar, he's knocked down with a bottle to the head and taken to a room to be threatened by four burly thugs, who want to know why he's looking for him. They go on to describe the sound a man makes when his balls are cut off, and are about to demonstrate, when Sydney bursts in to tell the gang that Jackson is actually seriously mentally ill and has just got out of hospital. Jackson plays along for a few moments before unleashing his full fury and kicking ten shades of shit out of all four.

After a tip from Kid Sable, Jackson heads to Dee Love's Barbershop, as apparently Dee (Armelia McQueen) knows everything: and true to his word, she does. She tells him via the medium of beat poetry all about Dellaplane being mixed up with a guy called Enzo Catelli, who has an elite group of bodyguards called 'The Invisible Men'. She explains that they have an 'almost demonic ability to remain completely undetected' – apart from when you can hear them moving around on the floor above you, obviously. Dellaplane had Catelli killed, and he's now the master of this band of blokes who can't even keep quiet when they break into an office. The Invisible Men have been responsible for all the union deaths, and Dellaplane is calling the shots. She leaves him with one last piece of wisdom: he can find Oliver O'Rooney late at night at a club called the Red Devil. She compliments Jackson on his reputation, and, oh, would she have gone mental if she'd seen that flip over the taxi he did earlier.

Back at the hotel, Jackson catches Sydney with Mr Quick (Sonny Landham), a sweaty hulk of a man who was clearly about to give her a lethal fix. After a brief exchange of punches and bad language, Jackson injects him with his own product and then flings him through his window, and into another window across the alleyway. Damn, if I'd been there, I would've applauded.

At the Red Devil club, Sydney goes in alone to pick up O'Rooney, who is drunk at the bar. She lures him to a local factory under the pretence that he's meeting Dellaplane. Instead, he gets a big dose of Action Jackson and immediately confesses that Dellaplane is holding a big party that night at his house, where he will kill the leader of the union, and O'Rooney will be installed in his place, with the kicker being that Jackson will be doing the murder. However, before Jackson can ask what the fuck he's talking about, the Invisible Men (with David Glen Eisley sporting the kind of mullet that would stop traffic) arrive and capture our hero.

Jackson is topless, tied between two posts, with a liberal amount of grease smeared over his massive chest. Dellaplane reveals his entire plan to him: he wants to be a kingmaker and install people into power, so he can gain influence. He then confesses to all the murders, considering them necessary steps on the way to achieving his goal. He now intends to kill Jackson and send one of his men, dressed as him, to kill the union leader. The real Jackson's charred body will be put in a burnt-out car, and the case will be very much open and shut – just another murder by an obsessed man. Jackson's face suggests that he agrees with the audience at this point: the whole thing sounds so deeply flawed and absurdly convoluted, it's exhausting. Dellaplane then departs, telling him that Sydney will die of an overdose, but he'll 'fuck her one last time', which really seems beyond the pale. As he saunters into the lift, Jackson tells him that 'one of these days, you're gonna really piss me off' and the Invisible Men prepare a large industrial blowtorch to toast him.

With the villain now gone, his supermen set about chargrilling our hero, and things are looking very bleak. Fear not. From out of nowhere, Sydney's giant bodyguard, Mr Edd, who spotted her in the Red Devil earlier, loudly introduces himself before jumping down from a high walkway, a move that would, undoubtedly, have broken every bone in his body. He and Jackson now work in unison to make the Invisible Men the Unidentifiable Men, with each one either being blown up, electrocuted, or set on fire, just as karma would demand.

Cut to the barbecue at Dellaplane's exclusive party. The tycoons mingle among the fountains and ice sculptures while a string quartet peppers the night air. Jackson's double gets in place up a tree. He's fixing a silencer to his gun, ready to perform one final act of murder on behalf of his boss. Dellaplane takes to the stage and asks for the crowd's attention; it's union leader Raymond Foss's birthday, and he wants him to come up and say a few words, so he can be murdered. As Foss begins his speech, Jackson appears in the crowd, wearing a sexy tuxedo. He scans the area for the potential sniper, finally spotting him in his tree. As he's about to pull the trigger, Jackson pulls at some lights and swings Tarzan-style over to the sniper, causing him to miss his shot and merely clip the union leader in the shoulder. He then falls out of the tree and impales himself on a fence, meaning that his presentation to Dante Fires will surely be cancelled.

As the guests run around in panic and Mr Edd and Kid Sable despatch everyone, O'Rooney decides it's the perfect time to point at Dellaplane and announce that he's the one responsible for everything and should be arrested – a courageous, albeit late, gesture that leads to him having a knife plunged into his chest by a henchman. Dellaplane makes a break for it and heads straight for Sydney, putting a gun to her head and locking her in a room, with the intention of giving her that one last fatal overdose. Not to be outdone, Jackson jumps behind the wheel of a fancy sports car and guns it straight into the house, killing another henchman as he does, driving up the stairs and bringing it to a screeching halt right under Dellaplane's nose. Round of applause, please. It's almost as if Michael Carroll, the Lotto lout, started his own series of *Junior Kickstart*. It's at this point that you have to admit that if your house is able to furnish a half-arsed demolition derby, then maybe it's just way too big.

It's the final showdown. Dellaplane has his gun to Sydney's head, and Jackson has his pointed at the villain. Not wanting to die like a punk, Dellaplane puts his gun down and indicates that he'd rather have death by hand-to-hand combat, like the king of white-guy karate he truly is. After getting a few lucky kicks and punches, and putting Jackson's cranium through a car window, he's made to regret it. Like Popeye before him, Jackson gets his second wind and declares, 'Now you've pissed me off,' before treating Dellaplane like a punchbag full of warm piss. When it's clear he's losing the fight, the baddie goes for his gun, but even in that race he comes second, and Jackson blows a hole in his chest, sending him sprawling to the floor in satisfying slo-mo.

Captain Armbruster arrives on the scene and tells Jackson he wants a report on his desk first thing in the morning, and when he protests, Armbruster tells him again, but adds the sweet addition of 'in the morning, Lieutenant', which leads to wild celebration and Sydney joyously declaring she's now an ex-junkie. She's going to go 'cold turkey' and Jackson can have her for Thanksgiving – eeugh, wait till she sees dead babies crawling across her ceiling. Nevertheless, Jackson thinks it's good news, and as they kiss, the Pointer Sisters sing about how someone 'turned them out' (is that a good thing?), and all is well with Jericho Jackson. Action by name, and very much Action by nature.

SIXTEEN

1988

MOSCOW'S TOUGHEST DETECTIVE. CHICAGO'S CRAZIEST
COP. THERE'S ONLY ONE THING WORSE THAN MAKING
THEM MAD. MAKING THEM PARTNERS.

A STEAM SAUNA, SOMEWHERE in the Soviet Union. A place
where men are real men, like they've taken lesser men, swallowed
them, and now stride around like socks full of snooker balls. It's
so hot in this steel foundry of machismo that they only wear tiny
pinnies to cover their bits, and, dressed accordingly, in walks
Captain Ivan Danko (Arnold Schwarzenegger), a tough Moscow
cop who's working undercover in literally the only place on Earth
where he will fit in – that isn't the inside of Liberace's mind.

He approaches a man who looks like he has Maradona on
his shoulders, and looks at him intensely. He is then handed
a red-hot stone to hold, which is somehow seen to be an act
of manliness. Danko grasps it purposefully and then punches
Maradona with it, sending him flying through the window and
tumbling into deep snowdrifts outside. Danko then wrestles with
the other heavy in the room (Sven-Ole Thorsen, bodybuilding
pal of Arnold, who pops up in most of his films), and this ends
in them both falling out the same window, with only their tiny
pinnies for cover. After pummelling them both, he grabs Thorsen

by the throat and asks him where he can find Viktor Rosta (crime kingpin of Moscow). Eventually, he gives up the information that Viktor left and went to the Druzhba Cafe. Danko then lands one final blow, knocking him out and into the snow, where he will surely either die of exposure or be dragged away by horny bears.

The police swarm outside the cafe. Danko is sitting in his patrol car with his partner, Yuri Ogarkov. Yuri warns Danko that the drug problem in Moscow is getting so out of hand that it'll be like Harlem in a few years. He then breaks the bad news to Danko that his nickname used to be 'Iron Jaw', but since the naked tussle in the snow, it's 'Roundhead', which sort of underlines what a hard, unrelenting country the Soviet Union is. You fight *one* man in the nude, and your reputation is toast.

A man sounding like the Russian Randy Newman is playing a knackered piano in the corner of the café to a baffled-looking crowd of extras. Danko walks in alone, with the heightened sense of confidence that being a massive brick shithouse dressed in full militia uniform and a furry hat offers you. A waiter tells him there are no problems today, but Danko begs to differ, as he spots Viktor Rosta (Ed O'Ross) and his gang at a table at the back. 'Let's go, all of you,' he intones, in his best Russian, but Viktor accuses him of hassling good Georgian people. His cohorts also protest at why he is hassling them when they're just trying to enjoy a drink and listen to Comrade Randi Newmanski murder a piano. Danko punches one of them, throws him to the floor, and pulls his leg off. The cafe screams as one, but their horror is soon allayed when it transpires the man has a wooden leg that is full to the brim with cocaine, and you can tell by the way he uses that walk, he's a cocaine man, no time to talk.

As Danko barks the brilliant line 'Cocainum', chaos breaks out as Viktor and his men begin shooting and running into the streets. Danko takes out one, but sadly Viktor murders Danko's partner with a hidden sleeve pistol and flees the scene. At Yuri's funeral, Danko's superior officer tells him that Viktor has fled the country with two accomplices. It seems they packed up their leather jackets, drugs and guns, and fled to Chicago. He tells Danko that they will pay for their crimes against the Motherland.

Chicago. A bustling metropolis of busy streets, high-pitched saxophones and fast-moving cars. Viktor is in a phone box. He has plans of lucrative drug deals with a kind of cool Muslim Brotherhood/Black Panthers-type gang called the cleanheads, a name that refers to the fact that they all shave their heads. After some subterfuge involving a torn $100 bill, Viktor returns to his two comrades waiting in the car and tells them the deal is on.

Meanwhile, Detective Art Ridzik (James Belushi) is in a patrol car with his partner Max Gallagher (Richard Bright – Al Neri in Godfather 1-3), whiling away the time by objectifying women ('fun-bag patrol'), and talking about whether their breasts are fake or 'home-grown'. Their colleague, Lieutenant Charlie Stobbs (Larry Fishburne), becomes so bored of Ridzik's misogyny that he leaves the car altogether. Gallagher tells Ridzik that maybe he should tone down his personality a bit, they're not sitting in that car to look at boobs; although they are on another kind of bust. They're planning to arrest some cleanheads, after Gallagher got a tip-off from his snitch, 'Streak'. They bust in and catch three of them in the act, surrounded by cocaine, guns and money. There's shouting and protesting, but nothing our boys can't handle, that is until Ridzik opens a door to find another gang member standing there with a shotgun. He blasts a hole in the door and makes a run for it, only to get snagged by Ridzik at the bottom of the fire escape, where Ridzik tells him he reminds him of Marvin Hagler, and that he lost money on Hagler. With the cleanheads sorted and the drugs seized, Viktor is left hanging in that same phone box from earlier, with no deal.

A telegram is received at Moscow Militia HQ, informing them that Viktor Rosta has been arrested in Chicago for a minor offence. Danko is immediately asked to go to America and bring him back to Moscow. The militia know why Viktor is there: he was in the process of arranging a $5m drug deal that he would then use to 'pollute their children' (sort of like The Beatles did in the sixties), and Danko is told in no uncertain terms that he must not tell the Americans anything about it, as the poisonous West must not know their problems. Oh, how times have changed.

O'Hare Airport, and Ridzik is waiting for the Moscow flight, eating nuts and looking bored. 'How are you doing, honey?' he asks an approaching woman. 'Blow yourself,' she says in reply. 'Thank you, thank you very much, good thinking,' he says, packing more peanuts in his mouth – an exchange I will never not find funny. Gallagher arrives to tell him their visitor will be out any second, and, sure enough, here he is – Captain Ivan Danko, a vast pillar of a man, dwarfing everyone around him and parting the crowds like a red Sea Line ferry. They put him in the car, and on the journey, Ridzik asks why he's been sent all this way to pick up Viktor. Just what crime did he commit back home to demand a personal envoy? Did he take a leak on the Kremlin wall? This irreverence earns him daggers from Danko. He asks where Viktor was arrested, and is told that it was at the Garvin Hotel, a breeding ground for pimps and drug pushers who enjoy the sultry sound of a saxophone and the rattle of the L trains. Despite the fact that they have him booked into a posh hotel in the city, he asks to be dropped off there.

Danko approaches the front desk and stares at the hotel owner (Pruitt Taylor Vince). 'Danko,' he barks. 'You're welcome,' the owner replies, laughing at his own joke and clearly missing his true calling. Danko asks for the same room as Viktor Rosta and then heads upstairs. To say Room 302 is a dank, shabby, disgusting hovel is doing it a disservice. Words have yet to be invented to adequately describe it, but one thing you can say for sure is that the guys on *Four in a Bed* would all have an aneurysm if they had to try and score it. Danko turns on the TV, and it immediately pours out porn, which he isn't too impressed by. He blames capitalism – yet I can imagine he'll soon take some comfort from it, during those long, lonely nights ahead.

The next morning, Danko arrives at the police precinct to curious glances and a comment that he looks like a glorified postman from World War II, which isn't far off the mark. He's introduced to Commander Donnelly (Peter Boyle), who hands Danko Viktor's extradition order. He was arrested running a red light, had no valid driving licence, and was carrying a gun, so they brought him in. He didn't ask for asylum, and is apparently resigned to going home. (Aren't we all?) Donnelly, who's about to have a heart bypass, then shares some of his stress-relief tips with Danko – nice fish in a tank, plants, deep breathing and soothing music – making him very much the Alan Titchmarsh of police officers, minus the writing of erotica. He then summons Ridzik and tells him that he and his partner are to take Danko to the jail to pick up Viktor, and then take them to the airport.

Viktor is in no mood for small talk, and you can tell this because his immediate answer when asked questions by Danko is 'kiss my ass'. Among his many personal effects, Danko finds what looks like the key to a locker, but Viktor refuses to divulge exactly what it opens. Getting nowhere, Danko asks Ridzik to try, but he's quickly told to 'go kiss his mother's behind'. Danko pockets the key as they leave the prison, and they all head to the airport. Ridzik says his goodbyes, and leaves Gallagher and Danko with Viktor. However, once Ridzik has gone to buy his racing tips paper, things don't go smoothly. The cleanheads intercept the party, there's a shootout where one of Viktor's accomplices is shot and wounded, and Gallagher is sadly killed. Danko fights valiantly but is knocked out, and the cleanheads take Viktor with them as they escape from the incoming sirens. Danko's huge fist closes around the key on the floor.

At the hospital, Danko's massive X-rays show he only has concussion, and Viktor's comrade is wheeled into Intensive Care. Ridzik tells Stobbs that he thinks it was the cleanheads who did it, and Stobbs agrees: they all walked out of jail yesterday morning. Later, Danko is visited in his hospital bed by two Soviet liaison officers from Washington, who look a bit like the USSR's answer to Little and Large. They tell him he has embarrassed the Motherland (though not via the medium of Deputy Dawg impressions). Thanks to him, Viktor can now do his big deal and poison all of Moscow with drugs and Baby Ruths. It is all *so* humiliating. He is ordered to take the first plane home and report to his superiors, who are not happy with his work.

Ridzik pops in to visit Danko, to find him fully dressed and loading an enormous gun, which he managed to keep hold of on the flight over thanks to diplomatic immunity. Ridzik says he shouldn't really have a massive cannon, but he'll let him keep it if he tells him what's going on with Viktor. Danko isn't quite ready to share this, but he does inform his visitor that he'll work undercover to find Viktor, despite the fact that he looks like a public library on legs.

Ridzik takes him to Donnelly, who is not best pleased, as he now knows, thanks to the Russian Embassy, that Viktor is not just a red-light runner, but in actual fact a major drug trafficker, currency speculator, rapist, kidnapper, murderer and fan of *Mrs Brown's Boys*. Danko says he had no authorisation to tell him before, but he's not leaving the country until he gets Viktor. He asks for co-operation, which Donnelly happily accepts with the proviso that he stays away from the press and doesn't roll through Chicago like the Red Army. Stobbs questions the decision, but Donnelly can see no downside: Danko is a loose cannon, and if he fucks up, he's Russian, so it's not his problem.

Ridzik takes Danko to see Gallagher's snitch, Streak (Brion James), for some information about the cleanheads, but warns him beforehand that in America all people have rights, no matter how awful they are, and tells him all about the Miranda Act. However, it quickly becomes clear that Ridzik is happy to bend the rules; he plants drugs on Streak in order to get him to talk. When this doesn't work, Danko steps in with a more Soviet style of interrogation and tries to break Streak's fingers. In doing so he gets the information they were after: the leader of the cleanheads, the self-described political revolutionary (and bank robber) Abdul Elijah is running things from prison, and a big shipment is coming in the next couple of days, but he doesn't know where to.

Next stop, the cleanheads' playground, an area of prison so intimidating and scary that even the guards won't enter (think Blobby Land on steroids). Ridzik and Danko are there to speak to Elijah and find out what they can about their missing Georgian.

Danko speaks to the charismatic Elijah alone, and tells him he has Viktor's key. This, it turns out, also means he has Viktor's money. He says he'll give Elijah the key in exchange for Viktor, and Elijah agrees, after a brilliant Marxist monologue on his scheme to sell drugs to every white man, and his sister, on the planet. He'll arrange a meet between the two of them, as he wants his money, but he warns Danko that he's just another motherfucker to be dealt with.

Cat Manzetti may sound like a feline private eye, but in this case she's Viktor's girlfriend (Gina Gershon). She's holding a dance class for lots of people in headbands, Lycra and long socks when she notices she has two intriguing visitors: Ridzik and Danko. It's immediately clear she won't co-operate, and after revealing that she's actually married to Viktor, she storms out during one of Ridzik's many accusations. Danko reassures him that it's fine; they can use her to get to Viktor. They decide to stake out the dance studio, so Ridzik heads off to get some coffee and doughnuts.

After Danko pulls the car away too quickly, to follow Cat in a yellow cab, hot coffee is spilled all over Ridzik's lap, allowing him to do a small skit about having a burnt penis, hard-boiled nuts, etc, etc. Cat leads them to a parking garage and a massive, heavily armed cleanhead ambush. A gun is put to Ridzik's head, and Danko is sent away to speak to Viktor. They approach one another in the dark lot, and exchange comradely greetings. Viktor tells him he'd be dead if he had a gun and that drug dealing in Moscow is fine, as any country that survived Stalin can survive a little dope, and then there's some random chat about looking forward to death – standard Soviet-style small talk. Danko refuses to give him the key (by now concealed in Ridzik's pants), even after being offered eye-watering sums of money, and Viktor calls him a fool then walks back into the darkness.

News comes in that Viktor's buddy is coming out of his coma, so they rush to the hospital to question him, only to find the other accomplice there, dressed fetchingly as a nurse, murdering him. Ridzik is about to shoot him as he makes his escape, but Cat jumps out from nowhere (as they often do) and tells him not to shoot. The man doesn't listen, though, and begins shooting, but he's quickly wasted by Danko, whereupon he flies through multiple glass doors and sprays blood all over the message boards. Cat runs, and Danko corners her in a stairwell. He tells her she is stupid, and that Viktor has ten women at home just like her, either dead or in prison – so is he counting the dead ones? Is this where the Conservative government gets its ideas? Either way, Cat's scared, and says she didn't mean for all this to happen and doesn't know what to do, so Danko kicks open the door and tells her to run – but knowing cats, she'll be back later for dinner.

Donnelly and Stobbs burst into the treatment room where Art is being patched up, demanding answers, but Danko is tight-lipped, even when he's required to hand over his gun. I mean, it doesn't look good politically if a Soviet militia man, who's built like a football stadium, is running around town with one. After telling Ridzik he needs a full report, Donnelly dismisses them both.

While filling out endless paperwork detailing the death and destruction of the last few hours, Ridzik bonds with Danko in a coffee shop. They actually have lots in common in terms of family (both parents are dead, so not a lot of Christmas shopping required) and life in general (they like women and are not gay, OK?), and it just goes to show that deep down, aren't all humans just the same? Can we not just have world peace? Can we not all just get along?

Ridzik drops Danko off at the Garvin Hotel and heads to the precinct to type up his report. Danko arrives to lots of messages from Cat. She tells him that the drugs are coming in that evening and, if she gives him this information, she wants her freedom. She only married Viktor because she earns $5.84 (she's a woman for detail) an hour teaching kids to dance and he gave her ten grand, which is nearly as much as *Hello!* would pay for a wedding back then. Danko promises to help her, once he gets Viktor.

Danko goes up to the room he shares with bacteria, cockroaches and semen stains, and places the key in the lightshade, which would have been an excellent place to hide it, were it not for the fact that Viktor and the cleanheads are watching him with binoculars from across the street. Danko has himself a lovely, refreshing shower as the baddies make their way purposefully to the third landing. When they reach the corridor, Viktor points the cleanheads to the wrong room and slips off. After they murder an innocent man in his shower, they realise Viktor's set them up. Danko hears the shots and proceeds to murder all the cleanheads with ease. While he's having fun jumping out and firing, and hiding from bullets, Viktor sneaks into the right room, smashes the lightshade, and runs off with the key.

In the morgue, Stobbs and Donnelly look mournfully down at a clear plastic bag that contains the remains of Catherine Manzetti. She's been strangled and dumped in the river, literally a case of the cat being pulled out of the bag (sorry). What with the multiple hotel murders and now this, Stobbs tells Ridzik he's 'riding a desk' from now on (which will be murder in traffic) and that Danko is going home – back behind the curtain where he belongs. After their reprimand, Ridzik takes Danko to Pat's key shop, and while he argues with Pat about the bouncing alimony cheque payments for his sister, Danko studies some books about keys. Luckily, he wrote down the serial number, so he's able to determine that it's for a bus terminal locker.

Viktor slips the key to the cleanhead seated next to him in the bus terminal cafe. He retrieves the large suitcase from the locker and retreats to the Men's to check the money. As he's thumbing the cash to check everything is OK, Viktor drifts in through the door, looking as shifty as ever. The cleanhead tells him everything's good and the drugs are coming in on the 9.30 from El Paso, but before he can wish him a pleasant journey home to sell all his drugs to children, Viktor shoots him dead with his sleeve pistol.

As Viktor concludes his transaction in the bus terminal, up pops Danko from behind a departing bus telling him that he has failed and pointing a gun at him. However, before we can all break out the vodka and caviar, Ridzik emerges from a doorway and tells him to back off: Viktor killed a Chicago cop and should be arrested. There's a spot of argy-bargy between the unlikely partners, and Viktor takes advantage of the confusion to jump behind the wheel of a parked bus and speed off. Danko commandeers another bus, and Ridzik jumps in, they give chase through the wet streets of Chicago, ploughing through cars, breaking windows of shopping precincts, and decimating a Chicago landmark in the process – probably leading to many a tourist becoming lost.

Eventually, down by the railway tracks, the two buses face one another. The two Russians decide to play chicken (proving that *Footloose* must have made its way behind the Iron Curtain at some point). Ridzik cannot believe what he is seeing; at the last minute he yanks the steering wheel, causing their bus to crash and tumble, while Viktor's is hit by an oncoming train. As they crawl out of the wreckage, Danko reprimands Ridzik for saving their lives, much to Ridzik's chagrin, but their argument doesn't last long. Viktor is stumbling, miraculously, out of his own wrecked bus and kills the driver of the train that hit him. 'I take care of this,' Ivan declares, looking coldly at the battered figure of Ridzik. 'I give up. This whole thing's very Russian,' Ridzik replies as he watches Ivan walk away, holding his Magnum .44.

Viktor stands waiting amidst the smoke pouring from the crashed train and fires wildly at the oncoming Danko, but he doesn't figure on Danko being a better shot. He's sent flying as Danko replies with deadly accuracy, many times, pumping him full of lead. As his body slides down the side of the train in a snail trail of blood and guts, Ridzik arrives to ask, with some irony, if he got him. Viktor is dead, and the drugs will not be heading to Moscow after all, though they will probably end up in Liberace.

Danko is watching baseball on TV in the airport with Ridzik. He announces – to much nodding from the rest of the world –

that he doesn't understand baseball. After some excellent banter about Russian vs American sport, Danko hands Ridzik his watch, as it is customary in the Soviet Union to exchange an article as a sign of friendship. Ridzik is deeply touched, and gives Danko his $1,000 watch in exchange, but soon realises he's actually received a very cheap East German one in this transaction. Danko stands to his feet and reminds Ridzik that they are police officers, not politicians, so it's OK to like one another, even though a few seconds ago he admitted that he probably would have shot Ridzik back at the bus terminal. They bid a fond farewell, and as Danko reaches the gate, he turns and salutes his American ally, before a hard cut to Danko in full uniform standing in Red Square (the shot of which was achieved illegally as they were refused a filming permit). He then marches off to join his fellow militia officers and show them his awesome new watch while telling them all about the capitalist porn he saw on a TV once.

SEVENTEEN

DIE HARD

1988

40 STOREYS HIGH . . . WITH SUSPENSE,
EXCITEMENT AND ADVENTURE ON EVERY LEVEL!

NERVOUS FLIER JOHN McCLANE (Bruce Willis) is landing in LA. He's been receiving advice from a fellow passenger about the best post-flight relaxation techniques: basically, take off your shoes and socks, walk on a carpet, and make fists with your feet. A glimpse of his gun as he removes a huge teddy bear from the overhead locker leads to his revealing that he's a cop.

Chauffeur Argyle (De'voreaux White) meets McClane in his awesome limo. He's totally excited; it has a telephone, CDs, VHS, Run DMC cassettes, the works. He's taking McClane to meet his estranged wife, and McClane being McClane, he insists on sitting in the front. Argyle is utilised as a device to tell us all about McClane and how he and his wife have separated – but not in a climbing Buckingham Palace dressed as Spider-Man way, more in a not wanting to leave New York sort of way. So that's OK.

Meanwhile, over at Nakatomi Plaza, Joseph Takagi (James Shigeta) is giving a speech to the staff, congratulating them on an amazing year for the corporation, wishing them all a merry Christmas, and mentioning that he's not expecting any terrorist attacks, but should there be one, the fire escapes are at each corner of the room. As the crowd applauds, McClane's wife Holly (Bonnie Bedelia) is still busying herself with work, preparing for John's visit, when she's accosted by Ellis (Hart Bochner), who offers ancient cheese, mulled wine and a roaring fireplace, and may as well present us with a business card that informs us that he will be the sleazy yuppie man in this film, thank you very much. As his invitation falls on deaf ears, he departs, so Holly calls home and speaks to the housekeeper, asking if John has called – he hasn't – and to make up the spare bedroom just in case – the one with the blow-up bed and jazz mags. As she hangs up the phone she turns to a family portrait of happier days and lays it down flat, as many people did with their copies of *Hudson Hawk* a few years later.

Nakatomi Plaza: the most memorable skyscraper in cinema history (that King Kong hasn't climbed) and the setting for, let's face it, the greatest action film of all time. McClane leaves Argyle with the understanding that if the talk with his wife goes well, he'll leave him to it, and if it goes bad, he'll take him to a hotel, to presumably take wild advantage of the adult movie channels. He steps into the foyer of the plaza, and is greeted by a touch-screen computer (probably borrowed from *Tomorrow's World*) to locate which floor Holly is on. He sighs when he sees that she's going by her maiden name of Gennero, which seems to suggest that this reunion is already off to a shaky start.

As McClane joins the Christmas drinks reception, all string quartets and champagne, and mutters 'California', he's greeted by Joseph Takagi, who takes him to Holly's office. There, they find Ellis making use of the desk to hoover up some cocaine, which McClane isn't very impressed by. Holly arrives, and the awkwardness in the room is soon dissipated by the longing look they give one another, one that seems to linger with a sweet refrain, until Ellis sabotages the moment by telling Holly to show her husband the Rolex he bought her, like a total douchebag.

As the suits depart, McClane asks to use the bathroom to wash up, and he and Holly chat as he gets down to his vest and trousers. He warns her Ellis has his eye on her, and she says that he could stay at the house – the kids would like it, and she would too. He takes this comment onboard, and then decides to bring up why she's going by her maiden name, which then leads to an argument, and before they can finish it, Holly is called to do a speech for the staff and has to leave. McClane looks in the mirror and castigates himself for ruining a nice moment – so it is definitely Christmas, then.

The Pacific Courier truck looms over the horizon as the sun begins to set. It trundles ominously into the underground garage of Nakatomi Plaza, followed by a Mercedes that drives up to the front of the building and comes to a halt. Theo (Clarence Gilyard Jr) and Karl (Alexander Godunov) swagger out of the car and into the foyer, and before the guard can ask why they're there, Karl shoots him dead. Theo brings out his walkie-talkie and communicates to the truck that they're in, so it backs into position, opens the back door, and releases a gang of mercenaries led by Hans Gruber (Alan Rickman on iconic, career-defining form).

Theo, cheerfully humming 'Singin' In The Rain', disables loads of electrical stuff, and a big blond guy muttering 'left' and 'right' in German disconnects cables.

With a delicate ping, the elevator doors slide open and the baddies calmly drift into the celebration, then begin firing warning shots into the ceiling. McClane, busy doing his foot-relaxation exercises, hears the shots and screams, and races to the door to see the terrorists pulling people, and a half naked woman – obviously, it's obligatory in the eighties – from the offices, but before they can reach Holly's office, he makes a dash for the fire escape, barefoot, in his vest and trousers.

Gruber calmly silences the screams of the assembled Nakatomi employees like Mike Ashley at a corporate do. He tells them that he's only after one man, Joseph Takagi, and then he silkily glides around the crowd listing his credentials, like some sort of terrorist version of *This Is Your Life*. But before he can get into the real meat of what Takagi has achieved in his life, and much against Holly's wishes, Takagi steps forward and tells Gruber he has his man. Gruber coldly shakes his hand before whisking him away from the area, getting daggers from Holly as he does so.

They take Takagi to another floor, and as Gruber admires the construction models and makes small talk about suits, McClane enters the neighbouring room, watching from a distance as the conversation develops into something more serious. Gruber wants Takagi to give Theo the code key for the vault and the $640m of bonds that are sealed within it.

Takagi is mildly taken aback by this demand to steal his money, as he clearly had a different idea in his mind about what terrorists actually are, but Gruber laughs it off and tells him that they need the code, and as he brings out his pistol, he tells him he will count to three.

As McClane skulks around, trying to get a better viewing position under a table, he watches as Takagi refuses to hand over the information to Gruber and his men, and warns them that there are seven safeguards to the vault, and the key is only one of them. This turns out to be a lamentable error. Gruber happily shoots him, spraying the wall behind him in regret. As his body falls to the floor, and Gruber orders his men to dispose of it, Theo reassures Gruber that he can break the code, but it'll take a few hours. He can break six of them with a machine, but the seventh lock is out of his hands, as it has an electro-magnetic seal and can't be cut locally. As they depart the office, McClane hides, shocked, in the stairwell, knowing full well that this Christmas will be a bit more stressful than usual.

He then goes back to the floor under construction and curses himself for not trying to stop them, while also noting that he'd be dead if he did. He wonders exactly what he can do to alert the authorities, short of holding an illegal rave or posting an incendiary tweet. Thinking on his bare feet, he notices sprinklers in the ceiling and decides to set off the fire alarm.

At the window, he celebrates wildly as he sees fire trucks roaring down the road toward the building, but he quickly has to cancel the party, as the trucks kill their sirens and slowly turn away. Before he can comprehend why, the elevator doors ping, and he is not alone. In walks Tony (Andreas Wisniewski, Necros from *The Living Daylights*), dressed in tight grey joggers like an Instagrammer, carrying a shoulder bag and a machine gun. He taunts the room, telling whoever it is in there that their plan has failed and they should come out and join the others. However, McClane has other ideas. He leaps from the darkness, pressing his gun into his face, telling Tony that he's a cop and he should drop the gun. Tony smugly remarks that McClane won't hurt him as he's a policeman and will follow the rules – boy, do I have some news for you. McClane punches him in the face, which leads to a scrap that ends with them both tumbling downstairs (where you can see a stuntman wearing pretend-feet shoes). Tony's neck breaks, killing him instantly.

After checking that he's dead, McClane begins to loot his body and shoulder bag, and as he poses Tony on a chair in the lift, channelling Dennis Nilsen, he thinks of something: what could be worse than a corpse in a lift sitting on a chair and wearing a Santa hat? Why, a corpse in a lift sitting on a chair and wearing a Santa hat, with the message 'Now I have a machine gun Ho-Ho-Ho' written on him with red pen.

As the lift reaches Gruber's floor and the door opens, it's met with shrieking horror by the staff and a deeply unimpressed Gruber. What he doesn't realise, as he's chattering away in German to his men, is that McClane, much like a serial killer visiting the scene of a crime, is on top of the lift, watching and listening in an effort to gather intel. Meanwhile, Gruber has to break the news to Karl that his brother is dead, and even worse than that, he is now a meme, which Karl doesn't take well. Gruber reassures him that the most important thing is to get that vault open and plant the detonators on the top floor, and after that's done, he can have his revenge and try to stop sales of T-shirts celebrating his brother's death.

However, before Karl can contact Redbubble to complain, McClane decides to throw further shit at the fan by heading to the roof to contact the police via his stolen walkie-talkie. The police dispatcher doesn't believe his story of multiple terrorists and death, but Gruber, overhearing the message, decides to send Karl and his boys up to the roof to make sure that he doesn't say anything too controversial, like how it's probably the 5G that's making them do it. As the dispatcher tells him that if he doesn't stop barking at her he'll be in trouble, gunshots ripple in McClane's direction from Karl and the boys, the noise of which causes her to be alarmed enough to alert a policeman to do a drive-by – but not just any policeman.

Down at the mini-market below, Sergeant Al Powell (Reginald VelJohnson), a jolly, rotund patrol cop, is buying some essential sweets and treats, and being fat-shamed by the even more rotund cashier, when he gets a call to investigate a code 2 over at Nakatomi Plaza, so he gets in his car and slowly drives over.

Meanwhile, McClane has escaped from Karl and the boys by slinking into the air vents and talking to himself about how Christmas is essentially a shit time and how he should have stayed at home – a sentiment that I think every family can wholeheartedly agree with. However, while he's using a lighter to see where he's going, Karl spots the light and heads down to the relevant floor to pop some caps in that ass, only to have his search interrupted by the arrival of Sergeant Powell.

McClane emerges from the air vents to watch, hoping that the police officer will stumble upon a hill of bodies, a bloke with a machine gun and an awkward situation involving a gerbil, but he doesn't. In fact he sees nothing suspicious at all. Infuriated by the lack of action, McClane decides it's time to begin smashing a window with a chair, a loud and risky action that causes some of Gruber's men to spring into action and burst into the room as McClane is rebooting Windows.

After a firefight, McClane runs to the window again to see Powell leaving, so he decides to offer him a parting gift: the corpse of one of the bad guys, which lands squarely on the car's windshield and causes machine gunfire to rain down on him as he hurriedly reverses away from the plaza and crashes into a ditch. Welcome to the party, Al Powell.

Dick Thornburg (William Atherton – Walter Peck from *Ghostbusters*) is a slimy reporter, an awful man. In fact, he's so slimy and awful that his funeral catering would probably be a solitary Kit-Kat. Tonight, he's at work at TV station KFLW-TV, sitting in the corner, sliming, whining and being awful over a telephone, trying to get a table for dinner at Spago (a top restaurant on Sunset Strip) – where, presumably, he'll ruin everyone's evening by being a prick – when he hears something interesting over the police scanner: Powell's urgent request for back-up.

The police arrive in heavy numbers, which initially panics Gruber's men, but he reassures them that this is all part of the plan; it's just happening earlier than he would have liked. However, before he can bring out the team-building exercises where they make a tower out of balloons, his radio crackles into life. It's McClane, who, buoyed by the police presence, decides to roll out a carpet of swagger and comedy chops. He tells Gruber all about the men he just killed, and how he's not a security guard, but a simple fly in the ointment, a monkey in the wrench, a pain in the ass, that bloke in the cinema who orders nachos and sits next to you. Gruber tells his men to check who's missing and resumes his chat with McClane, asking him if he really thinks he has a chance against him and his men, and accusing him of being just another American who saw too many John Wayne films as a kid, and thinks he can save the day.

McClane tells him he was always partial to Roy Rogers, before putting a final stamp on their chat by uttering the immortal phrase 'Yippee ki-yay, motherfucker', giving birth to a catchphrase that will live on his shoulders for a further four instalments of his cursed life.

The news that the bag of detonators is missing concerns Gruber, and just as he's about to wrap his head around this inconvenience, the radio crackles into life once again. This time it's Powell, radioing in to try to find the person who called for help. McClane replies and explains the set-up: thirty-odd hostages, all on the thirtieth floor, an arsenal of weapons (enough to orbit Arnold Schwarzenegger, apparently), mostly European terrorists (owing to the clothing labels and cigarettes), and he's got them down to just nine now. He adds that they must have good financing as their fake IDs are *really* good.

Gruber's men begin to panic about what he's telling Powell, but Gruber remains calm: he's waiting for the FBI to arrive, and until then they can chat all they like, but they must get the detonators back. Powell asks McClane for his name, so he tells him to call him Roy, and says he'll leave the rest of the situation to him.

Unfortunately, McClane's confidence in the LAPD is about to be severely tested. A car pulls in at speed, and out steps one prize-winning dickhead, Deputy Police Chief Dwayne T. Robinson (Paul Gleason – one of the best assholes in Hollywood). He demands to know what the terrorists want and rubbishes Powell's claims that the person he's been talking to isn't a terrorist himself, especially as Powell doesn't know who the person actually is. Robinson has his own ideas: that maybe Roy's a terrorist essentially doing a prank call like Steve Penk, or he could be a bartender. Yeah, maybe. Powell knows better.

Holly has a request for Gruber. It might be prudent to let the hostages go to the toilet, because it would seem they're all moments away from pissing all over the room, and maybe let the heavily pregnant woman have a chair to sit on, as sitting on an architectural rock is doing her back in? Gruber agrees, and compliments Holly on her business acumen and negotiation skills. He asks her name, and after briefly looking at her downturned family photo frame, she tells him it's 'Gennero, Miss Gennero', clever girl.

Thornburg grasps his microphone and stands in a spotlight as he reveals to camera what has happened in the skyscraper behind him: terrorists have seized control of the building and sealed off all entrances and exits. While this isn't news to anyone in the building, it certainly is to someone in the car park below it. Argyle pauses as he pours himself a drink in the back seat of the limo and sits open-mouthed as his in-car television explains what has happened. It's like living in a flat below Charlie Sheen. However, he's not as clueless as Dwayne T. Robinson, who, much to Powell's incredulity, is sending in a team of armed police to take out the terrorists.

The massive searchlights fire up and point towards the edifice, burning determinedly into the windows. McClane reaches for his walkie-talkie, and Powell tells him to pray. The SWAT team edge their way towards the entrances, and Robinson nods at his tactical officer, telling him to 'kick ass', once again proving that he's not a man overly burdened with self-awareness.

Within seconds, the game is up. Bullets ping through the windows and doors like angry bees, taking out the searchlights and wounding the team, and forcing the uninjured to retreat like the bunch of spanners they are. The police then employ an armoured response vehicle that mounts the entrance to the building, but it's quickly fired on by a rocket launcher from another floor. As Gruber orders it to be hit again, McClane jumps on the radio and tells Gruber that he's made his point, but he's ignored. Gruber's acting like a British politician who feels slighted by a European trading community and decides to blow up his own house. As Gruber's men race in to announce the police are using artillery on them, he dismisses them, knowing all too well that it's that fly in the ointment.

Thornburg's nipples nearly explode from under his shirt when it's confirmed that his cameraman caught the entire thing. He pats himself on the back for trusting his questionable instincts, safe in the knowledge that although everybody hates him, his subterranean morals will ensure he does very well as a journalist.

Back on Radio McClane, he's asking if the building is on fire, and Powell confirms that he took out another two terrorists with the blast, which McClane enjoys greatly. Robinson, however, isn't so happy; he rushes in from the smoke to grab the radio from Powell and basically act like he's just phoned into Five Live to complain about lockdown. McClane basically tells him to fuck off and reminds him that he just 'got butt-fucked on national TV', which is a keeper, and gets a hearty laugh from Argyle, listening down in the car park.

After pushing some more Colombian marching powder up his hooter, Ellis decides he's had enough of being a hostage. He thinks it might be time to put his incredible schmoozing skills into practice with the Euro trash next door. He stands up, straightens his tie, and asks if he can chat to the big cheese. As Gruber sits there, quietly scrutinising him like a pigeon being taught philosophy by Stanley Unwin, Ellis breaks out his version of *The Art of the Deal* and tells Gruber he knows who's running around the building ruining everything for everyone.

Bored, and basically inventing social media, McClane comes on the radio again to tell Powell he's eaten a very old Twinkie. As Powell lists the ingredients, thereby inventing Wikipedia, they begin to share a touching conversation about their children, mercifully stopping before they can sing a song together and send a poke.

Gruber breaks into the brotherly chat and offers his own tale: he knows exactly who McClane is, and not only that, he has with him the person who brought him to the party. As his name is read out over the airwaves, Thornburg and his team burst into action, and the world listens as Gruber hands the radio to Ellis. He explains that Gruber just wants his detonators back, and if he hands them over, everything will be OK, but McClane ruins this play slightly by telling Gruber he doesn't know Ellis, he only met him that evening, and as Gruber pulls out his gun Ellis smiles weakly. He tries to smarm his way out of it, and let's see how that plays. A gunshot rings out, and Ellis is left to negotiate his way into heaven with a PowerPoint presentation. Gruber broadcasts the screaming hostages and demands that McClane bring him his detonators, only to be told to go forth and multiply.

As Robinson and Powell go head to head over the merits of morality, Gruber delivers his manifesto over the radio. He proceeds to demand the release of (basically) every political prisoner in the world, from Northern Ireland to Sri Lanka, in an effort to waste time. He may as well have included all cancelled celebrities and demanded that they put on a TV extravaganza hosted by Kevin Spacey doing his traditional Christmas Eve message of eldritch word salad. Once he's finished confusing the badges, he tells Karl to hunt McClane down and get the detonators.

An excited Robinson buttons up his jacket on the arrival of the FBI, the wonderful sight of the two Johnsons (the wonderful Robert Davi and Grand L. Bush – both mainstays in 80s cinema) strolling through the carnage. They look up at the skyscraper and coldly tell Robinson that they are now in charge. They quickly assess the situation and announce that it looks like an 'A7' scenario – presumably meaning it'll need really small paper. Powell reminds them that McClane is in there, and he's the reason there are only seven terrorists left, but they seem uninterested.

Gruber wanders through some dry ice, torch in hand, investigating the many charges in place throughout the ceiling. As he checks the wiring and fittings, fumbling through the many plugs and cables, he slowly climbs down and sets his feet on the floor, only to see another pair of feet – without any shoes on. Without a moment's hesitation, he bursts into character and begins to play lost hostage as McClane points a gun in his face.

After listening to Gruber's performance, McClane asks his name. Gruber goes for 'Bill Clay', a name he can see listed on the wall behind him. McClane tells 'Bill' that he's a cop from New York who was invited to the party by mistake, which will ring alarm bells with everyone in the Nakatomi events planning team. After a brief chat and the offer of a cigarette, McClane hands 'Bill' his gun and asks him if he knows how to use it. As he turns to leave, 'Bill' melts back into Gruber, and begins to talk German into his walkie-talkie, pointing the gun at McClane's back as he does so. However, McClane is no fool. As Gruber demands his detonators back, it quickly becomes clear that the gun is empty. As McClane snatches it back from him and tells him he's not stupid, the lift pings disconcertingly and Karl and two more men come steaming out. A firefight begins, and McClane takes out two more, but is pinned down by Gruber's clever idea of shooting out all the glass in the room onto the floor. McClane has to abandon his bag of detonators and run the gauntlet towards the exit, over a vast floorspace of shattered windows – which may or may not be a new game show on ITV in the near future. As the smoke clears and McClane has vacated the room, Gruber stoops to retrieve the detonators. He tells Karl they're back in business.

The bathroom door slowly opens, and as McClane crawls inside on his back, a stream of red follows him. His feet are cut to ribbons, so he perches himself on a sink and runs water over them, wincing in agony. The radio crackles into life, and it's Powell, asking how he's doing. After a few slices of banter are handed out like sandwiches at a picnic, they get into the heavy stuff. Powell recounts the reason why he's a desk-bound police officer: when he was younger, he accidentally shot and killed a child who had a toy gun, and since that day he's never been able to draw his gun on anyone, and this could all be an awful metaphor for something else. McClane says it's very sad and all that, but at the moment he's a bit sad himself, as he's stuck in a building with armed men, and his feet look like someone's put a Hobbit in a threshing machine. Powell decides to lift his mood by telling him that the LAPD aren't calling the shots any more, the FBI are in charge, which may be good news on paper, but in reality it's like inviting Hulk Hogan into a china shop run by Randy Savage.

At last, Theo has news for Gruber. He's got through all the locks on the safe, but the electro-magnetic seal can't be broken, which in any usual situation would be very bad news, but right now is music to Gruber's ears. He knows that now the FBI are on the scene, their first order of business will be to cut the power to the building, thus bringing down the last obstacle in their way. As the lights go off, and the Johnsons laugh into their sleeves, Gruber and Theo watch in wonder as the doors majestically open to the sound of Beethoven's *Ode To Joy*, and the treasure inside is plundered by the terrorists like pirates with erections.

McClane gets on the radio to deliver one last message to Powell: when this is all over, he wants him to tell his wife he loves her, that he's been a jerk, and that he should've been more supportive of her career, and he's sorry. But after delivering his heartfelt message, he suddenly has a thought about what Gruber was doing where he found him, so he limps away on his patched-up feet to find out what he was up to.

In the air shafts where he last saw Gruber, he sees exactly what's waiting for the FBI when they arrive: a vast ornamental garden of C4 and beeping lights, with the capacity to blow the roof off the building ten times over and leave it looking like the *Blue Peter* garden in 1983. He jumps down to the floor and begins to tell Powell that it's a double cross, but a full stop is provided by Karl's gun being thrust into his face. McClane, though, offers his own full stop by punching Karl's face very hard.

As the FBI helicopters approach, Gruber steps away from his office and tells Holly to gather her people, but he notices that she's transfixed by what's happening on the television behind him, and it isn't an episode of *Naked Attraction*. It's her own children being exploited by Thornburg for ratings. Gruber remembers the downturned photo and lifts it to see the McClanes in happier times. He orders his remaining men to take the hostages to the roof and then grabs Holly, telling her she's coming with him by way of insurance.

Meanwhile, McClane is still rearranging Karl's face and telling him all about the time he murdered his brother, before leaving him hanging on a chain noose and racing to the roof to help the hostages.

The door is flung open and McClane downs the terrorist guarding it, then runs to meet the hostages. He's told that Holly's been taken to the vault. He barks a message for them all to run as the roof is about to blow, but no one can hear him, so he begins to spray machine gunfire into the air. This panics them sufficiently that they race back down the stairwells – and this is something that should really be trialled with people who won't leave parties when they're over.

Gruber gives the order to blow the roof, and up it goes, just as McClane manages to tie a fire hose to his waist and jump off, like someone leaving a fireman's convention that's got out of hand. The FBI choppers are engulfed in flames, and as the explosion rattles out, Robinson suggests that they're 'gonna need more FBI guys, I guess', which is one of the finest lines in movie history. As McClane plummets down the side of the building, he manages to shoot out a window and swing himself back inside.

Down in the car park, Argyle notices some movement. Theo's backing an ambulance out of the big truck. So, Argyle rams the limo into the side and knocks Theo out with one punch, in a move that is reminiscent of baggage handler John Smeaton kicking a flaming terrorist in the balls at Glasgow Airport.

As McClane approaches the vault, he realises his options are very limited: on the one hand he has two guns, but on the other, he only has two bullets. Spying some gift-wrapping tape abandoned on a trolley, a lightbulb appears above his bloodied head. He calls out Gruber's name as he staggers into the vault, machine gun in hand, and Gruber instantly grabs Holly and puts a gun to her head, while Eddie, his last remaining cohort, reaches for his gun. Holly is, understandably, surprised to see her husband, who she last saw cleaning himself in the bathroom and now looks like he ran through an abattoir on fire. McClane's clearly a bit annoyed that this was all just about a robbery, and asks why it was necessary to destroy the entire building, which is a very British reaction, if you ask me. Gruber explains that if the authorities think he's already dead, no one will come looking for him, which is fair enough. He tells McClane to throw down his gun or he'll kill Holly, so he does. Gruber them recalls what he said to him earlier, and as he points the gun at McClane, he recounts the immortal cowboy line, which when coming from him serves to send the room into hysterics.

However, the laughter is a cover for McClane's excellent plan, and as the chuckles continue, he quickly reaches for the handgun taped to his back and fires his last two rounds: one into Eddie, the other into Gruber. As Gruber staggers back towards the now bullet-holed window, McClane coolly blows the smoke from his now empty gun and wishes him 'Happy trails'. The window shatters, and Gruber falls out, still holding Holly's wrist as he does so, and McClane races to set her free. As Gruber grimly looks up at them and slowly pulls up his gun, McClane uncouples the Rolex Holly got from Ellis, and Gruber loses his grip. What follows is not only an incredible stunt, but also an incredible moment captured. Alan Rickman was told by the director that he would be dropped 40 feet onto a crash pad on the count of three, but was actually released on one, making his shocked expression utterly genuine.

With John and Holly reunited and walking out of the building in, mostly, one piece, they're greeted by Al Powell, who McClane is understandably very happy to see. They embrace lovingly while Holly wonders in horror if they'll all be living together now. As Robinson approaches, demanding a debrief and sounding like a flaming ball of arse pain, McClane readies a thump, but before he has time to clench his fist, a scream is heard from behind, and they all turn to see Karl, throwing off a blanket and wielding a large machine gun.

As the crowd disperses in panic, the music score does an odd thing, switching from Michael Kamen to James Horner's 'Resolution And Hyperspace' cue from *Aliens*. This was due to the filmmakers using it as a temporary track while editing, but liking it so much and feeling that it fitted the moment perfectly, they left it in. Who could disagree?

Karl's machine gun is raised, his face is contorted in rage, but before he can let a round off, he's taken down with five loud shots. Powell stands holding his pistol, the one he thought he'd never use again, and takes in what he's just done. He's got his mojo back, and can once again go out on the streets and shoot people. I love a happy ending.

There's another surprise, too, as Argyle's limo bursts through the gates of the car park and pulls over to take the McClanes away. But before they can climb in and relax, Thornburg breaks through the crowd and pushes a microphone in their faces, asking for their feelings after the whole ordeal. Holly punches him hard in the face, live on TV, and laughter rings out as Thornburg asks if his cameraman got it. And the world applauds in a shared sense of karmic poetry.

The happy couple then speed home to celebrate Christmas together. Though how much celebrating McClane will be able to do is up for debate, seeing as he's a half-dead man held together by gaffer tape, with shredded feet.

Thus ends the greatest action film of all time, and so say all of us.

EIGHTEEN

Road House

1989

THE DANCING'S OVER.
NOW IT GETS DIRTY.

THE BANDSTAND CLUB: THE sort of sophisticated joint where the men are the most awful of men, and women are essentially cleavages on legs that make the place look prettier. Frank Tilghman (Kevin Tighe) strolls in and is delighted by what he sees. While on the surface it looks like one of the worst places on Earth, to his eyes it is paradise – and that's all because of one man, James Dalton (Patrick Swayze). Dalton is the Pele of 'coolers', the Buddha of bouncers, and when he's in charge, people know their place. As Tilghman observes the well-run club, a little fracas breaks out, with a drunk customer slicing Dalton's arm and announcing to him that he thinks he can beat him up. Rather than making a scene and smashing the place up, Dalton coolly tells him to come outside; once in the car park, he wanders back inside while the drunk stews in his own warm piss. This is how it should be done; this is the cool world of Dalton.

As the Lord of Order is sewing up his small arm wound in his office, Tilghman walks in and makes him an offer. He has a club just outside Kansas City called the Double Deuce. It used to be nice, but now it's a proper shithole – the kind of place even Wayne Lineker would consider rough. He needs someone to help him clean it up and he needs the best. Dalton tells him he'd want $5,000 up front, $500 a night, in cash, and that he gets to run the show completely – though he does want some help with medical expenses. Tilghman doesn't bat an eyelid. Dalton has himself a deal.

Upon arriving at the Double Deuce, Dalton essentially acts out an episode of *Ramsay's Kitchen Nightmares*, in that he uses this first visit as a chance to observe the service and get to know how the joint runs. He's not a fan of what he sees. There's staff doing drug deals, money being stolen from the till, random violence breaking out, and worst of all, a head bouncer who's not interested in what's going on and totally preoccupied with scoring hot chicks. Dalton stands at the bar like an eagle, shaking his head and smiling wryly as he calculates just what he will have to do to get this place into shape. A nice waitress, Carrie Ann, introduces herself to him, and when he tells her his name is Dalton, it's clear that he's well known in the industry, and she's suitably impressed.

A band plays MOR rock behind a screen of chicken wire, but it's not just any band, it's Jeff Healey's band – or 'Cody', as he's known in this film. He and Dalton go way back, and have a bit of banter about the good old days of working in shit bars. Cody tells him this is the worst joint in America and there's blood on the floor every night. Word is out among the bouncers in the Double Deuce that Dalton is in, and they begin to tell tall tales about how cool he is, how he once killed a guy by ripping his throat out, and how he can beat up your dad, even though he's a fireman.

Once again, the place erupts into a bottle-smashing brawl, where all the staff join in and cause more damage than necessary. Dalton has seen all he needs to see.

Next day, he buys himself a cool old car and rents a room in a barn from Emmet, a man who looks like he belongs on a Scrumpy label. The view from his new home is lovely, with an idyllic, tree-lined river flowing under a bright blue sky, but suddenly a helicopter flies over aggressively, disturbing Emmet's horses, before it lands outside a gaudy mansion on the opposite riverbank. It belongs to Brad Wesley (Ben Gazzara), and he will be the villain of our story. Wesley has a tight grip on the town, and I, for one, think he may not care very much for Dalton's ways.

Back at the Double Deuce, Tilghman reveals his new plans to the gathered staff, telling them that what Dalton says goes. Straight off, Dalton fires Morgan, the head bouncer, because he doesn't have the right temperament for the trade. Morgan doesn't take this well, and tells Dalton that he will kill him. Next to go is the waitress who was selling all the drugs in plain sight, and then Dalton warns the rest of the staff that everyone has to cut out their bad behaviour: people who want to have a good time won't come to a slaughterhouse. He points out that the clientele is no good – too many felons, power drinkers and drug users – and they need to clean it all up. One of the staff points out that most of the customers who come there are very aggressive and difficult to handle, so Dalton lays out the rules of how to deal with them:

1. Never underestimate your opponent and expect the unexpected.
2. Take it outside.
3. Be nice . . . until it's time to not be nice.

And with those simple rules learned, the first night of Dalton's job can begin. It gets off to a nice start, but he quickly notices the barman still pocketing money, and then he has to deal with a knife-wielding drunk. He immediately breaks two of his own rules when he thumps the guy's face through a table. He then catches Steve the bouncer in the store room having weird, bouncy intercourse, and tells him he's fired. Then there's the small matter of the barman, whom he tells to 'take the train', which we can assume means he's fired too and is being asked to leave; that, or he's trying to get some of his green initiatives over to his men. This is a provocative move, as Pat, our light-fingered barman, is a relation of Brad Wesley.

Tilghman is pleased. It was a good night, and no one died, but before he can pop the cork on his champagne, Dalton warns him that it will get worse before it gets better, like the sage that he is, and saunters out to the car park to find his car trashed.

Back in his cosy barn room, Dalton is enjoying the silence and reading a book (Jim Harrison's epic trilogy, *Legends of the Fall*, trivia fans, and not Sid Little's autobiography), but his peace is soon shattered by the racket from across the lake. Wesley is having one of his legendary sexy parties, where middle-aged men dance like they're being held at gunpoint and topless ladies cavort in swimming pools and whoop. Dalton regards this decadence with disapproval before going back to reading his great book.

The next morning, Carrie Ann arrives with coffee and breakfast, and has to witness the great hunk getting out of bed naked. Her mouth falls to the floor as his toned arse is exposed, and I'm pretty sure she immediately falls pregnant. She tells him how firing Pat the barman may well come back to bite him, as he's very well connected, and Dalton, being Dalton, isn't bothered in the slightest. He has bigger fish to fry. He takes his car to Red Webster's Auto Parts (Red is memorably played by Robert 'Red' West, one-time bodyguard of Elvis) and is paying for a new aerial when in walks Brad Wesley. Wesley introduces himself to Dalton and wishes him luck in cleaning up the Double Deuce. There's something sinister in his tone, though, and as Dalton leaves, he catches the steely expression of Brad's henchman, Jimmy (who looks like an out-of-work porn actor), and they lock eyes like the sexy alpha dogs they are.

That night at the Double Deuce, Dalton is called to the office, and when he gets there, he finds Pat and two friends looking threatening. They inform him that there's been a mistake and Tilghman's changed his mind. But we know he hasn't. They say that Pat's back on the job, and Dalton's fired. There's also the fact that all the booze in the Double Deuce is supplied by Brad Wesley, who is Pat's uncle. Pat brings out a knife and threatens Dalton with it, which is a bad idea, as Dalton karates his ass through a window and beats the other henchmen unconscious.

During the contretemps, he is mildly stabbed, so he takes himself to the hospital, bringing his own medical records, of course, and claiming the wound is due to 'natural causes'. He's tended to by Red Webster's niece, Dr Elizabeth 'Doc' Clay (Kelly Lynch), who tells him that the Double Deuce sends a lot of business her way. He tells her he'll change that, and she seems doubtful. She offers him a local anaesthetic, as she needs to staple him up, but he informs her he doesn't want it, as 'pain don't hurt'. She asks why he carries his medical records, and he tells her it saves time. His file also shows that he has a degree from NYU, which it turns out is in philosophy. Which also explains why he couldn't get a proper job.

Back at Wesley's place, Pat and his sorry beaten-up pals (one of whom drives a Bigfoot truck) arrive to break the bad news that their plan failed, and Wesley doesn't take it very well. He asks for an apology from one of them, but he doesn't believe one, saying he's a 'bleeder', which he then proves by punching him in the nose twice and making it bleed. He then declares that he's a piece of shit coward, and instructs his men to get him out of there.

Dalton arrives at Red's auto shop to find that the place has been smashed to bits. It would seem that Wesley is running a protection racket and that Red hasn't paid his ten per cent this week. Wesley has all the businesses in town under his protection, and it would seem, increasingly, that he's not a very pleasant man. Of course, Dalton, possessing a degree in philosophy, is less than impressed. Knowing that he may have his hands full, and with some time to spare while washing his smalls in a laundrette, he decides to call an old friend for a heart-to-heart. Wade Garrett (Sam Elliott), who looks like a Hells Angel crossed with a celebrity chef, is the other best bouncer in the business, and Dalton is comforted by his soothing words.

Carrie Ann can sing, and she's belting out 'Knock On Wood' on the newly refurbished stage at the Double Deuce. No more chicken wire, and the wall is rich with neon signage, making this truly a Ramsay-style makeover. Dalton watches from the bar and likes what he sees, but his happiness is short-lived. Sexy Denise asks him if he wants to come back to her house and fuck, but Dalton tells her he's shy. It turns out she's the girlfriend of Jimmy (Brad's top muscle), who doesn't take too kindly to her offering herself to the new man in town. He drags her outside, signalling to his men to go in and start trouble, which they do, before being flung outside and beaten up again.

As the dust settles, Dalton notices Doc has arrived, dressed entirely in red gingham, like a tablecloth has gained sentience and possessed a human. He takes her to a diner, and they chat long into the night about the human experience of being a bouncer. After a sufficient level of sensual chat has been endured, she takes him back to his car, which has been vandalised again, and, after a chaste kiss, he heads home.

The following morning, Dalton has visitors at the barn – Wesley's men – who tell him Wesley wants to see him. As they enter the mansion, Dalton notices Denise doing aerobics and failing to hide a black eye, which makes me think that maybe Jimmy isn't very nice, either. Wesley welcomes him and offers him some breakfast, which Dalton refuses, although a vintage photograph of a good-looking man on Wesley's table catches his eye. 'My grandfather,' Wesley confirms. 'He looks like an important man,' Dalton says. 'He was an asshole,' Wesley says, while looking like he's eaten a bad egg. He goes on to tell Dalton how impressed he is with him and how he worked his way up from the streets in Chicago and was in Korea and how he built the town and how all the big shops are coming soon . . . so he'll get even more rich. Dalton isn't buying it, and doesn't like how he's got all his money by exploiting people, a suggestion that Wesley happily admits and laughs at. He knows all about the man Dalton killed in 'self-defence' in Memphis, and asks him if he'd come and work for him. It seems he likes the cut of his jib and is all for men that can rip throats out. Dalton doesn't even flinch; he says that there's no amount of money that would interest him, and he leaves with his dignity intact (if you forget about the haircut).

Business at the Double Deuce is now booming. A queue of excitable punters is round the block, the car park is full of fancy-looking cars, and the giant neon sign is a welcoming beacon to all the good people out there who would like to get drunk and listen to some godawful, diluted dad rock. Dalton can't help but smile, but Tilghman's joy at the joint being full is mitigated by the fact that booze supplies are running low. Wesley's put the squeeze on, but Dalton, ever the provider, tells him he'll take care of it, and gets on the phone to Oddbins.

Doc appears at closing time to give Dalton a lift back to his barn. He takes her up to his room and shows her the beautiful view, before telling her that the horses let him know if anyone is around, which doesn't sound weird at all. After a sufficient amount of small talk, Dalton tunes the radio into a slow, sexy Otis Redding number, and the love-making commences in the moonlight. But across the water, the scheming eyes of Wesley are watching.

Wade Garrett pulls up to the Double Deuce on his motorbike, fighting a continual battle to stop his long hair flopping into his face. He observes the majesty of the club, murmurs, 'The Double Douche,' to himself, and walks into the joint. He is met with gasping faces and wide smiles – like Elvis stopping at a provincial tearoom in Kent to use the phone. 'I know you,' Tilghman drawls, like he wants him to sign his tits. Garrett says he's looking for a skinny little runt called Dalton, who he's told is out back helping with a booze delivery. Garrett finds Dalton being beaten up by a troop of Wesley's numpties. What they don't realise is that Garrett is the best dang cooler in the business, and within moments they are all either face-planted on the floor or in a bin. As the dust settles, Dalton greets Garrett like a monkey seeing his old keeper in a viral video, then excitedly tells him he wants to introduce him to his new friend.

At a dingy table in a dark bar, Garrett holds court over Dalton and Doc, telling tales of the various injuries and scars he's collected over the years, before finally showing off a nasty one he has pretty close to his penis, which feels a bit like a soft porn remake of *Jaws*. After dancing flirtatiously with Doc, he tells Dalton to stop beating himself up about what happened in Memphis. But what happened in Memphis? Well, it would appear that Dalton was seeing a lady who was married, but she didn't tell him. And one day, the husband came to kill him, and Dalton ripped his throat out. So, rather than being an awful act of brutal murder, it was self-defence, your honour. Whatever the story, the fact remains that Dalton is haunted by what happened and carries it around with him everywhere he goes, much like Wade's penis scar.

That night at the Double Deuce, business is booming, but that's not the only thing booming, as Red's place across the street is on fire. As the club empties to watch it explode, Dalton is relieved to see Red arrive in his truck to witness the chaos. When Dalton and his staff file back into the club, they find Brad Wesley at the bar with his entourage, faux-mourning the fate of Red's business. Wesley then demands the band play 'something with balls' (and they immediately abandon their idea of playing a Black Lace medley) and watches Denise doing a striptease. Jimmy does a karate show with a pool cue, beating up some of the Double Deuce staff and Garrett, which kicks off a big, messy brawl that culminates in a fight with Dalton. Just as that's really getting going, Wesley fires a gun and puts a stop to it, such is his power.

The town elders gather at Red's house; Dalton and Doc are there, too. They bemoan the fact that they all got poor while Wesley got rich and that they can't go to the police as he owns them all. Tilghman tries to lift the mood by telling the room that Dalton scared Wesley last night, but Dalton is not convinced. He's seen fear, and he doesn't see it in Wesley's eyes – and this is coming from a man who rips throats out.

Later, in a further show of strength, Wesley has his men destroy the car dealership of one of the elders with a Bigfoot truck. When Doc tells him he's gone too far, he warns her that she should stop seeing Dalton, as he's going down. He then reminds the old men that this is his town and that they should never forget it, much like Noel Edmonds did to the poor and humble townsfolk of Crinkley Bottom.

Dalton blames himself for bringing all this heat onto the elders, so he retires to his barn to practise his martial arts by thumping a board of wood. Garrett arrives to talk some sense into him, but he won't listen. He urges his little amigo to leave with him, before it's too late, but Dalton wants to stay and fight. Garrett wishes him luck and takes off.

That night, Doc tries to talk some sense into him, and after some passionate arguing about why Dalton's so committed to taking out Wesley, Wesley sort of proves his point by blowing up Emmet's house next door. Luckily, Emmet is unharmed, but as Dalton carries him from the burning building, he spots a cackling Jimmy whizzing away from the scene on a motorbike.

Dalton gives chase, like a leopard hunting a Sinclair C5, and as he dives onto Jimmy, pulling him from his bike, the ultimate fight begins between two men who could easily be in the *Top of the Pops* audience during the number one performance at the end. After many hours of high kicks, low punches and homoerotic banter, Dalton gets the better of Jimmy, and in a move that everyone saw coming, rips out Jimmy's throat in one quick swoop. He then boots the body into the river and calls out to Wesley, who watches, helpless, as his henchman floats towards him. Regrettably, Doc witnesses this absolute horror and runs away, mentally scarred for life, although, as a health professional, she must have marvelled at the ease with which Dalton performed such a complicated medical procedure.

The next day, Dalton arrives back at the Double Deuce, and as he walks through the doors, the phone rings. It's Wesley. He tells Dalton that he has to choose between Wade or Elizabeth:

one of them will have to die. As Dalton has no real comeback, other than to tell him he's sick, Wesley says he will just have to flip a coin. As Dalton puts the phone down, Garrett lurches through the door, bloodied and battered. He props him up on a bar stool and tells him Wesley wins, and that they're leaving as soon as possible. After unsuccessfully trying to persuade Doc to join him in his escape, sort of forgetting that she's just witnessed him brutally murder someone, he returns to the Double Deuce to find Garrett very dead, with a knife jammed into his body carrying a note that reads: 'It was tails'. As Dalton fights back the tears and pulls the knife from his friend's body, it's clear that Wesley is a dead man.

At Wesley's mansion, his goons are waiting, heavily armed, and they shoot wildly as Dalton's silver Merc races straight towards the compound. It explodes in a ball of flames, and as they inspect the wreckage, they find the knife that killed Garrett stuck into the accelerator pedal. There then begins a game of cat and mouse, with Dalton slowly taking out the mice (culminating in a room full of stuffed animals) one by one, like Batman with a mullet.

At last, Dalton has Wesley to himself. After a fight that is essentially an old man hitting a ballet dancer with a stick, Dalton pins him down and prepares to carry out another throat-rip, before deciding that Wesley isn't worth getting blood all over his nice white blouse. Satisfied he has the moral high ground, Dalton turns his back and goes to walk away, but Wesley isn't interested in morals, or indeed any kind of ground, and pulls out a gun, only to then find Doc, her uncle and the entire town of elders in his living room, armed to the teeth. They then take turns pumping him full of lead, sending him crashing through a glass coffee table in a splatter of blood and viscera.

Before the police arrive to assess the damage, the elders dispose of all their weapons, and then tell them they didn't see what happened, and giggle away to themselves, forgetting that it would be incredibly easy to prove that they all did it and send them to jail, where they can share a wing with James 'Throat Ripper' Dalton.

214

As some bland soft rock blares out, Dalton and Doc frolic naked in a river, splashing each other playfully and seeming perfectly happy with the grisly murder they've both been a part of, and merrily kiss like Netflix won't one day make a documentary called *The Town That Murdered as One.*

NINETEEN

1989

THE MAGIC IS BACK!

MAKING A SEQUEL TO a gritty, dark action film with undertones that explore mental-health issues can be a tricky proposition. A fine line needs to be walked, and there's a responsibility to ensure that things don't . . . Oh, hang on, is that the *Looney Tunes* theme, I hear?

As the spray-painted number 2 rushes over the chrome words 'Lethal Weapon', and all you can hear is Riggs hollering and whooping as he and his partner pursue a suspect in a high-speed chase, the tone has already been set. We're doing a sequel, yes, but we're going to explore the fun side of things, too, and as any viewers alive at the time who saw Mel Gibson's very silly video diary from the set of this film will know, a lot of fun was had making this one.

Riggs (Mel Gibson) wants Murtaugh (Danny Glover) to floor it so they can catch up with the suspect, but Murtaugh delicately explains that he can't. He's driving his wife's brand new station wagon, and she'll kill him if anything were to happen to it, and I am sure nothing will. As they emerge from a tunnel, they overhear the suspects communicating with one another over the radio in a language they don't understand. Some officers think it may be German, but Riggs and Murtaugh decide to make a joke about how it may be Japanese because they own everything (I wouldn't have opened with that one, lads). After a long, frantic pursuit, where Mrs Murtaugh's car takes the brunt of the carnage, the red car they are pursuing crashes into the front of a shop, and by the time our heroes arrive, the occupant has disappeared without a trace. In the boot, they find a large haul of pure gold coins; so, either this villain is a pirate, or he runs a local arcade and was just cashing up for the day. The coins, it turns out, are Krugerrands, and, as Murtaugh points out, it's illegal to have them in the country, which would mean that the men who have been shooting at them, blowing up bits of the city, and avoiding the police, may actually be criminals. Mind blown.

Captain Ed Murphy (Steve Kahan) is not impressed with the previous night's antics. He tells Murtaugh it will be coming out of the department's budget, a fiscal fact that is always a fascinating insight when brought up in action movies. It's good to know how budgets work. He was told it was just a simple drug bust, but Murtaugh explains that it got a bit out of hand, which feels like an understatement.

However, their conversation is killed stone-dead as they happen to walk in on Riggs in a straitjacket, bouncing around the room as the rest of the squad (a perfect array of faces you know from elsewhere: Hank from *Breaking Bad*, Dominic from *Casino*, Vasquez from *Aliens*, and our old friend Grand L. Bush from everything else) wave cash at him. No, this isn't a commentary on mental-health issues; this is a bet to see if he can get out of the jacket and win their money. He wriggles, writhes and hops around the room, and just when it looks like he'll never get out, he announces that they shouldn't try this at home, and then pops his arm out of his shoulder. It turns out that he dislocated his shoulder once and can do it whenever he wants. They ask if it hurts, and he says it doesn't, but it does when he has to put it back in, which he demonstrates by banging himself against a wall – and the room winces as one. Doctors around the world suggest that such a feat can only be achieved with a good deal of anaesthesia and recovery, but who gives a shit, really. Stay with it, it'll pay off later.

Riggs then asks Murtaugh if he fancies going out for dinner in the evening, in a deeply platonic way, obviously, but he can't. His daughter, Rianne, who is now an actor, has her commercial on Channel 8 that evening, and the family will be watching. Ignoring Murtaugh's pleas not to tell anyone in case she's rubbish, Riggs tells the whole room to watch it and flashes her photo around to some of the men, who make odd, growling noises.

The Riggs and Murtaugh vehicles arrive home in unison to witness Murtaugh's builder working on his house extension, and it's at this point one has to ask where he's getting all this money from. He has a fishing boat, a massive, detached house and now a giant 'hobby room' (wanking den) *and* a double garage being bolted on the side. It's really no surprise that Internal Affairs look at him twice in the next film, to be honest.

The builder, who is a bit of a smartass, makes them both jump by firing his nail gun, which causes them to drop to the floor and pull their guns on him, in a perfectly normal way. But they all laugh it off, and I'm sure that nail gun won't be important later.

The family are gathered, and the TV is tuned to the right channel, with the classic 'And All Through the House' episode of Richard Donner's *Tales from the Crypt*, featuring Mary Ellen Trainor (Dr Woods from *Lethal Weapon*), playing in the background as everyone chats about the picture quality. After a brief chat about how dolphins are dying in tuna nets, the commercial begins, and it's immediately apparent that it's an ad for Ramses Extra, and you're left wondering why Rianne never thought to tell her obviously puritanical father that she was doing an advert for condoms. A shocked and embarrassed Murtaugh sends the kids away and begins to pace the room, cursing the fact that his colleagues will never let it lie and how it will be a banter apocalypse at work from now on. Riggs, however, reassures him that it'll be fine, because, with policemen, it's 'in one ear and out the rubber', which is a fine joke and no mistake.

A dark, foreboding, sparsely furnished room is lit by a small yet efficient desk lamp and a giant, refulgent fish tank. Arjen Rudd (Joss Ackland) is sitting behind his desk, tucking into a hearty dinner, while his henchman Pieter Vorstedt (Derrick O'Connor) enjoys a cigarette in the corner. Clearly, there is no banter in this room, as they are angry South Africans from the eighties, and no one ever met a nice one of them. There's a knock at the door, and in walks Hans, the driver who escaped from the red car earlier. He's welcomed with open arms and asked to not mind the plastic sheeting on the floor as he is having some painting done. Rudd wants to know what happened with the car crash: he lost a million dollars' worth of Krugerrands, which is a bit sloppy. Hans apologises, then explains that these things can happen occasionally, and Rudd agrees, giving the nod to Vorstedt to put a bullet in Hans's face. As Hans is rolled up in plastic and ready to be put somewhere sensible, Rudd bemoans the police sticking their nose into his affairs, pointing out that they have become an 'intolerable nuisance', so Vorstedt suggests warning them off. Rudd then shows him the file of the officer in charge of the investigation, Roger Murtaugh, leading to Rudd dropping an ethnic slur for no extra charge. Be in no doubt, ladies and gentlemen, these are our villains.

Riggs is preparing chilli for the family – and for some reason is putting crushed Oreos in it (am I really supposed to root for this man?) – while chatting to Trish Murtaugh (Darlene Love) about life. She tells him she found a gold pen in the laundry and wondered if it was his. He explains that it was a gold pen he found the night his wife died, and goes on to explain how she died in a car crash returning from a dinner he'd forgotten they were supposed to be having. As he got the call informing him that she had died, he dropped to his knees and found that gold pen under the couch. He later used it to sign her death forms, and thus ends this exciting, and emotional, bit of exposition.

It's night-time in the Murtaugh house, and not a creature stirs, apart from the small band of South Africans in balaclavas who break in and gaffer-tape Murtaugh and his wife's mouths up while issuing a warning about backing off. He's told that, if he keeps his nose out, this will be it, but if he carries on, things will get bloody, and then they run away into the night – and this is what happens when you stop buying Milk Tray.

The next day at the station, Murtaugh is consoled and offered support by the guys on his team for suffering horrible trauma, before being given a special assignment from the Captain: babysitting a federal witness who will be testifying before a special inquiry on drugs and money laundering. It's an all-expenses-paid job, so Riggs and Murtaugh can order whatever they want and watch all the blue movies they like. The guys aren't too happy with this, but the Captain tells them they're the most qualified for the assignment (in what way?) and feels it will be a good distraction for Murtaugh, which is very thoughtful.

Leo Getz (Joe Pesci) stands on his tip-toes to look through the peephole of his hotel door. He's wrapped in tax payer-funded silk pyjamas, robe and slippers, and is enjoying his cushy lifestyle, until Riggs and Murtaugh burst in and tell him to shut up. He tries to break the ice by running his name by them and telling them that 'whatever you need, LEO GETZ', but it's not really buttering any parsnips. They give him the coldest of shoulders as they inspect the lavish suite, and inform him they'll be taking his room after mildly slapping him about when he wants to look at their guns. He finally agrees to hand it over, and employs his machine-gun 'OK-OK-OK' catchphrase at every opportunity. Getz is a man who just wants to be loved, and his release into this film is like a little comedy bull at a rodeo. Room service arrives, and it's evident that Getz didn't order it, or the gun that's thrust in his face by the hotel porter. Riggs senses the danger and leaps at the assassin, which inevitably leads to all three of them going out of the window and falling seven floors down into the swimming pool (with a nice view of Nakatomi Plaza in the background). The would-be killer escapes as Riggs drags Getz to the side of the pool – he can't swim – and has to ask why someone would take such a huge risk to kill him, whereupon Getz lets slip that he laundered half a billion dollars in drug money.

Back at Murtaugh's place, Getz explains how the entire grift and laundering scam works. He concludes that, with all the money that he embezzled, who would miss it? But he's then forced to agree with Riggs and Murtaugh when they point out that the drug dealers would. They then ask him for information on who the dealers are, but Getz says he never met them, only the couriers. He can, however, remember the name 'Hans' and the address of a very distinctive house on stilts where he was once taken, so off they go for a road trip.

Before too long, they arrive at said house, and as luck would have it, it's full of strident South Africans counting money. They shoot at Riggs as he pokes around outside while pretending to be a pool cleaner (Clouseau he is not), and when one of the bad guys makes a run for it, Riggs recognises him as the room-service guy who tried to shoot them at the hotel. The angry, apartheid-supporting assailant commandeers a tow truck, with a car still on the back, and tries to make a break for it, obviously not counting on Riggs being a mix of rabid dog and Spider-Man. With Riggs clinging to the back of the speeding vehicle, Murtaugh and Getz give chase in his wife's station wagon, and a thrilling chase ensues, which inevitably ends with the truck getting into a crash with a car carrying a surf board that flies through the windshield and decapitates the driver. Don't you hate it when that happens?

Later, at the house on stilts, Riggs, Murtaugh and their squad return to raid the place, with it being full of drugs and money and so on. However, they are met there by Rudd and Vorstedt, who are not pleased with the police showing up. Rudd reminds the officers that he is the Minister of Diplomatic Affairs for the South African Consulate and therefore has diplomatic immunity, which, in this instance, appears to mean they can all do whatever they like. During their tense chat, Murtaugh uses Riggs's name, and Vorstedt is very interested; he asks if he is *the* Martin Riggs, for reasons unknown at present. As Rudd puts his paperwork back in his pocket, he reminds the officers that they couldn't even give him a parking ticket and the house they're standing in is owned by the South African government, which goes down well with our heroes. After calling them dickheads, Rudd tells them to leave, and on the way out, Riggs bumps into Rika van den Haas (Patsy Kensit), Rudd's consulate secretary. There's an instant sexual frisson and flirting, so she's probably not long for this world.

After some top-level stalking and gurning at Rudd at various points around the city – all standard police procedure – Riggs returns home to find Getz hoovering and finding horrible things under the refrigerator of his man-cave trailer, which he finds beyond the pale. He's about five minutes away from staging a dirty protest, when he gets a phone call from work informing him that Murtaugh hasn't shown up and can't be reached on the phone. He races over to chez Murtaugh to see if everything is OK with his friend. His mind is racing as he breaks down the door and hears Murtaugh informing him that he's upstairs. Has he been tied up? Beaten? Covered in silly string? No. He's on the toilet, and he can't move – and I think we've all been there. He laments the fact that, for the first time in ages, he had the house to himself and duly sat on the throne, in peace and quiet, to read an excellent feature on marlin fishing, when he found himself unable to move (again, we've all been there). However, this wasn't a bodily malfunction: it was a message written on his toilet paper informing him that there was a bomb under the khazi. Riggs pokes about, and it is indeed true. The device isn't triggered to go off if Murtaugh stops pooing, like some sort of awful *Speed* sequel; it's triggered to go off if he *stands up*. So, for now, he's stuck on the bog, and things are about to get worse, as Riggs will need to call in the bomb squad to defuse this explosive thing, and I don't mean his arse.

With the street and house now very much full of busy people, and Murtaugh stuck trouserless on the pooper, like some sort of hellish nightmare, it's time to try to get him out of his predicament. The squad inform them that the only way to do it is to spray some liquid nitrogen on the device to postpone the detonation temporarily and to pull Murtaugh into the bathtub to protect him from the blast. Without even a moment's hesitation, Riggs says he'll stay and do the pulling, and it makes my heart soar to see how beautiful this friendship is. Might I, one day, have a friend who will love me enough to free me from an explosive toilet and pull me into a bath? As the room clears of helpers and watchers, it's just Murtaugh and Riggs, and after a small bit of banter, they have a beautiful moment together of unspoken love, and then, after careful consideration, and on the count of three, Riggs tugs Murtaugh off into the bath (stop it), and after the vast explosion, amidst the smoke and debris, there's the comforting sound of laughter and life.

With tensions high and the very concept of diplomatic immunity stretched to breaking point, our lads decide the best idea is to break into the consulate and rattle cages. Getz messes with an immigration official about a friend of his who wants to emigrate to South Africa, the joke being that he is a black man – Murtaugh. They create enough fuss and disruption to allow Riggs to slip into Rudd's office, whereupon he tells him and all his men to pack up their tents and fuck off home, before then shooting out his fish tank, which in diplomatic terms is known as 'No-Deal Brexit'. Before leaving under a cloud of bullets, though, Riggs manages to snag a note with the mysterious words 'Alba Varden, Thursday' written on it. This could be a real clue.

At the supermarket, Rika is tum-te-tumming among the fresh veg when she happens to bump into Riggs. He admits that he followed her from the consulate and then invites (well, sort of drags) her over to his place for dinner and drinks. Astoundingly, this approach works, and she doesn't seem perturbed in the slightest. Back at the static home, he shows her how he lives and gives her a beer, and they discuss how vile her boss is and how he's hiding behind his credentials, like a nudist at an antiques fair. Their courtship quickly moves on to heavy petting as doo-wop music chirrups out of the speakers, and the scent of erotica is sweet in the air.

Meanwhile, across town, Riggs and Murtaugh's colleagues are being offed one by one, some more creatively than others: one is shot, one succumbs to a bomb under the diving board of her swimming pool, and the rest are exploded while playing poker. The only officers unaccounted for are our Riggs and Murtaugh, with the latter at home with Getz, puzzling as to just what or who Alba Varden could be. Murtaugh suddenly remembers where he saw the name. It's the name of a ship in one of his home-made fishing videos. But before he can jump for joy at his eureka moment, his house is suddenly full of two bad bastards with guns, and a fight breaks out, ending in Murtaugh dispatching them with the nail gun he played with earlier. Thank God for his curiosity in tools. If this police thing doesn't work out, he's got a job on *Ground Force* for life. After proclaiming to thin air that he 'nailed them both', he runs out the front to find that his car, and Getz, are gone.

Riggs and Rika are nude in bed when the eerie sound of an evil chopper approaches, and not for the first time that night. As Sam barks a warning, Riggs dismounts and checks where it's coming from. Soon the trailer is perforated with bullets. Rika hides in his truck, and Riggs takes down the bad guys with his pistol, Three Stooges impressions and cunning guile. However, it's all for nothing: after he drops her off at home – yes, he takes her home after surviving a double helicopter assault, it is a first date, after all – they are both captured, and Riggs is knocked out.

He awakes at the docks, groggy and dressed in a sack, covered in chains and with the pleasure of Vorstedt's company. He offers Riggs a drink, but says he knows that he's on the wagon these days, which leads Riggs to enquire how he knows so much about him. Lo and behold, it turns out he's the man who changed Riggs's life. Four years ago, he handled a contract on Riggs's life when the detective got too close to their drugs operation, and he ran his car right off the road, except he wasn't driving – his wife was. He takes great pleasure in informing Riggs that she took some time to die and he was there to watch it. Riggs considers this news for a moment, before trying to go for the dastardly racist. However, he's held back and then thrown into the sea to die. Vorstedt is happy with his work and drives away to be racist somewhere else. Riggs sinks to the bottom and takes a moment to pop that shoulder out again. As he swims out of the jacket, he turns to see the rather alarming sight of Rika drowned at the bottom of the sea, looking a bit surprised herself. He power-swims to the surface and viciously murders the two goons who threw him in the water, before smashing his shoulder back in place by using the side of a car. It's safe to say, he's a bit annoyed.

Murtaugh's phone rings, and Riggs tells him Rika's dead and that he's not a cop tonight. It's personal, and he's on the way to the house on stilts to 'fuck them'. Murtaugh tries to explain that the whole squad are dead and they're under orders to not do anything else with the South Africans, but Riggs won't listen. He is totally off on one now. Murtaugh hangs up the phone, puts his police badge in his desk drawer, and stands up to join his friend.

Getz is in a bit of bother. He's tied to a chair, face all bloodied, and he's being beaten to a pulp by men who fail to see the subtle irony in Alf Garnett. They want their money back and they want him to tell them where it is. But before he can give them his PIN number, the house starts shaking. At first, they think it's an earthquake, but it's not. It's Riggs. He's tied his truck to the stilts, and he's pulling as hard as he can. In the middle of this chaos, Murtaugh bursts in shooting and manages to rescue Leo, just before the house slides down the hill like a half-cooked pizza, much to everyone's delight. However, Vorstedt has got away in all the confusion, and as Murtaugh explains to Riggs what the *Alba Varden* is, they send Getz back to the precinct – allowing him to sound the siren – and race to the docks to finish this thing.

The vast *Alba Varden*, out of Hamburg, sits at the docks, next to a large container waiting to be loaded, guarded by three men who can't wait for GB News to launch. After murdering the guards, Murtaugh and Riggs open up the container and find it full to the brim with dirty drug cash. Enough to fund three *Waterworlds* and half a *Heaven's Gate*. As they contemplate just what you could do with all that money, the doors are closed behind them, and Rudd tells his men to put it on the ship, mentioning that the next time they see the light of day, they'll be in Cape Town. But what Rudd should know by now is that our two heroes are as cunning as a pair of foxes with a Machiavellian degree in adaptability. Inside the container is a limousine, and as that shoots through the battered container doors and money rains down like the proverbial, our boys come out shooting, with a fine performance of abseiling. The boat bursts into gunfire, and as Riggs and Murtaugh take different decks, the bodies pile up, with one notable moment when Riggs dispatches a bad guy while internally shouting the names of all his fallen loved ones and colleagues, like he's making a shopping list for funeral flowers. Eventually, Riggs comes face to face with his nemesis, and a shadowy, white-guy karate battle comes to life, with our hero finding himself with a knife jammed deep in his thigh. Things are looking bleak, until he eventually finds a switch and drops a giant container right on Vorstedt's stupid Aryan face, putting an end once and for all to his extreme views.

Murtaugh joins Riggs, and is about to whoop and cheer, only to then witness our old friend Rudd pumping four hundred rounds into Riggs. Murtaugh turns to point his gun at the Minister and tells him to drop it, only to be met with yet another round of 'diplomatic immunity', which one presumes he thinks will play well here with an attempted murder witness. Murtaugh takes aim, cricks his neck, and then puts one right in Rudd's smug head. 'It's just been revoked,' he says as he watches the envoy slump to the ground, thus ending this round of political debate with a nice full stop.

As Murtaugh cradles his fallen friend in his arms, it doesn't look good, and one suspects that if he gave Riggs a glass of water, he'd become an errant garden-sprinkler system. 'Knocking On

Heaven's Door' plays out quietly as Murtaugh tells him he's not going to die and won't be dead until he tells him. Riggs looks up at his friend and tells him he's going to quit smoking and that he's not going to die, which comes as something of a relief. Laughter echoes in the empty ship as Murtaugh confirms that the bad guys have been 'de-kaffirnated'. As police sirens approach and difficult questions will be asked about what the hell's just happened, it's comforting to know that even though Riggs has more lead in him than a giant pencil case, the banter remains strong. The camera drifts away into the night, George Harrison tells us to 'Cheer Down', and we're left with the warming knowledge that there may well be further adventures in store for our delightful *arme mortelle* after all.

TWENTY

Tango & Cash

1989

TWO OF LA'S TOP RIVAL COPS ARE GOING TO HAVE TO
WORK TOGETHER . . . EVEN IF IT KILLS THEM.

LIEUTENANT RAY TANGO (Sylvester Stallone) is no normal, run-of-the-mill Hollywood cop. There's no doughnuts, cowboy boots, mental-health issues or booze problems here; instead, we have Armani suits, expensive shades and a detailed knowledge of the stock market. He's a yuppie with a badge, but still one hell of a police officer – to the point that when he arrests someone, it gets in the papers, for some reason.

Today, he's cruising on a California highway in his open-top Cadillac, in hot pursuit of a tanker truck driven by 'Face' (played by Robert Z'Dar, the man with the biggest face in the world), but he's being told by overhead air support that they'll handle it from here. Tango voices his concerns, telling them he's been working this case for three months. He flashes on his red light and decides to take the truck himself. As he speeds ahead, air support tell him it's out of their jurisdiction and whatever he's going to do, he'll need to do it fast. Tango overtakes the truck, pulls over, steps out of his sexy car, in his immaculate, dove-grey, three-piece suit, and takes his gun from his holster. For some reason, he dumps all the bullets and reloads, spinning the cartridge as he does so, and then takes aim at the truck slowly rising above the horizon. As it nears, Tango fires three shots into the cab, causing Face to tell his passenger that 'this guy is crazy' before he jams his foot hard on the brakes. As the huge vehicle comes to a perfect stop, Face and his companion fly through the windshield and down onto the road below.

This entire set piece is supposedly an homage to Jackie Chan's *Police Story*, where Jackie's character Chan Ka-Kui does the same thing – the gun reloading and firing into the windshield of an oncoming bus driven by baddies – but, as I'm sure you can imagine, it's carried out competently in that version.

'Glad you could drop in,' Tango says, with a smile on his face that only serves as a further punch to the gut. 'Fuck you,' the furious Face says. As air support lands, Captain Schroeder (Geoffrey Lewis in a wig) steps out and approaches Tango, asking him just what the hell is going on, telling him all about the damage he's just caused, and enquiring why he stopped the truck. Tango tells him it's not a truck, it's a 'major moving violation', much to the confusion of Schroeder and everyone else.

The Sheriff's department arrive and aren't entirely convinced by Tango's unconventional methods. They've checked inside the truck, by putting a stick in it, and can only find gas, so one deputy storms into Tango's face, calls him an asshole, and asks just exactly who he thinks he is, and then another deputy drops the almighty clanger of a line suggesting that Tango 'thinks he's Rambo'. As the laughter dies down and the paying cinema audience look around slack-jawed to check that what they're seeing is actually happening, Tango slurs out the line, 'Rambo is a pussy,' before firing a round into the tanker, which causes a long trail of white powder to snake out. Tango grabs a handful, dips a finger in, and confirms that it is indeed cocaine, like all policemen did in the eighties, before that smug smile returns and he leaves the entire police department scratching their heads and wondering how this here city type is so doggone smart.

A limousine slowly crawls by the scene of the incident as Face and his pal are loaded into police cars and Tango stands looking like a cat that shot the cream. 'Ray Tango has done it to us again,' Yves Perret (Jack Palance) tells his business partners, Quan and Lopez (James Hong and Marc Alaimo), who obviously all fancied a day out. 'And if it isn't Tango, it's Cash,' he says with maximum ham. He tells his companions that something has to be done, as, frankly, they are a massive pain in his balls (I'm paraphrasing); he has an idea in mind that will take the pair out of the equation. Then they all drive off to get Happy Meals.

Gabriel Cash (Kurt Russell – Patrick Swayze turned down the role, fact fans) may look and act like Martin Riggs, but he isn't, OK? To the sound of jaunty music, he arrives in his modest – and let's be honest, shit – apartment, with a pack of beers, a sandwich and a cheeky smile on his face. He picks up his newspaper and checks the headline, only to see his Westside rival Ray Tango on the front cover again. 'Armani with a badge,' he scoffs. He then tries to cheer himself up by looking at himself in the mirror and pulling in his stomach, you know, like any normal person does when they get home. Except today this is no normal mirror, as behind it stands an armed killer, who shatters the glass with his pistol and fires two shots into Cash, sending him flying through an open window. Luckily, Cash has a gun in his cowboy boot – no, not tucked into the boot, actually part of the boot. His shot misses, but the attacker decides to run anyway, jumping through another window and legging it along the street below. Cash gives chase and reaches an underground car park, where he draws his revolver. It's a Ruger GP100, with an experimental laser sight – and I can only conclude that this, along with the weaponised cowboy boots, were purchased from wish.com. Cash's attacker appears behind the wheel of a car, so Cash commandeers another and gives chase again, with the clear intention of causing as much automotive damage as possible, probably ending in a mass freeway pile-up, stuff on fire, and Cash catching up with his would-be killer, with hilarious consequences, because he is so cheeky.

Tango arrives at his precinct, strutting through the corridors as his colleagues pass him copies of the newspaper and pat him on the back. There's no doubt that his claimed three months of hard work has paid off, and he's loving the attention a front-page splash gets him. The only fly in the ointment to his perfect day is that his sister, Katherine (Teri Hatcher), has stopped by, so he'll need to discourage her from chasing her dream of going on a dance tour. Katherine lives with her brother, and I am guessing that their parents both died of pride/shame, so Tango has decided to take on the role of father figure/patronising arsehole. He tells her she doesn't need to travel and everything she could ever want is in their city, like any middle-aged dad would, but she wants to broaden her horizons, see new things, maybe get a straw donkey. However, before Ray can give her a speech about responsibility, he gets a message that his stockbroker is on line three to talk about a 'margin call', which he must deal with immediately to carry on this whole yuppie thing, and I for one hope his Dow Jones falls off. Katherine dashes off, much to Ray's displeasure, announcing that she has a plane to catch.

Over in a grimier part of town, Cash is in a lift with his buddies, bragging about how excellent he is while removing his bulletproof vest and lamenting that his shirt, that cost him all of $9, now has a hole in it. He snaffles a slice of pizza from a colleague and makes his way to his messy desk, where he finds that something is up with the gun that he keeps in his even messier drawer. He loudly asks the room if anyone has been fucking with his gun, as the sight is off, and I so want someone to put their hand up and say that they've been putting it up their arse for weeks. But no one says anything, and before he can focus on this issue too much, he sees his Captain, who tells him that the guy who tried to blow him away doesn't speak English and even the interpreter could only get a request for a lawyer out of him. Cash asks if he can try. The Captain says no, but Cash decides he will anyway, because rules are for fools.

The man is standing at a urinal, but not just any urinal – a urinal in a locker room. Cash wanders in and stands looking as his near-murderer does a wee. When he's finished, Cash tells him that they're at something of an impasse, what with him not knowing how to speak English and he not knowing Chinese, so he decides to break out the analogue version of Duolingo, which involves putting a chair over someone's neck while you sit in it and strangle them. Unconventional, but anyone who has looked into the eyes of that desperate translating owl will know that attempted murder is the only real course of action.

It's mere seconds before the man divulges the identity of who is behind this attempt (Quan) and tells Cash about a big drug deal that's going on that night, so while his methods may be questionable, there's no denying he gets results.

Tango is reading an interesting article in the paper, with the headline 'Cash Makes Another Bust, 200 Kilos Seized', an article that just happens to be below the one about his recent exploits, which leads one to question just what the rest of the police force think about these two officers being in the papers each and every time they do their job. It makes you wonder what other features are in this paper: do the firemen get a fluff piece, too? The Captain arrives to let him know they've just been given a big tip about a drug bust happening that night, and then, upon seeing the paper, asks if it's 'Downtown clown versus Beverley Hills wop?', a statement Tango, with an ego the size of Belgium, finds incredibly funny.

Over at Perret's compound, the man himself is watching the footage of Cash foiling yet another drug deal and laughing about how many times he's stopped him. Requin (a ponytailed Brion James) joins Quan and Lopez as they all watch a video of Tango being equally awesome. 'Ray Tango, how he loves to dance. He waltzes in and takes my drugs,' says Perret, mirthlessly, before producing a small maze, which makes one wonder if he's been snorting his own product. He tells his men they can't kill Tango and Cash because they're too well known. He then pulls out two mice called Tango and Cash – yes, this actually happens – and puts them in the maze. He goes on to explain that, instead of killing these supercops, it's better to disgrace them and put them in jail, and this needs to happen before the huge weapons deal that's going down in the next two weeks. Quan and Lopez look on coolly, like they get what's happening, but internally they must know this guy is paddling without both oars in the water.

Tango makes his way into a grotty warehouse, having already seen Requin handle a suitcase and wander by his eyeline. Cash, meanwhile, is also skulking around and following shadows, dressed in a T-shirt that's three sizes too big for him, with his big laser-sight gun drawn. As Requin purposefully strides along, he's fully aware that his shadow is marked, and as he leads his quarry a merry dance, it's not too long before Tango and Cash come face to face, or rather gun to gun, like two massive wallies. They briefly exchange banter about just who is the best cop in town, like two one-legged men at an arse-kicking contest, before deciding to investigate the scene together.

What they find isn't good: it's a corpse wearing a wire, and before they can decide who is the best at looking at corpses, police officers burst in and find Cash's spare gun on the floor. How do they know it's his spare gun, you ask? Well, he tells them it is when they pick it up. This is one of the best cops in the world, folks. The police tell them they're going down for this and lead them away in handcuffs; meanwhile, Requin hands a copy of the doctored recording to an FBI agent and tells him to use it. The tape is played to Tango and Cash's superiors, and it's not good. Listeners can clearly hear that they both took great pleasure in killing the suspect, even though it sounds like they read the lines drunk at 3 a.m.

The trial begins, and tape expert Floyd Skinner (Michael Jeter) says in no uncertain terms that it sounds genuine; he even ran it through his professional equipment, so there can be no doubt. More evidence arrives from attending officers, and none of this looks promising for our heroes. Tango's lawyer tells him that it may be time to cop a plea, as minimum-security jail time is all but guaranteed. Tango asks to speak to Cash and, after the requisite amount of banter, tells him that he's not fond of him but he's going to cop a plea. They have to do it together, and what's more, while they figure out who set them up, he'll be making the closing statement in court.

The judge listens to the defendants' announcement that they're changing their plea. Tango approaches the bench and makes his statement, and it's subdued and eloquent, detailing how he's proud to be a cop and hopes the department is not tarnished by what they're accused of. Cash, on the other hand, stands up and says the whole thing 'FUCKING SUCKS', so he's gone for a more Joe Kinnear approach to defence pleas. As the court erupts in high fives, the judge calls for order and the lawyers announce they're pleading guilty to involuntary manslaughter, which will put our boys inside for eighteen months, without any chance of a quip.

Perret is in the mood to celebrate, but Lopez and Quan are not so happy. As they rightly point out, in eighteen months they'll have the same problem when Tango and Cash get out – if they're actually still allowed to be police officers. Perret laughs off their concerns, telling his business partners that they're never getting out – before presumably putting a couple of chickens in a larger maze and mumbling to himself, as per normal.

End of the line. The prison truck arrives, and it's immediately clear that this isn't a minimum-security facility with a gym: in fact it's the direct opposite. As Tango and Cash limp through the gates in orange suits and manacles, it's clear that they may need to rethink some of their repartee. But before all that can begin, we have a very, very, very long scene where the lads take a shower, which involves them walking into the block naked and then cracking jokes about picking up soap and penis size while they try to figure out who's pulling the strings, as it were. Cash is worried. He thinks they'll be put in general population. But Tango eases his concerns: cops don't get put in general population. You can guess what happens next. As they walk through a corridor of cells, with flaming paper, piss and insults raining down upon them, the jokes still come, with Tango stopping to tell Face that he loved him in *Conan the Barbarian* – all of which makes me wish someone would remake this film with Jackie Mason and Rodney Dangerfield.

They meet their new cellmates. Cash is bunked with a giant guy who won't let him use the broken toilet; Tango is housed with Slinky (Clint Howard), an oddball who constantly plays with a Slinky while boasting about the friends he's killed. As night falls, Cash is struggling to sleep beneath a snoring lump, and Tango is happily resting, with Slinky tied up in his namesake. Their rest is rudely interrupted when they are snatched from their cells by burly men and beaten as they are dragged away to the laundry room.

Perret and Requin step from the steamy shadows, the latter with a knife. Requin begins to utter words in an accent akin to Dick Van Dyke attempting Ray Winstone, words which stumble, tumble and eventually topple over. Cash takes umbrage with his threats and demands to be killed by an American rather than whatever the fuck Requin is. And then out strides Face, with a jaw so big it needs its own weather system. Cash tells Tango they're about to get 'FUBAR' but refuses to explain what that means as Face monologues about how they're both going to die very soon. However, before he can get more words out of his pumpkin head, our heroes thump him and valiantly try to beat their way out of trouble, but it's all to no avail. There are simply too many baddies (half the prison seems to be in the laundry at this point) and they are soon overpowered. Just as they are about to be lowered into a water tank fizzing with electricity, the assistant warden arrives with his men – and it happens to be Matt, an old buddy of Cash. He tells them they're in deep shit and they have to escape, or they'll be killed. Tango suggests tunnelling out with a spoon, but Matt shows them the plan of the prison's ventilation system.

Tango, though, has doubts, and after hearing what 'FUBAR' means (Fucked Up Beyond All Recognition), he tells Cash he won't be joining him on his great escape. He doesn't trust the plan, so Cash decides to go it alone, hoping to form another double act on the outside with someone called Ian Card.

As the rain falls hard on the prison complex, Cash makes his way out on the pre-decided route, getting inside the ventilation system and slinking through the stopped fan that Matt said he would turn off. However, he finds Matt's dead body in the tunnel, and then guards heading his way, with Face's giant head leading the charge.

As the fan comes back on and Cash is cornered, things look bleak, but Tango arrives in the nick of time to hold the fan and help them both escape by getting to the roof. Their only escape route is to run through some electrical pylons, jump onto a power cable, and then zipline their way to freedom with their belts, which they're allowed to wear in prison. Cash makes the jump and glides away, but Tango is caught by Face before he can leap. An epic battle ensues, with Face sadly coming a cropper when pushed into a set of pylons. Tango makes the jump and escapes to victory, meeting Cash on the grass outside the prison walls. 'What did you do, stop for coffee and a Danish?' Cash barks. 'I hate Danish,' Tango responds, a barbed dig at Brigitte Nielsen, who he had not long divorced, which is very grown-up and clever. Our two heroes then part ways and slide away into the night, but not before Tango tells Cash that if he gets into trouble, he's to go to a club called Cleopatra's and ask for a dancer called Katherine. She'll know how to find him.

Perret takes a call from Lopez and Quan. They're worried about the fugitives, but Perret reassures them that they won't be a problem; he has everything under control. As he hangs up on them, Requin brings him his two mice, so he can talk to them again – only this time he tells them they're beautiful. This bloke isn't right.

Owen (Michael J. Pollard), an idiot savant who seems to be serving as Cash's very own Q branch, but with a $40 budget, sees the newspaper headline about the killer cops on the run and wishes them well. Suddenly, Cash appears in his face, telling him he needs a change of clothes, and can he throw in a big gun? Owen gives him what he wants and then shows him his new, senior-citizen home-protection invention: a stuffed dog with a gun in it, which explodes. We dwell on this for a second as Owen shrugs in a sort of oh-dear-what-am-I-like? gesture, and Cash gives him a cheeky thumbs up as the audience speculate on who, exactly, this film is aimed at.

Federal agent Wyler (Lewis Arquette) goes to his fridge for some leftover spaghetti, which looks awful, but before he can enjoy it, he finds Tango in his kitchen, and as UB40 once wisely asked, just what is he to do? Well, he could admit that he was involved in the set-up that put them away, given that he switched the weapons and planted the evidence. That might be worth a try. Tango asks for more information about who is behind it all and who paid Wyler, but he doesn't know. All he does know is that one of them was that rare breed of limey who talks like English is their second language. After offering to split his fee with Tango, Wyler tries to make a run for it, but when he reaches his car, it explodes.

Floyd Skinner arrives at S&S Soundlab for just another day of soundlabbing, but the mild-mannered nerd finds someone sitting in his chair, Gabriel Cash, and he has a shotgun. He's been going through Floyd's tapes, and he doesn't like what he's heard. It would seem Floyd has lots of tapes of our boys, taken over many conversations, and he has been a bit of a wizard with the editing. I await the compilation CD of their best jokes. Floyd doesn't know who hired him, either, but he has tapes of their phone conversations, as any well-organised soundlabber would.

Cash needs to find Tango to tell him all about his latest news, and as he saunters through the crowd at the Cleopatra club, as any wanted fugitive would, Katherine begins her dance routine to the upbeat tones of 'Don't Go' by Yazoo. Her act consists of her walking through one of those string screen curtains that your nan has and then banging a drum machine as men look on and whoop. However, Cash can't enjoy the show for too long, as the police are filing into the club looking for him, so he runs backstage and, surrounded by a lot of dancers' boobs, meets up with Katherine in her dressing room. He asks for her help to escape and then has a brainwave.

A biker in full leather gear strides out the back of the club, visor down, and is immediately stopped by the waiting police. When they lift the helmet, they find Katherine beneath it, of course. 'Hey, Lynn, let's go,' she says as she mounts the bike, and as the saxophone dribbles out a horny lament, we see a pair of stilettos step into the light – and we slowly, painfully, realise that this is Cash, caked in make-up and in full drag. As he approaches the motorcycle, a watching policeman proposes a three-way, only to be given the middle finger as the two women ride away into the night, flicking away their cigarette butts contemptuously. And the audience looks away in disbelief, thinking, is this an actual film?

The camera slowly pans around the room, which is strewn with clothes. Katherine is straddling Cash's back, massaging him into action. They talk about Tango, how obstinate he can be, and how she lives her own life. Meanwhile, the door handle turns just as the innuendo goes full-blown *Carry On*. Tango pauses, thinking he's watching his sister having sex, but before he can do a Kenneth Connor impression, he notices someone at the back door. He races through the room and rugby-tackles the figure through the screen door, and it turns out to be his captain, who may or may not have been wanking. While the sight of renowned character actor Geoffrey Lewis being squashed under a screen door is something of a distraction, it doesn't deter Tango from threatening to punch Cash for trying to have sex with his sister. After our comedy heroes clear up the confusion, and Cash shows Tango the tape he has, the Captain reveals that he has the address for Requin, and that they have 24 hours to clear their names.

Requin is next seen hanging upside down from the top of a building, with both feet being held by Tango and Cash. They're trying to scare him into talking, but he's made of stern British stuff. He mangles out the word 'bollocks' when they try to put the squeeze on him and announces that he loves the view. 'Up yours, arsehole, you ain't worth a toss,' he slurs, sounding more like Crocodile Dundee in a rap battle. It's clear that Plan A isn't going to work, so Tango launches Plan B, which is gaffer-taping a grenade to the limey's face and holding the pin. As Requin stands there looking bored with a bomb on him, Tango and Cash play the good cop–bad cop routine, with amazing amateur dramatics about ethics and conduct, and, astonishingly, it works. Requin is suitably scared, and as they remove the tape, he reveals his boss's name and the location of his top-secret compound. This allows our heroes to wander off high-fiving and making jokes about how Cash wants to have sex with Tango's sister. Thank you once again, England – our special relationship has brought further misery.

At Owen's lab, which has previously only been capable of delivering exploding fluffy toys and cowboy boots with guns in them, he's very proud. As the lights come on, he unveils a bulletproof Chevrolet K-3500 Silverado van that looks like something your mad uncle who loved *The A-Team* a little too much would build himself and drive to car boot sales for a laugh. Our boys are very impressed by Owen somehow pulling something useful out of the bag, and can't stop touching it and whooping like seals. 'The RV from Hell', as Cash christens it, impresses Tango so much that he actually begins to emote like a human. As they climb aboard, they assure Owen that they won't put a scratch on it. As they roar off into the dry-ice night, Owen has his doubts, as do we, and wanders off to invent a block of cheese that turns into gas.

On a hill overlooking Perret's compound, the lads pull out their binoculars and carry out some surveillance. It's quiet, maybe too quiet, but before things get noisy, Tango mournfully tells Cash that, whatever happens, he's the best cop he's ever worked with – and I'm going to need receipts that prove how he came to that conclusion. Cash accepts the compliment whole-heartedly, and then says he's definitely going to shag Tango's sister, thus pouring warm piss on this intimate moment. Tango explains that the reason he is against their union is that he doesn't want Katherine to get that 2 a.m. call telling her that something's happened to him. Awww. Cash explains that nothing will happen to him, he's charmed – though I would add that if he keeps using Owen as his weapons provider, he's less likely to die via a deadly assailant and more likely to die while taking his boot off and shooting himself in the clock weights.

I think Perret speaks for us all when he says, 'Oh, my God,' at the sight of the ridiculous clown car leaping through the front gates of his compound and steaming into his property. 'Come on,' he murmurs, looking as confused as the audience when his defence team of pick-up trucks, dune buggies and construction vehicles try to take on the Twat Mobile, which is roaring around firing its onboard machine guns and careering wildly over mud ramps.

It's not too long before pretty much everyone is dead and our heroes are inside the compound to stop Perret and his evil mouse-based plans. As they throw around more banter and find many tables piled high with assault weapons, an alarm begins to sound . . . The self-destruct sequence for the facility has begun, and Tango and Cash have 12 minutes to save the day. On the way upstairs they bump into Quan and Lopez, who they immediately murder, before reaching Perret's weird office, which, aside from a note saying 'boom', is empty.

Suddenly, the banks of TVs come to life with an image that concerns them both: Requin has Katherine, and there's a razor to her throat, and for some reason it turns out he's literally standing behind them, so it's not clear who's filming him or why. He tells them both to drop their guns, which Tango does immediately. Cash, on the other hand, refuses. He has a good shot and wants to take it. Requin has a trick up his sleeve, though. A grenade is taped to Katherine's neck. The 'English' villain then brings in his 'mate', who is good at the karate and announces that he wants to kick their 'arses'. So, with Requin holding all the cards, he then decides to throw Katherine to the floor and fight Cash. After a few slaps and kicks are dealt, Tango kicks Karate Man through a table, and Cash tells Requin about his new plan, which involves stuffing a grenade down his trousers and booting him down some stairs, whereupon he blows up, mercifully bringing an end to the biggest mangle seen this side of the Industrial Revolution.

It's been clear for some time that Yves Perret is a deeply disturbed man. He fondles mice, he rides about in limos watching his men being arrested, and he materialises in the dark corners of prison laundries. Now it appears that he's been cultivating a hall of mirrors in a secret room behind his office, for emergencies, and this is one such emergency. He's faced with the very real prospect of his own death, and he's clearly decided that he's going to go out in the only way he knows how: being fucking mad. He has Katherine and a gun, and decides to taunt our heroes. His one problem is that they immediately know – mystifyingly – which one of the multiple reflections is really him, and before he can show them his mice, they shoot him twice in the head – one from Tango's hidden pistol, the other from Cash's boot gun. As he falls dead to the floor, one can only hope that among the very last things going through his mind, aside from the bullets, was an overriding sense of regret about the choices he made in his last few days on Earth, and how he was really, really good in *Shane* and should have stuck to westerns.

With Katherine saved, and a good distance reached before the compound explodes, our heroes look on the burning wreckage with glee, before quickly returning to inanities about just who is the best cop in LA. Katherine suggests that maybe they should admit that they work well together, which causes them to grin and high-five as jubilant Harold Faltermeyer synth pop rings out into the night.

Before we leave them to argue about just how Cash will date Katherine, without even asking if she wants to, we're left with one last image: another headline clipping from the over-excited local rag telling us some important breaking news – 'Heroes again . . . TANGO AND CASH BACK ON THE FORCE'. We can all sleep safely in our beds again, knowing that Los Angeles will forever be crime free, for whenever there's injustice and evil, Tango and Cash will be out there.

And before you ask, no, there isn't a sequel. Yet.

EPILOGUE

'THERE HAS BEEN TOO MUCH VIOLENCE, TOO MUCH PAIN'
THE HUMUNGUS

WE COME TO THE end of our brief escape from reality, and as we all stumble battered and bruised from the wreckage, I hope that this serves as a little time landmark – a reminder that cinema, even in its crudest form, can still peel the mind away from the horrors of the outside world, and deliver us fantastic, and in some cases 'stupid', realities where the perturbations and horrors of 2020 and 2021 dissolve away, albeit only temporarily.

The last eighteen months have been about as bad as they could have been, for far too many awful reasons. The world has lost so much, but it if you disregard the grifters, the weirdos, and the craven maniacs, it's also showed itself to be capable of kindness, and supreme fortitude in the face of what we've somehow managed to live through.

With that in mind I would like to also leave one last thank you to the NHS and key workers who put so much before themselves, and showed the world what true heroism really looks like.

Here's to a better future for all, and I thank you for reading this, and for the support you've given me to get it done.

See you on the next one.

'And so began the journey north to safety, to our place in the sun.'

JR
2021

THE WORLD OF BOND ACCORDING TO
SMERSH POD

'Beautifully observed and a
laugh-out-loud joy'
KATHY BURKE

THUNDERBOOK
JOHN RAIN